Total Quality in
HIGHER
EDUCATION

The St. Lucie Press
Total Quality Series™

OTHER BOOKS IN THE SERIES:

For more information about these books call St. Lucie Press at (407) 274-9906

Series Editor • Frank Voehl
Series Development Editor • Sandy Pearlman

Total Quality in

HIGHER

EDUCATION

By
Ralph G. Lewis
Associate Professor
Florida International University
Miami, Florida

Douglas H. Smith
Associate Professor
Florida International University
Miami, Florida

S^t_L

St. Lucie Press
Delray Beach, Florida

Library of Congress Cataloging-in-Publication Data

Lewis, Ralph G., 1935–
    Total quality in higher education / by Ralph G. Lewis and Douglas H. Smith.
      p. cm. — (Total quality series)
    Includes bibliographical references (p.) and index.
    ISBN 0-9634030-7-9
    1. Education, Higher—Administration. 2. Total quality management.
    I. Smith, Douglas H.   II. Title.   III. Series.
LB2341.L46 1994
378'.1—dc20   93-23440
                                                    CIP

Direct all inquiries to St. Lucie Press, Inc., 100 E. Linton Blvd., Suite 403B, Delray Beach, Florida 33483.
                           Phone: (407) 274-9906
                           Fax: (407) 274-9927

S_L^t

Published by
St. Lucie Press
100 E. Linton Blvd., Suite 403B
Delray Beach, FL 33483

CONTENTS

SERIES PREFACE

THE NEW DIRECTION

The St. Lucie Press Series on Total Quality originated when it was recognized that the rapidly expanding field of Total Quality Management was neither well defined nor well focused. This realization, coupled with the current hunger for specific, how-to examples, led to the formulation of a plan to publish a series of subject-specific books on total quality, a new direction for books in the field to follow.

The essence of this series consists of a core nucleus of seven titles, around which the remaining twenty or so revolve:

- Education Transformation: *Total Quality in Higher Education*
- Respect for People: *Total Quality in Human Relations Management*
- Speak with Facts: *Total Quality in R & D*
- Customer Satisfaction: *Total Quality in Marketing and Sales*
- Continuous Improvement: *Total Quality in Information Systems*
- Supplier Partnerships: *Total Quality in Supplier Quality Management*
- Cost-Effective, Value-Added Services: *Why Quality Systems Fail*

As we move toward the mid-1990s, we at St. Lucie Press are pleased to witness a true convergence of philosophy and underlying principles of total quality, leading to a common set of assumptions. One of the most important deals with the challenges facing universities and schools in how to manage for quality.

This book introduces the reader to the relevance of total quality for universities and colleges. The objective is to provide managers and practitioners in higher education with a ready guide to implementation issues as they relate to quality management techniques and practices, as well as to the broader themes presented in the organizational sciences and systems technology fields. The central message is that a framework for total quality can be derived from business experience, but it requires more than adoption; it requires a major adaptation in order to work.

What this means to the university is that total quality is a means of assuring quality and standards by providing a philosophy as well as a set of tools. The premise is that excellence can be achieved through a singular focus on customers and their interests as the number one priority, a focus which requires a high degree of commitment, flexibility and resolve. However, no book can tell an organization how to achieve total quality; only the customers and stakeholders can.

As Series Editor, I am delighted with the manner in which the series is developing and am pleased to contribute in many small ways. Of particular interest to me has been the production of the abstracts contained in the books. I am indebted to my son, Chris Voehl, for all his help in the research and writing of selected abstracts. Finally, the work on the Academic Quality Consortium and its focus on continuous improvement in higher education deserves mention.

The Academic Quality Consortium is a collaboration of the American Association for Higher Education and the William C. Norris Institute. It was created to provide the following advantages to those committed to implementing continuous quality improvement (CQI) in higher education: an opportunity to work collaboratively by exchanging information, building on each other's experiences, expanding on the assessment practices already being utilized, and sharing with the wider higher education community the results of their work. Participating colleges and universities are committed to institution-wide implementation of the principles of continuous improvement to maximize learning. The Consortium provides leadership for the transformation of higher education by innovation, implementation, and shared learning.

Strategically, the Consortium intends to start with a small group of institutions that have already gained experience in pursuing continuous quality improvement or to provide a learning laboratory for sharing among the most advanced practitioners. It is the commitment of the Consortium to broaden its membership as it gains experience in its own operation and as resources become available to support a larger effort. In order to share their own learning efficiently and to accelerate the understanding and application of quality practices in higher education, the Continuous Quality Improvement Project has been created. (Contact Steve Brigham of the AAHE for more information at 202-293-6440 phone or 202-293-0073 fax.)

Finally, the need for more books on total quality in higher education was highlighted in the September 1993 issue of *Quality Digest* and the October issue of *Quality Progress*, both of which were entirely dedicated to quality education. This book casts a wider net, while developing a mosaic of knowledge surrounding this all-important topic.

Frank Voehl
Series Editor

AUTHOR PREFACE

Question: *Why total quality in higher education?* Answer: *Because it is right.* We believe that it is right because:

- It builds on the tradition of concern for quality that has characterized higher education in the United States and throughout the world.
- It recognizes the need for continuous development of the people who are part of the higher education system, whether students, faculty, or administrators.
- It involves principles applicable to institutional administration and classroom teaching, thus providing a bridge between traditionally separated parts of the system.
- It will help us meet the challenges of the 1990s and build effective universities and colleges of the twenty-first century.

Many individuals in higher education question the need for a renewed focus on quality in higher education and/or the appropriateness of applying the concepts of total quality to such an effort. We believe that they are wrong on both accounts. The need for a renewed focus on quality stems from several sources. First, over the past decade numerous books, reports, and commentaries have expressed an increasing dissatisfaction with the performance of our higher education system. We do not agree with all of the criticism, but we also do not believe that the general defensive, closed-system response of attacking the critics and ignoring the critique is the appropriate response. In fact, we believe that this negative mode of response contradicts the intellectual heritage and ideals of colleges and universities. A focus on quality, on the other hand, complements and enhances this rich heritage.

Second, the world in which institutions of higher learning operate is changing dramatically. Higher education is experiencing substantive shifts in student enrollments. If present trends continue, by the year 2000 over fifty percent of the student body will be over 25 years of age. Meeting the needs of the older, and increasingly part-time, student will require new approaches in the delivery of educational services.

The third reason for a focus on quality involves increased market forces and competition in higher education. Students who believe that higher education will provide the key to employment and career growth are increasingly assessing the value of a degree based on their perceptions of quality learning, service, timeliness, and price. Sensitivity to these criteria was not critical in a rapidly expanding economy, in which a premium was placed on a college degree even if the value added by the educational experience was minimal. The expected limited growth of the coming decade will encourage students to assess the value of their educational experiences by something more than a piece of paper. This will encourage greater competition among educational institutions to provide the quality of education desired by today's students.

Fourth, competition among colleges and universities will be encouraged by technological developments and the reality of long-distance education. Geographical location as a barrier to the size of the area served by an institution will be eliminated. Institutions in Boston will compete with institutions in Florida or California for students and for faculty. Increased competition will also emerge from the private sector. Corporate America already spends billions of dollars on training programs (over $48 billion in 1992), in part in response to their dissatisfaction with the products and service received from colleges and universities.

Finally, projected conditions of the general economy strongly suggest a continuation of limited economic growth for the foreseeable future. Thus, fewer funds will be available for a variety of human services including higher education. Moreover, there is reason to expect increased competition for funding with other human service areas such as health and public safety.

In sum, the fact is that (1) the environment of higher education is changing and (2) competition for both students and funds will continue to increase, at a time when (3) we are going to have to accomplish more with less. The result is that colleges and universities in the coming century will not be the same as they are today. Thus, the question that must be addressed is how we as members of the academy will respond to these (and related) trends. Will we respond in a proactive manner and initiate positive, quality-focused, learner-centered programs, or will we respond in a defensive manner, attempting to preserve the past at the expense of the future?

Just beyond the mid-point in the writing of this book (the point of no return), Alexander Pope's phrase "Fools rush in where angels fear to tread" came to mind. It occurred particularly when seeking our colleagues' opinions about the application of total quality management and continuous improvement (TQM/CI) to higher education. Although we, through our collective experience in both teaching and administration (the total years, if combined, would put a person near retirement either as a full-time university academician or administrator), are convinced of the need to implement TQM/CI within colleges and universities, the core of the academy—the faculty—have and will continue to question and resist its implementation.

We believe, to the contrary, that the adoption of the principles associated with total quality management will help create a superb future for higher education. We also believe it is appropriate to apply total quality to higher education because total quality emphasizes principles that are firmly enshrined in the halls of academia. These include an emphasis on knowledge and education, experimentation and management by fact, continuous improvement, and respect for and the ongoing development of people. A brief discussion of these concepts is warranted.

Ardent practitioners of total quality share an emphasis on the importance of knowledge and education with the academy. W. Edwards Deming, one of the founders of total quality, includes education as one of his "Principles for Transformation." In discussing this principle, Deming writes, "Encourage education and self-improvement for everyone. What an organization needs is not just good people; it needs people that are improving with education." (from *Out of Crisis*, Massachusetts Institute of Technology Center for Advanced Engineering Study, 1986, p. 86). Mary Walton also quotes Deming: "How do you help people to improve? What do you mean by improve? If you asked me, I would say that I find a general fear of education. People are afraid to take a course. It might not be the right one. My advice is take it. Find the right one later, and how do know it is the wrong one? Study, learn, improve. You never know what could be used, what could be needed. He that thinks he has to be practical is not going to be here very long. Who knows what is practical?" (from *The Deming Management Method*, Putnam Publishing Group, 1986, p. 85). It would be difficult to find a stronger statement in support of knowledge and broad-based education from any academic in any field than provided in these statements.

The basic total quality model for action is compatible with the scientific model espoused by higher education. The total quality model is based on the Shewhart cycle, consisting of a four-step process: (1) plan (study the situation and/or process), (2) do (carry out appropriate tests), (3) check (assess the results), and (4) act (implement and study the results of the implementation). The scientific model is also based on four steps: (1) analyze, (2) experiment, (3) review, and (4) implement–evaluate. Despite differing terminology, the espoused process is the same for total quality and the academy.

Practitioners of total quality and the academy also share a belief in the need for continuous improvement. The academicians may identify it as continuous learning or research, but for both it is a belief in learning appropriate concepts, processes, and skills and applying these skills to appropriate problems and projects. For both it is a commitment to quality, initiated with a dedication to a shared mission (a body of learning) and vision and the empowerment of everyone (students and employees) to incrementally move toward the vision.

The academy has a historical tradition as the champion of individuals and their rights. This tradition is also reflected in the principles of total quality (see Chapter 3) and is demonstrated in at least two ways: (1) an emphasis on individual education and development and (2) empowerment of individuals through independent thought and decision making. These principles certainly are espoused by and aspired to in the academy and also comprise one of the pillars of total quality.

With these similar concepts in mind, this book was written for our colleagues, both academic and administrative, who are interested in initiating total quality efforts and need a framework to help guide these efforts. Our approach assumes some knowledge of total quality and related principles. We have included a variety of concrete examples and instruments designed to help the reader translate these total quality concepts into practice. These materials are found at the end of Chapters 4 to 7.

We believe that the novice to total quality will also profit from reading this book, even though he or she may not be immediately ready to apply the principles and/or use the instruments. The novice would benefit greatly from thoroughly reading the first three chapters. Chapter 1 elaborates on the question "Why total quality?" and includes some warnings as to why implementing the principles of total quality in colleges and universities will not be easy. Chapter 1 also introduces material on the Malcolm Baldrige National Quality Award, sponsored by the U.S. Department of Commerce and the American Society for Quality Control. At the present time, educational institutions are not eligible for this award, but the categories assessed in the review process merit attention by members of the academy.

Chapter 2 provides an overview of the history of the total quality movement. It is particularly valuable for those interested in understanding the historical, intellectual, and personal connections in the development of the total quality movement.

Chapter 3 describes the House of Quality, the basic framework for Chapters 4 to 8. It is based on the work of Frank W. Voehl, the editor of this series. This chapter describes (1) the social, technical, and management systems (the superstructure of the House of Quality), (2) the four pillars of quality (serving the customer, continuous improvement, managing with facts, and respect for people), and (3) the four cornerstones of quality.

These cornerstones comprise the next four chapters: strategy management (Chapter 4), process management (Chapter 5), project and team management (Chapter 6), and individual and task management (Chapter 7). Collectively, these chapters provide the guidelines and strategies for implementing total quality efforts at each of the cornerstone levels.

Chapter 8 provides guidelines for the potentially difficult and complicated process of initiating a quality improvement program. It describes various quality implementation models and then provides a specific model and supportive framework to assist in the implementation of TQM/CI.

The final chapter focuses attention on an emerging development in the field of total quality—ISO 9000. ISO 9000 began in Europe with the work of the International Organization for Standardization. It was originally focused on the need for minimum international standards for quality control in manufacturing companies. Based on its success in manufacturing, it has been expanded to address quality issues in the service industries and most recently in training and education. Thus, it is likely that we will hear more about ISO 9000 in the coming years.

In closing, we want to acknowledge and express our gratitude to Oregon State University in general, and Nancy Howard, OSU's Quality Manager, in particular, for allowing us to use their experiences in the implementation of total quality as the primary case study for this book. As stated in Chapter 4, the selection of OSU was based on the extensive documentation they prepared, which is perhaps the best record of total quality implementation in a still sparse area of published examples in higher education.

We trust you will find this book beneficial and usable. We wish those readers who attempt to implement total quality improvement efforts at their colleges or universities maximum success and minimal constraints. We encourage you to contact us, sharing your successes and your concerns.

Ralph G. Lewis
Douglas H. Smith

CHAPTER 1

WHY
TOTAL QUALITY?

Why read a book about Total Quality in higher education? There are at least four possible answers to this question. First, it may be a matter of intellectual curiosity. The terms *total quality management, continuous quality improvement,* and *quality improvement* are currently very popular. Why not find out what they are about and how they might apply to higher education? Second, someone may be involved in a field concerned with the management and productivity of organizations or, third, may be concerned about conditions and changes in the organizational environment of colleges or universities. In fact, one may be motivated to read this book because such changes are viewed as threats to the academy. Finally, this book may be read in the search for a better way to help create a more effective and efficient educational system for the twenty-first century.

Whatever the reason for reading this book, one of its goals is to help establish that a need exists to recreate the academy for the twenty-first century. Change may be viewed as an opportunity, not a threat, and the principles and practices of total quality can aid in this transformation.

THE ENVIRONMENT OF HIGHER EDUCATION

Four assumptions reflect the environment in which higher education operates, now and in the future: (1) conditions and conventions within the environment are changing, (2) they are changing faster than they have changed in the past, (3) changes will continue to rapidly occur as we progress into the twenty-first century, and (4) sensitivity to these changes is imperative and their implications for colleges and universities must be anticipated.

Why *should* someone read a book about quality in higher education? Those involved in higher education believe that quality is already being practiced. However, there are at least six factors within higher education which question the assumption that it is quality driven.

First, more than at any previous point in history, the perception of *quality* in higher education is increasingly becoming a problem for many outside the academy. Within higher education a tradition prevails that colleges and universities are the preservers, transmitters, and generators of knowledge and that, except for a few established professions such as law, medicine, the clergy, and more recently the arts and sciences, higher education should not directly relate to the world of business and provide employers with employees. Many members of the academy—perhaps most members—still hold this view.

This view, however, conflicts with the opinions held by some involved in higher education. At the most basic level there is disagreement over the priorities assigned by the academy to the traditional triad of teaching, research, and service. At a recent conference, Elaine Hairston, chancellor of the Ohio Board of Regents, summarized the situation as, "We are buying instruction and higher education is selling research."[1] Chancellor Hairston's assessment is shared by the governing bodies of other state higher educational systems and many private institutions.

The general public also seems to have greater expectations for the job-related value of higher education than is recognized in the traditional view. According to policy analyst Daniel Yankelovich, 88 percent of the people feel that "a high school diploma is no longer enough to qualify for a well-paying job," and 73 percent "agree that having a college degree is very important to getting a job or advancing in one's career."[2]

Commenting on the relationship between the products of colleges and universities and the expectations of employers, Seymour[3] concludes, "The disconnect is real between what our colleges and universities produce in terms of learning and outcomes in their graduates and what industry requires. And the longer we refuse to address the gap, like the budget deficit, the more drag it will be on our economy and global competitiveness."

Boards of regents and/or trustees, students, parents, employers, and the general public are the constituents who fund higher education. If there are disagreements between them and the academy concerning the role of higher education, then it is likely that disagreements also exist as to whether institutions of higher education are pursuing and achieving quality. (For additional information, see Abstract 1.1 at the end of this chapter.)

Second, economic conditions in the United States have generated increasing concern about career opportunities and economic well-being. According to Yankelovich, the historical trend of increasing economic well-being has been reversed. "Today we are a people who are living at the 1965 level, in terms of real wages."[4]

Third, the general public is increasingly concerned about access to higher education as a means toward employment and economic security. Real concerns exist about the ability to pay for a college education. During the past decade, student tuition and other costs associated with higher education have increased substantially. The response of the public is pessimism about the potential access to higher education in the face of an increased conviction that a college education is a critical means to employment and economic security. Yankelovich[5] summarizes his findings in this area:

> Eighty-seven (87) percent feel that college costs are rising at a rate that will put college out of reach of most people. Seventy-nine (79) percent feel that it is getting harder for average families to provide a college education for their kids. Only 25 percent say that most people can afford to pay for college education. And pessimistically, 89 percent believe that ten years from now, it will be even more difficult to afford college....It will become more of a need, but also more out of reach.

Fourth, students, parents, legislators, and employers have increasing expectations of higher education and are willing to commit funds to evaluate the performance of colleges and universities in light of these expectations. Many believe that these constituent groups are bringing an educated consumer orientation to their assessment of higher education. While the following statement focuses on students, it is applicable to all constituent groups.

> Today's students expect of colleges and universities what they demand elsewhere: better service, lower costs, higher quality, and a mix of products that satisfy their own sense of what a good education ought to provide. They want the enterprises that serve them to be efficient—not for efficiency's sake, but because efficiency promotes the flexibility and adaptability they seek in the marketplace.[6]

At a minimum, the consumer orientation has helped support the *outcome assessment* movement in higher education, and this development is expected to continue during the coming decade.

A fifth factor is a decrease in the levels of esteem and trust associated with institutions of higher education. As summarized by Chaffee and Sherr:[7]

> Every U.S. college or university is for quality. Every accreditation self-study documents quality. Every set of admission requirements promotes it. Every faculty member grades for it. Every promotion and tenure committee screens for it. Everyone is for quality....Yet the last decade has brought unprecedented public demand for higher quality in colleges and universities....External agencies and the public have lost confidence: We might be "for" quality, but in many eyes we do not "do" quality.

A more dramatic assessment was recently made by Cornelius Pings, provost of the University of Southern California, who said that in the current situation universities "are at best regarded with indifference, and at worst looked upon with disdain and contempt."[8]

The reasons for this loss of confidence are complex. In part, colleges and universities suffer from the general decrease in trust in all social institutions which occurred during the liberal 1960s and 1970s and the conservative 1980s. It is also aided by several academics who wrote books attacking higher education and their faculty colleagues. Whatever the reasons, many groups inside and outside the academy believe that the primary focus of most colleges and universities is to protect disciplines and the culture of the academy, often to a fault. The result is a loss of confidence, which many argue is not deserved. Whatever the reasons, the loss of confidence is real and seems likely to continue over the coming decade. One need only look at the growth in "accountability" legislation recently passed in several states to affirm that the rules—the guidelines of the game—have changed.

The sixth and final factor in questioning the assumption of quality is the decrease in funding for higher education during the past decade at both the federal and state levels. Many academics believe that this is a temporary aberration, primarily associated with a short-term drop in the economy, and that funding will be increased in the future. They contend that this short-term decline can be managed with a combination of judicious economizing and vigorous budgetary lobbying until the inevitable recovery occurs.

Others believe that the present economic conditions will not improve and that the current funding problems will not disappear. As stated by Ewell:[9]

> First, we appear to be up against a fundamental structural condition. In growing numbers of states, 80–85 percent of the budget is now tied up in entitlements, court ordered spending, and restrictions of one kind or another; in this context higher education has become the "budget balancer"— the last-in-line piece of discretionary spending remaining after mandatory expenditures are accounted for. A second element of the problem is that taxpayers simply will not support further increases, however worthy the cause. This was demonstrated convincingly by a series of bleak state electoral results last November. These conditions, together with more general trends in the economy, suggest strongly that higher education will need to do what it does for less for the foreseeable future.

For additional information, see Abstract 1.2 at the end of this chapter.

TOTAL QUALITY AS AN OPPORTUNITY

The Chinese symbol for crisis combines the characters for *threat* and *opportunity*. If the preceding analysis of the environmental conditions impinging upon higher education is accurate, then there is no questioning the conclusion that the academy is facing challenges of an unprecedented nature and scope. The question to be asked instead is whether these challenges will be viewed as a threat or an opportunity. Colleges and universities defining their worlds in terms of a threat may engage in defensive actions, focusing on preservation of the past. In contrast, institutions defining their worlds in terms of an opportunity focus on the future, carrying forward the best of the past and bringing the two together in innovative activities.

The principles and practices associated with total quality provide a framework consistent with the best existing practices in higher education, but one that allows a positive response to conditions in the environment, viewing them as opportunities, not as threats.

To help understand total quality, a summary of the major concepts and principles of total quality and continuous improvement is provided in Table 1.1. The first column presents the House of Quality (Figure 1.1), the framework around which this book is organized.[10] The roof or superstructure consists of three subsystems: the management, social, and technical subsystems of the organization, within which the actual work of any organization takes place. Support for the superstructure is provided by four pillars of quality: customer satisfaction (meeting needs and expectations), continuous improvement, managing with facts, and respect for people. This is more fully described in Chapter 3.

The second column in Table 1.1 presents the seven categories and core values and concepts of the Malcolm Baldrige National Quality Award. The Baldrige criteria are included in this book for three reasons. First, the seven criteria are sound, providing a reliable basis for organizational self-assessment. Second, the award and its criteria are well known in the manufacturing, service, and small business sectors. Knowledge and use of the criteria would enhance communication between these sectors and the academy. Third, some version of the Baldrige Quality Award, such as presented in Chapter 3, may be expanded to include all levels of education in the near future. Thus, colleges and universities familiar with the Baldrige criteria will have greater opportunity to participate in the competition if they so desire.

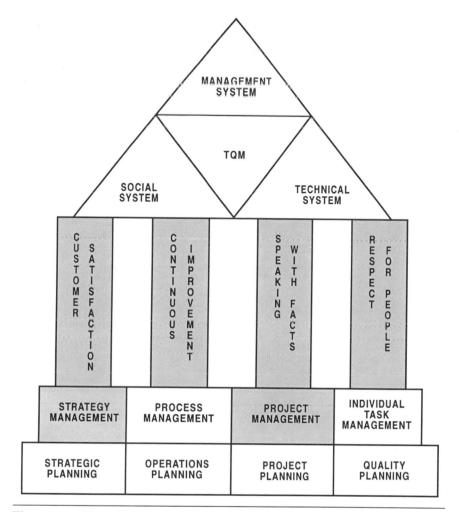

Figure 1.1 House of Quality.

The third column in Table 1.1 presents an abridged listing of the principles and concepts developed by W. Edwards Deming; a complete listing, edited for applicability to higher education, is presented in Chapter 3. Deming's beliefs are included for two reasons. First, Deming was an early practitioner of total quality, and much of the work in the field is directly or indirectly influenced by his ideas. Second, they are provocative; his Fourteen Principles stimulate exploration of their implications for individual institutions. (For additional information, see Abstract 1.3 at the end of this chapter.)

Table 1.1 A Comparison of the House of Quality with the Baldrige Categories and Deming Principles

House of Quality[a]	Baldrige Categories[b]	Deming Principles[c]
THE ROOF		
Management system	1 Leadership	1 Create constancy of purpose
1 Systems, process	3 Strategic quality planning	2 Adopt the new philosophy
2 Leadership	* Long-range planning	7 Institute leadership
3 Strategy		
4 Mission, vision, values		
Social system	* Employee development	* Western style of management must change
1 Structure	* Partnership development	* Transformation can only be accomplished by people, not hardware
2 Culture, climate	* Responsibility and citizenship	
3 Teams		
4 Values, norms		
5 Relations		
Technical system (operations?)	5 Management of process quality	9 Break down departmental barriers
1 Work plans	* Fast response	
2 Job descriptions	* Design quality	
3 Problem-solving tools		
4 Work processes		
5 Decision making		
6 Tools and job aids		

THE PILLARS

Customer satisfaction	7 Customer focus and satisfaction		* Aim quality at the needs of the consumer, present and future
Continuous improvement	2 Information and analysis 5 Management of process quality 6 Quality and operational results		3 Cease dependence on mass inspection 4 End price tag wars 5 Improve the system constantly
Speak with facts	2 Information and analysis * Management by fact		* In God we trust, all others bring facts
Respect for people	4 Human resource development and management * Employee participation and development		14 Involve everyone in the transformational process 6 Institute training on the job 8 Drive out fear 10 Eliminate slogans and targets 11 Eliminate numerical quotas 12 Remove barriers to workman's pride 13 Education and retraining

a Voehl, Frank (1992). *The House of Total Quality.* Coral Springs, Fla.: Strategy Associates.
b 1993 Award Criteria, Malcolm Baldrige National Quality Award, Milwaukee: American Society for Quality Control.
c Walton, Mary (1986). *The Deming Management Method.* New York: G. P. Putnam's Sons.

In-depth analysis of Table 1.1 reveals many points at which the principles and concepts of total quality are compatible with the best traditions and practices of higher education. The various guidelines and instruments presented in this book are provided to encourage similar individual analysis. There are, however, two points that must be emphasized.

First, the premise here is that the underlying philosophy, values, and norms reflected in total quality and continuous improvement are appropriate to higher education. These include (1) an emphasis on service; (2) anticipating and meeting the needs and expectations of the constituents; (3) recognizing and improving transformation processes and systems; (4) implementing teamwork and collaboration; (5) instituting management based on leadership, knowledge-based decisions, and involvement; (6) solving problems based on systematic identification of facts and the use of feedback systems and statistical methods or tools; and (7) implementing a genuine respect for and development of human resources—the people who work in colleges and universities.

Second, the emphasis placed on quality-based systems and processes provides a framework for integrated institutional decision making and problem solving. The basic elements in an open systems model of an organization are (1) recognition that all organizations operate in an environment that can influence the success or failure of the organization, (2) an identified organizational mission (purpose), and (3) a transforming process that involves *inputs* to the organization from the external environment, *throughputs* or the actual techniques (methods) used to transform (add value to) the inputs, and *outputs* represented by the product and/or service provided to members of the external environment.

Figure 1.2 presents an open systems model of the core function of higher education—student learning. Student learning has been selected as the target issue for two reasons. First, it is the core function of colleges and universities and should be emphasized in all discussions of quality and quality assurance. Second, adapting the total quality approach to other functions of higher education will stem from the conviction that it can and should be applied to student learning.

As illustrated in Figure 1.2, the two traditional approaches to assuring quality in higher education are accreditation and outcome assessment. Accreditation focuses on the inputs of the institution, such as student achievement, faculty degrees, facilities, and physical resources (e.g., the number of library holdings). The basic assumption of

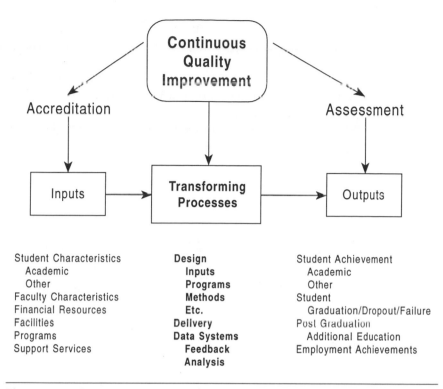

Figure 1.2 Continuous Quality Improvement: Integrating Quality Assurance in Higher Education.

this approach is that if high-quality inputs exist, high-quality outputs will result. This approach provides data on what goes into the system, but very little data on what happens in the system and what comes out of it.

Dissatisfaction with the focus on inputs led to the emergence of the outcome assessment movement, which emphasizes the importance of evaluating the outputs of higher education, such as student achievement, graduation, and employment. To the degree that it has been adopted by colleges and universities, the outcome assessment movement has made valuable contributions to institutions, their students, and the general public. Unfortunately, knowledge of educational outputs alone does not provide a basis for determining problems in the teaching–learning process. Assessment advocates recognize the importance of understanding the teaching–learning process, but this dimension has not received significant attention in most assessment activities. The net result has been a disjointed approach to quality assurance that essentially ignores the amorphous nature of what happens to students in the teaching–learning process.

The open systems approach of total quality improvement provides a means for developing an integrated quality assurance system for higher education. It emphasizes the need for quality at all three stages: inputs, transforming processes, and outputs. Such determinations are made from knowledge of the teaching–learning process.

SOME CAVEATS

It is important to provide a few cautions for those who attempt to implement total quality in all or part of their college or university. An initial general comment is that it is not easy to accomplish. This is a truism for any organization, because successful total quality and continuous improvement efforts require change over a fairly long time, e.g., three to five years. Some factors may make it even more difficult to successfully carry out these efforts in colleges and universities, particularly in those activities involving the academic areas. Three factors require further emphasis.

First, the organizational structure of colleges and universities presents difficulties in terms of developing a focused institution-wide total quality effort. This structural impediment includes at least three dimensions:

1. The *"dual" organizational structure* of colleges and universities (i.e., the division between administrative and academic functions).   These distinctions often lead to the creation of parallel worlds rather than a mutually supporting system, making it difficult to develop a shared sense of mission and vision throughout the institution. This separation is clearly unfortunate because it has become increasingly clear that the *total* quality of life has implications for the major mission of all colleges or universities—the academic performance and accomplishments of students.

2. *Intensive divisionalization.*   This encourages identification with subdivisions rather than the total institution. This centrifugal tendency is most obvious among faculties where loyalty to the discipline and/or department usually takes precedence over

loyalty to the college or school, not to mention the entire university. This is an important feature of total quality, which emphasizes interdepartmental, interdisciplinary, and even system-wide collaboration on problems and projects.

3. *Fragmented leadership.* This primarily involves the role of the college or university president. Often, there is a division of responsibility, with the president focusing on external issues and abdicating a leadership role within the institution. This has an adverse impact on organizational reform. Without active presidential support it is difficult to initiate and successfully implement an institution-wide total quality program.

For additional information, see Abstract 1.4 at the end of this chapter.

The second caveat addresses the culture of institutions of higher education. Various values, practices, and policies present conditions that may hinder the accomplishment of total quality and continuous improvement efforts. These cultural impediments include at least six beliefs, or "myths," prevalent in most colleges and universities:

1. *Difference and exemption.* As discussed earlier, this theory involves the belief that colleges and universities are different from other social institutions and are (or should be) exempt from the assessment and evaluation criteria applied to other institutions. They believe that as purveyors of knowledge, they already practice quality. This makes it difficult to initiate self-analysis and to appreciate and respond to the views of individuals and groups outside the academy, including those who provide the resources on which it operates. In fact, at the extreme, outside efforts to influence colleges and universities are viewed as unwelcome intrusions.

2. *Uniqueness* (i.e., the tendency for each college or university to view itself as unique or distinct). The result is that generalizations about the state of proposed changes to higher education either cannot be made or, if made, are perceived as applicable to a particular institution. This makes it difficult to develop the sense of urgency needed to initiate any change.

3. *Individualism versus the team.* Total quality improvement places great emphasis on teams and increases in productivity due to the synergistic effects generated by well-functioning teams. The general tendency of institutions of higher learning, however, is

to place emphasis on the accomplishments of the isolated individual rather than on team efforts. On the academic side this is characterized by a reward system which gives more credit to scholarly products that are the work of a single individual rather than the result of collaborative efforts. In both the academic and administrative arenas, promotions and salary increases are based on individual rather than group performance and productivity.

4. *The system versus the individual.* Total quality improvement focuses attention on the system (work processes) as the primary cause of problems. In fact, it stresses that as much as 85 percent of the problems in any organization are due to shortcomings in the system, as opposed to individual error. In colleges and universities, however, the emphasis may be reversed, i.e., problems are attributed to the behavior (mistakes) of individuals rather than the inadequacies of the system. For example, students do not perform well because they are not intellectually qualified, are not adequately prepared, or do not apply themselves. All these reasons may be true, but it is also possible that the students do not perform well because the teaching–learning environment (the instructional system) does not meet their needs.

5. *Continuous improvement.* All processes can and should be improved. This principle of total quality improvement appears to conflict with the belief systems of most colleges and universities. Within the academy the prevalent belief is that quality has been achieved and is being practiced. If this is the case, then there is no need to pursue quality and engage in efforts toward total quality improvement.

6. *Participation already exists.* A fundamental principle of total quality improvement is emphasis on respect for people and their involvement in the decisions relevant to their work. Members of the higher education community believe that because of a "culture of collegiality," high levels of participation already exist within the institution. Given this belief, in most institutions there is no perceived need to change the way and degree to which people are involved in the critical institutional decision-making processes. High levels of involvement may characterize some colleges or universities, but in most involvement in making substantive decisions is too often a process of superficial consensus gathering, with minimal weight given to the collective opinion.

The third caveat may best be designated as a linguistic factor. Some key words or phrases identified with total quality and continuous improvement do not always resonate well with members of the higher education community. These include:

1. *Customer and customer satisfaction.* The driving force for all quality improvement efforts is an emphasis on customers and meeting their needs and expectations. Resistance to these terms comes from many sources within higher education. First, many individuals find the term *customer* too commercial and simplistic to describe the relationship between students and the institution. Second, for many individuals the phrase *customer satisfaction* seems to imply a severely limited evaluation criterion and limited recognition of the knowledge of student needs vested in the discipline and institution. While neither may actually be the case, the concern is real. This issue is discussed further in Chapter 3.

2. *Control and management.* In higher education circles the terms *control* and/or *management* often generate opposition to any organizational improvement efforts. This stems from a tendency to assume that someone or something will limit an operation, process, or person. No one wants to be controlled or managed! In total quality improvement, however, the emphasis is on identifying and doing whatever is necessary to achieve what *we* want the organization to do. It is a team-centered control and management of the process in order to achieve the desired outcomes. This issue is discussed further in Chapter 3.

3. *Minimize variation, encourage standardization.* These phrases, which are a part of the language of statistical process control, also generate concern in segments of the higher education community. For some, they seem to imply limits on creativity and an overwhelming drive toward standardization and uniformity. In total quality improvement, however, they refer to deviations from desired and/or planned goals. Thus, it is quite possible to plan for positive variations within desired outcomes.

In conclusion, a strong relationship exists between the principles of total quality improvement and the best traditions and desired practices of higher education. The authors strongly believe that most colleges and universities are not presently operating at their best. The primary causes of ineffectiveness are based within the systems—the culture and the managerial and leadership styles of the administrators, beginning with the executive staff. The potential for change exists, and the degree of change required is dependent upon the existing incompatibilities with the principles of total quality improvement. These incompatibilities may be so severe that a radical transformation may be required. The intent of this book is to help sensitize individuals to these issues so as to take the initiative to develop total quality and continuous improvement efforts. (For additional information, see Abstract 1.5 at the end of this chapter.)

ENDNOTES

1. AAHE (1993). *Statewide Leadership of CQI Higher Education.* Session 36, Chicago: American Association for Higher Education.
2. Edgerton, Russ (1993). "The New Public Mood and What It Means to Higher Education." *AAHE Bulletin*, Vol. 45, No. 10 (June), p. 7.
3. Seymour, Daniel (1993). *On Q: Causing Quality in Higher Education.* New York: Macmillan, p. 25.
4. Edgerton, Russ (1993). "The New Public Mood and What It Means to Higher Education." *AAHE Bulletin*, Vol. 45, No. 10 (June), p. 5.
5. Edgerton, Russ (1993). "The New Public Mood and What It Means to Higher Education." *AAHE Bulletin*, Vol. 45, No. 10 (June), p. 7.
6. Zemsky, Robert, Massy, William, and Oedel, Penney (1993). "On Reversing the Ratchet." *Change*, Vol. 25, No. 3 (May–June), p. 56.
7. Chaffee, Ellen and Sherr, Lawrence (1992). *Quality: Transforming Postsecondary Education.* ASHE–ERIC Higher Education Report #3, p. 1.
8. McWilliam, Gary (1991). "Smaller Pie for Research." *Business Week*, May 20, 1991.
9. Ewell, Peter (1993). "Total Quality and Academic Practice." *Change*, Vol. 25, No. 3 (May–June), p. 50.
10. Voehl, Frank (1992). *Total Quality: Principles and Practices within Organizations.* Coral Springs, Fla.: Strategy Associates, pp. I, 18.
11. Figure 1.1 ©1992 Strategy Associates, Inc.

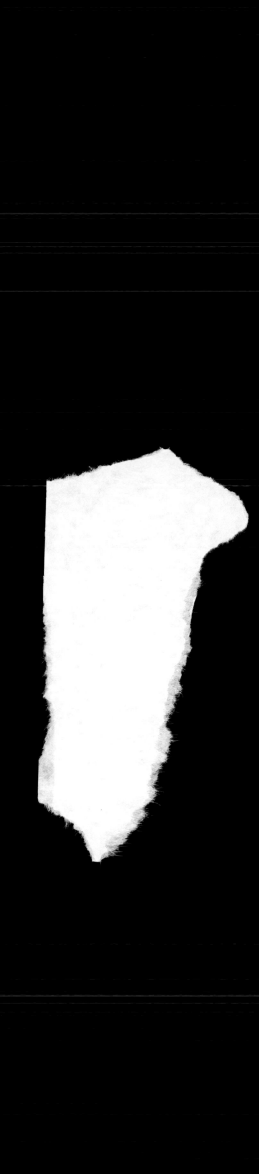

The third caveat may best be designated as a linguistic factor. Some key words or phrases identified with total quality and continuous improvement do not always resonate well with members of the higher education community. These include:

1. *Customer and customer satisfaction.* The driving force for all quality improvement efforts is an emphasis on customers and meeting their needs and expectations. Resistance to these terms comes from many sources within higher education. First, many individuals find the term *customer* too commercial and simplistic to describe the relationship between students and the institution. Second, for many individuals the phrase *customer satisfaction* seems to imply a severely limited evaluation criterion and limited recognition of the knowledge of student needs vested in the discipline and institution. While neither may actually be the case, the concern is real. This issue is discussed further in Chapter 3.

2. *Control and management.* In higher education circles the terms *control* and/or *management* often generate opposition to any organizational improvement efforts. This stems from a tendency to assume that someone or something will limit an operation, process, or person. No one wants to be controlled or managed! In total quality improvement, however, the emphasis is on identifying and doing whatever is necessary to achieve what *we* want the organization to do. It is a team-centered control and management of the process in order to achieve the desired outcomes. This issue is discussed further in Chapter 3.

3. *Minimize variation, encourage standardization.* These phrases, which are a part of the language of statistical process control, also generate concern in segments of the higher education community. For some, they seem to imply limits on creativity and an overwhelming drive toward standardization and uniformity. In total quality improvement, however, they refer to deviations from desired and/or planned goals. Thus, it is quite possible to plan for positive variations within desired outcomes.

In conclusion, a strong relationship exists between the principles of total quality improvement and the best traditions and desired practices of higher education. The authors strongly believe that most colleges and universities are not presently operating at their best. The primary causes of ineffectiveness are based within the systems—the culture and the managerial and leadership styles of the administrators, beginning with the executive staff. The potential for change exists, and the degree of change required is dependent upon the existing incompatibilities with the principles of total quality improvement. These incompatibilities may be so severe that a radical transformation may be required. The intent of this book is to help sensitize individuals to these issues so as to take the initiative to develop total quality and continuous improvement efforts. (For additional information, see Abstract 1.5 at the end of this chapter.)

ENDNOTES

1. AAHE (1993). *Statewide Leadership of CQI Higher Education.* Session 36, Chicago: American Association for Higher Education.
2. Edgerton, Russ (1993). "The New Public Mood and What It Means to Higher Education." *AAHE Bulletin*, Vol. 45, No. 10 (June), p. 7.
3. Seymour, Daniel (1993). *On Q: Causing Quality in Higher Education.* New York: Macmillan, p. 25.
4. Edgerton, Russ (1993). "The New Public Mood and What It Means to Higher Education." *AAHE Bulletin*, Vol. 45, No. 10 (June), p. 5.
5. Edgerton, Russ (1993). "The New Public Mood and What It Means to Higher Education." *AAHE Bulletin*, Vol. 45, No. 10 (June), p. 7.
6. Zemsky, Robert, Massy, William, and Oedel, Penney (1993). "On Reversing the Ratchet." *Change*, Vol. 25, No. 3 (May–June), p. 56.
7. Chaffee, Ellen and Sherr, Lawrence (1992). *Quality: Transforming Postsecondary Education.* ASHE–ERIC Higher Education Report #3, p. 1.
8. McWilliam, Gary (1991). "Smaller Pie for Research." *Business Week*, May 20, 1991.
9. Ewell, Peter (1993). "Total Quality and Academic Practice." *Change*, Vol. 25, No. 3 (May–June), p. 50.
10. Voehl, Frank (1992). *Total Quality: Principles and Practices within Organizations.* Coral Springs, Fla.: Strategy Associates, pp. I, 18.
11. Figure 1.1 ©1992 Strategy Associates, Inc.

INSTITUTIONS OF HIGHER LEARNING INVOLVED IN TOTAL QUALITY

The following is a list of over 200 institutions of higher learning that are reported to be involved in total quality, as reported in the October 1992 issue of *Quality Progress*. From 1991 to 1992, the number has grown from 92 to 220 and is expected to increase substantially during 1993 as well. See Abstract 1.5 for further information.

Colleges and Universities

Acadia University
Arizona State University
Auburn University
Augusta College
Babson College
Baylor University
Belmont University
Bismarck State College
Bradley University
Brigham Young University
California State Polytechnic University
California State University–Dominguez Hills
California State University–Long Beach
California State University–Sacramento
Central Connecticut State University
Clemson University
Cleveland State University
Colorado State University
Columbia University
Dallas Baptist University
Dickinson State University
Dominican College
Drake Business School
Drexel University
East Tennessee State University
Eastern Illinois University
Eastern Kentucky University
Eastern Michigan University
Ferris State University
Florida State University
Fordham University
George Washington University
Georgia Southern University
Georgia State University

Grove City College
Harvard University
Illinois Institute of Technology
Jacksonville State University
John Carroll University
Kansas Newman College
Kansas State University
Keller Graduate School of Management
Lamar University
Loyola University of Chicago
Mankato State University
Marian College
Marietta College
Marymount University
Mayville State University
McNeese State University
Metropolitan State College of Denver
Mid-America Nazarene College
Middle Tennessee State University
Milwaukee School of Engineering
Minot State University
North Carolina State University
North Dakota State University
Northern Illinois University
Northwest Missouri State University
Northwestern University
Oakland University
Ohio State University
Oregon State University
Pennsylvania State University
Portland State University
Purdue University
Purdue University–North Central
Rider College

Colleges and Universities (continued)

Rochester Institute of Technology
Roger Williams University
Rose-Hulman Institute of Technology
Rutgers University–Camden
Rutgers University–New Brunswick
St. Ambrose University
St. Cloud State University
St. John Fisher College
St. Michael's College
Samford University
San Jose State University
Southern College of Technology
State University College–Buffalo
State University of New York–Binghamton
State University of New York–Buffalo
Syracuse University
Tampa College
Temple University
Texas A&I University
Tri-State University
Union College
Universidad de Monterrey
University of Alabama–Birmingham
University of Alabama–Tuscaloosa
University of Alaska–Fairbanks
University of Arizona
University of Arkansas
University of Central Florida
University of Chicago
University of Cincinnati
University of Colorado
University of Hartford
University of Hawaii
University of Idaho-Idaho Falls
University of Idaho–Moscow
University of Illinois–Chicago
University of Illinois–Urbana/Champaign
University of Iowa
University of Kansas
University of Kentucky
University of Maryland

University of Maryland University College
University of Massachusetts–Amherst
University of Massachusetts–Boston
University of Massachusetts–Dartmouth
University of Massachusetts–Lowell
University of Miami
University of Michigan
University of Minnesota
University of Mississippi
University of Missouri–Kansas City
University of North Carolina–Chapel Hill
University of North Dakota–Grand Forks
University of North Dakota–Williston
University of North Texas
University of Pennsylvania
University of Phoenix
University of Phoenix–Southern California
University of Pittsburgh
University of Puerto Rico
University of Rochester
University of Scranton
University of the South
University of South Carolina–Aiken
University of South Carolina–Columbia
University of South Carolina–Spartanburg
University of Southern Colorado
University of Southern Maine
University of Tennessee–Chattanooga
University of Tennessee–Knoxville
University of Tennessee–Tullahoma
University of Texas–Austin
University of Vermont
University of Virginia
University of Washington
University of West Florida
University of Wisconsin–Madison

Colleges and Universities (continued)

University of Wisconsin–Milwaukee
University of Wisconsin–Stout
University of Wisconsin–Whitewater
University of Wyoming
Valley City State University
Vanderbilt University
Virginia Commonwealth University
Wayne State University

West Virginia University
Western Carolina University
Western New England College
Wichita State University
Winona State University
Worcester Polytechnic Institute
Xavier University

Community Colleges

Aims Community College
American River College
Austin Community College
Brazosport College
Broome Community College
Burlington County College
Catawba Valley Community College
Cagep de Jonquiere
Central Carolina Community College
Cincinnati Technical College
Colorado Technical College
Columbia State Community College
Community College of Vermont
DeAnza College
Delaware County Community College
Durham College
El Camino College
Fox Valley Technical College
Gateway Community College
Georgia Stone Technical Center
Glendale Community College
Grand Rapids Community College
Gwinnett Technical Institute
Hawkeye Institute of Technology
Jackson Community College
Lamar Community College
Lansing Community College
Lima Technical College
Lorain County Community College
Macomb Community College
Mid-State Technical College
Milwaukee Area Technical College
Mohawk College

Monroe Community College
Moraine Park Technical College
Northeast State Technical Community
  College
Northern Essex Community College
Okaloosa–Walton Community College
Owens Technical College
Palomar College
Pellissippi State Technical Community
  College
Pennsylvania College of Technology
Quinsigamond Community College
Rock Valley College
St. Clair County Community College
St. Louis Community College–
  Florissant Valley
Savannah Technical Institute
Sir Sandford Flemming College
South Seattle Community College
Spokane Community College
Suffolk County Community College-
  Technicenter
Triton College
Tulsa Junior College
Waterbury State Technical College
Waukesha County Technical College
West Shore Community College
Western Piedmont Community
  College
Western Wisconsin Technical College
Wisconsin Indianhead Technical
  College
Yakima Valley Community College

ABSTRACTS

ABSTRACT 1.1
THE MISSING ELEMENT IN HIGHER EDUCATION

Matthews, William E.
Journal for Quality Participation (QCJ), Vol. 16, Issue 1, Jan./Feb. 1993, pp. 102–108

The author presents a good basic view of why total quality is needed in the higher education field. His seven-step model is useful but falls short in not identifying the "customer" as one of the seven steps. The danger of teaching one thing and doing another is valid and needs to be addressed by university presidents. His section on "Barriers to Implementing TQM" is important. Matthews argues that the growing demand that U.S. industry become more competitive in world markets has led to pressure on academia to provide appropriate educational direction and support. Academia and total quality management meet in four basic areas: curriculum, operations, overall direction of the institution, and teaching and research. Because there seem to be many barriers to the utilization of total quality management in these areas, there is a very real danger of academia teaching one set of values and adopting a different set for itself.

In order to assume a real commitment to total quality management, academic institutions must follow seven steps: (1) identify the institution's primary stakeholders, (2) develop a specific competitive quality-based mission, (3) establish internal measures for quality and excellence in specific and identified areas, (4) determine who has to commit to the chosen standards, (5) establish motivation for those unwilling to commit to quality and excellence, (6) form quality progress teams, and (7) report, recognize, and reward success.

The author leaves us with a final thought. Academia has tackled the easy elements associated with the utilization of total quality management within its own walls. It is far easier to add courses to a curriculum or solve specific operational problems than it is to influence the direction of the institution as a whole or the behaviors of individuals.

ABSTRACT 1.2
DEVELOPING THE NEXT GENERATION OF
QUALITY LEADERS

Artzt, Edwin
Quality Progress (QPR), Vol. 25, Issue 10, Oct. 1992, pp. 25–27

The author wrote this article in 1992 in his dual role as Chairman of the Board of Procter & Gamble and Chairman of National Quality Month in October 1992. His opening remarks are startling: "I'm convinced that total quality is a survival issue for American business." Accordingly, he argues that total quality must be embraced so completely in the United States that it becomes an integral part of the way business is conducted, children are educated, and government is run. Partnerships between business and education can be a powerful catalyst in developing the next generation of quality leaders. Under his guidance, Procter & Gamble is involved in several of these partnerships, and its experience demonstrates to Artzt the significant benefits to all parties. Accordingly, a Leadership Steering Committee was formed to identify and recommend key objectives necessary to implement teaching total quality in college classrooms and researching and practicing it on college campuses. Artzt argues that a student's education is enhanced by meaningful field experience, while the schools and faculties have access to real-time business information.

He also speaks of bringing quality leaders together to forge strategic links with higher education. He offers many examples of the partnerships that are emerging and summarizes the framework for a Leadership Steering Committee working council. It needs to be understood that the partnering concept advocated by Artzt sounds good on paper but in practice is difficult to implement. In the 1980s, Florida Power & Light helped establish a "quality institute" at the University of Miami but never achieved the expected benefits for its investment. Others have had mixed success. The Center for Quality Management in Cambridge, Massachusetts is an outgrowth of a venture in this area between seven businesses and MIT and is one of the notable success stories.

Overall, this article is definitely worth reading. For additional information on the initiatives discussed or for reprints of the findings and recommendations of the Leadership Steering Committee and its working councils, contact Jean Kinney, Associate Director, Corporate Quality, Procter & Gamble, 2 Procter & Gamble Plaza, Cincinnati, OH 45202.

ABSTRACT 1.3
TOTAL QUALITY EDUCATION?

Bonser, Charles F.
Public Administration Review (PAR), Vol. 52, Issue 5, Sep./Oct. 1992, pp. 504–512

Dr. Bonser has over twenty years of senior administration experience at Indiana University. His background description of the condition of American universities following World War II is informative and excellent reading. It contains a concise description of the seven forces influencing the culture shift in society and what universities can learn from other organizations and settings. While his section on implementing Deming's Fourteen Principles as applied to education is satisfactory, his analysis of Constancy of Purpose as applied to the selection of a university president is noteworthy. He argues that the environmental situation in which American universities now find themselves, coupled with their philosophical–cultural approach to provision of their services, is making them less and less relevant to the needs of society and increasingly ineffective in accomplishing the missions for which they were created and have been supported.

Bonser goes on to answer the question he raised at the outset—higher education administrators *can* meet the new challenges of the 1990s *if* they adopt the total quality leadership (TQL) approach which has been so successful in other types of organizations. The principles of TQL, according to the teachings of Dr. W. Edwards Deming, offer what is essentially an integrated, internally consistent philosophy of management and leadership. Bonser concludes that although not all of Deming's principles may be directly applicable to higher education, a strong case can be made that enough of them are relevant. He argues that the total quality approach can be a vital component in the construction of a new philosophy by which higher education leadership can guide American institutions into the next century. Although the author provides a useful introduction and background for total quality in higher education, his article is noticeably lacking in how to accomplish it. Like Deming, he states why it is important, but the rest is left to individual analysis. Notes and references are provided.

ABSTRACT 1.4
THE NEW BOUNDARIES OF THE "BOUNDARYLESS" COMPANY

Hirschhorn, Larry; Gilmore, Thomas
Harvard Business Review (HBR), Vol. 70, Issue 3, May/June 1992, pp. 104–115

The opening lines of the first two paragraphs clearly set the stage for this interesting and thought-provoking article on the organizational boundaries which are meant to be defined in the eyes of the beholder: the institutional leaders and support staff. "In an economy founded on innovation and change, one of the premier challenges of management is to design more flexible organizations. For many executives, a single metaphor has come to embody this managerial challenge and to capture the kind of organization they want to create: the corporation without boundaries." From this vision of Jack Welch to the "data feelings" of the alert manager, a wide variety of challenging topics are covered: (1) challenges of flexible work; (2) remapping organizational boundaries of authority, tasks, politics, and identity; (3) the authority vacuum; and (4) downsizing with dignity.

The authors point out, however, that managers should not assume that boundaries may be eliminated altogether. Once the traditional boundaries of hierarchy, function, and geography disappear, a new set of boundaries become important and must be addressed. These new boundaries are more psychological than organizational; instead of being reflected in the structure of a company, they must be enacted over and over again in a manager's *relationships* with superiors, subordinates, and peers. The four new important boundaries are the authority boundary, task boundary, political boundary, and identity boundary. The article ends with a plea for getting started and is enhanced by an interesting mini-study on "The Team that Failed." A shortcoming is that references are not provided.

ABSTRACT 1.5
A HIGHER DEGREE OF QUALITY

Axland, Suzanne
Quality Progress (QPR), Vol. 25, Issue 10, Oct. 1992, pp. 33–38, 41–61

The opening statement says it all: "All at once it's like monitoring the flurry of swirling gasses and exploding matter during our earth's creation and like watching grass grow." Each year, *Quality Progress* performs a survey to determine how many universities and community colleges are both implementing and offering total quality principles, tools, and education. The explosion in interest, from 92 participants in 1991 to 220 in 1992, tells the story. The survey shows that an increasing number of educators are attending total quality management (TQM) conferences, seminars, and workshops, readings books by quality leaders, and becoming involved in state and community quality initiatives. State awards modeled after the Malcolm Baldrige National Quality Award are also driving quality in education.

The survey also shows that at least 65 districts and schools nationally are past their first year of awareness and actively implementing TQM principles and tools. School districts experiencing successful results in their TQM initiatives share the following attributes: visible leadership and a clearly articulated mission, a knowledge of customer groups and their needs, and a focus on process improvements. An alphabetical listing of colleges and universities is in matrix format and includes courses offered in engineering technology, total quality management, quality control, statistics, quality-related minor, and quality-related degree offerings for full-time students. The list is augmented by a list that provides the contact person for each school, complete with address and phone number. The American Society for Quality Control (ASQC) will continue to publish annual updates in the October issue of *Quality Progress*. In an interview given by Charles Aubrey II, ASQC president, he declared that one of his five strategic objectives was to "provide focus and leadership to educational initiatives in higher education." Can the *Academic Journal on Total Quality* be far away?

ARTICLES

APPLYING TQM PRINCIPLES IN THE CLASSROOM*

Robert S. Winter

About four years ago I was given my first undergraduate teaching assignment. I was going to teach future and current teachers about the use of computers. I faced this big challenge with limited teaching experience, a course description I found in the catalogue, the good advice of colleagues and several textbooks sent to me by interested publishing companies.

Although I knew very little about the students attending these types of courses, I decided on an approach and philosophy and prepared myself for an interesting semester. On the first day I introduced myself and the course to twenty-eight anxious students and a new phase of my life began.

It did not take too long to find out that my lack of knowledge about the students was a problem. I attempted to describe the computer's operating system, but I was interrupted continuously by students who had had little experience and were not prepared to move at the pace I thought the course required. Other students appeared either uninterested or bored. My lectures seemed to generate limited discussions and I was trapped in a typical model where the students are passively listening and applying methods.

I asked students to submit four exercises resulting from the application of computer software, and I gave a midterm and final exam to evaluate student's knowledge. With this information at hand I believed that I would be able to assess the effort made by each student. The semester ended and although, in general, students did well, I knew that much needed to be done to improve delivery of the course.

Throughout the semester I listened and observed. I knew that the course required active student involvement and more variety during each class session, but it became apparent that I needed to know more about the students.

* Reprinted from *Explorations in Teaching & Learning,* Vol. 3, No. 3, pp. 1, 7, January 1993. From the Academy for the Art of Teaching, Florida International University, Miami.

With that in mind, I began the next semester with a survey to determine the level of computer related knowledge of each student. This information allowed the establishment of teams that would bring together various levels of expertise. Each team was composed of students who already had computer experience as well as students who had none. Those with experience became the mentors and as such were an extension of the teaching process. My presentations moved at a quicker pace since questions were answered at the team level and did not always require that the lecture stop.

The establishment of teams provided a new classroom construct. The members of the teams began to work together and to find a team identity. I encouraged team work by asking each of them to lecture the class on various sections of the text book. I also added a team project ("The classroom of the future") to be presented at the end of the term. My role changed from expert to facilitator and moderator. The class sessions became louder and more active. Students became more involved in the course.

I increased the number of exercises to seven and altered the midterm and final exam to insure that I gathered information on the learning process of the students. The added information was useful in that I could assist students on a preventive basis and redirect their efforts. The changes proved successful. Students learned more and received better grades. My ratings as an instructor also increased.

Although I implemented these changes without TQM in mind, it is no coincidence that at the same time I was reading about this topic and attempting to apply it in a university setting. The principles of customer focus, management by facts, continuous improvement and participatory processes had been applied to the course with a significant degree of success.

I want to make one final observation. Students are not prepared to work in teams. All their experiences in the classroom stress individualism and competitiveness. If the organizations of the future stress team work, we must change our ways and incorporate TQM principles throughout the curriculum.

CHAPTER 2

OVERVIEW of TOTAL QUALITY

Frank Voehl

WHAT IS TOTAL QUALITY

Introduction

During the past five years, there has been an explosion of books in the field of Total Quality. Yet in all of the thousands of books and billions of words written on the subject, there is an absence of three essential ingredients: a good working definition, a comprehensive yet concise history, and a clear and simple systems model of total quality. This overview of total quality is intended to fill this void and provide some interesting reading at the same time.

Understanding the Concept of Total

Total quality is total in three senses: it covers every process, every job, and every person. First, it covers *every process,* rather than just manufacturing or production. Design, construction, R&D, accounting, marketing, repair, and every other function must also be involved in quality improvement. Second, total quality is total in that it covers *every job,* as opposed to only those involved in making the product. Secretaries are expected not to make typing errors, accountants not to make posting errors, and presidents not to make strategic errors. Third, total quality recognizes that *each person* is responsible for the quality of his or her work and for the work of the group.

Total quality also goes beyond the traditional idea of quality, which has been expressed as the degree of conformance to a standard or the product of workmanship. Enlightened organizations accept and apply the concept that quality is the degree of user satisfaction or the fitness of the product for use. In other words, *the customer determines whether or not quality has been achieved in its totality.*

This same measure—total customer satisfaction—applies through-out the entire operation of an organization. Only the outer edges of the company actually have contact with customers in the traditional sense, but each department can treat the other departments as its customer. The main judge of the quality of work is the customer, for if the customer is not satisfied, the work does not have quality. This, coupled with the achievement of corporate objectives, is the bottom line of total quality.

In that regard, it is important, as the Japanese say, to "talk with facts and data." Total quality emphasizes the use of fact-oriented discussions and statistical quality control techniques by everyone in the company. Everyone in the company is exposed to basic quality control ideas and techniques and is expected to use them. Thus, total quality becomes a common language and improves "objective" com-munication.

Total quality also radically alters the nature and basic operating philosophy of organizations. The specialized, separated system devel-oped early in the twentieth century is replaced by a system of *mutual feedback and close interaction of departments.* Engineers, for example, work closely with construction crews and storekeepers to ensure that their knowledge is passed on to workers. Workers, in turn, feed their practical experience directly back to the engineers. The information interchange and shared commitment to product quality is what makes total quality work. Teaching all employees how to apply process control and improvement techniques makes them party to their own destiny and enables them to achieve their fullest potential.

However, total quality is more than an attempt to make better products; it is also a search for better ways to make better products. Adopting the total quality philosophy commits the company to the belief that there is always a better way of doing things, a way to make better use of the company's resources, and a way to be more productive. In this sense, total quality relies heavily upon value analysis as a method of developing better products and operations in order to maximize value to the stakeholder, whether customers, employees, or shareholders.

Total quality also implies a different type of worker and a different attitude toward the worker from management. Under total quality, workers are generalists, rather than specialists. *Both workers and managers are expected to move from job to job, gaining experience in many areas of the company.*

Defining Total Quality

First and foremost, total quality is a set of philosophies by which management systems can direct the efficient achievement of the objectives of the organization to ensure customer satisfaction and maximize stakeholder value. This is accomplished through the continuous improvement of the quality system, which consists of the social system, the technical system, and the management system. Thus, it becomes a way of life for doing business for the entire organization.

Central to the concept is the idea that a company should *design quality into its products,* rather than inspect for it afterward. Only by a devotion to quality throughout the organization can the best possible products be made. Or, as stated by Noriaki Kano, "Quality is too important to be left to inspectors."[1]

Total quality is too important to take second place to any other company goals. Specifically, it should not be subsidiary to profit or productivity. Concentrating on quality will ultimately build and improve both profitability and productivity. Failure to concentrate on quality will quickly erode profits, as customers resent paying for products they perceive as low quality.

The main focus of total quality is on *why*. It goes beyond the *how to* to include the *why to*. It is an attempt to identify the causes of defects in order to eliminate them. It is a continuous cycle of detecting defects, identifying their causes, and improving the process so as to totally eliminate the causes of defects.

Accepting the idea that the customer of a process can be defined as the next process is essential to the real practice of total quality. According to total quality, control charts should be developed for each process, and any errors identified within a process should be disclosed to those involved in the next process in order to raise quality. However, it has been said that it seems contrary to human nature to seek out one's own mistakes. People tend to find the errors caused by others and to neglect their own. Unfortunately, exactly that kind of self-disclosure is what is really needed.[2]

Instead, management too often tends to blame and then take punitive action. This attitude prevails from frontline supervisors all the way up to top management. In effect, we are encouraged to hide the real problems we cause, and instead of looking for the real causes of problems, as required by total quality, we look the other way.

The Concept of Control

The Japanese notion of *control* differs radically from the American; that difference of meaning does much to explain the failure of U.S. management to adopt total quality. In the United States, control connotes someone or something that limits an operation, process, or person. It has overtones of a "police force" in the industrial engineering setting and is often resented.

In Japan, as pointed by the Union of Japanese Scientists and Engineers counselor and Japanese quality control scholar Noriaki Kano, *control* means "all necessary activities for achieving objectives in the long-term, efficiently and economically. Control, therefore, is doing whatever is needed to accomplish what we want to do as an organization."[1]

The difference can be seen very graphically in the Plan, Do, Check, Act (P-D-C-A) continuous improvement chart, which is widely used in Japan to describe the cycle of control (Figure 2.1). Proper control starts

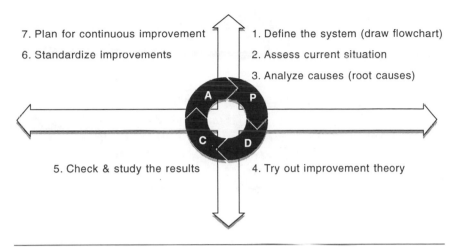

Figure 2.1 P-D-C-A Chart. System improvement is the application of the Plan-Do-Check-Act cycle on an improvement project.

with planning, does what is planned, checks the results, and then applies any necessary corrective action. The cycle represents these four stages—Plan, Do, Check, Act—arranged in circular fashion to show that they are continuous.

In the United States, where specialization and division of labor are emphasized, the cycle is more likely to look like Fight, Plan, Do, Check. Instead of working together to solve any deviations from the plan, time is spent arguing about who is responsible for the deviations.

This sectionalism, as the Japanese refer to it, in the United States hinders collective efforts to improve the way things are done and lowers national productivity and the standard of living. *There need be nothing threatening about control if it is perceived as exercised in order to gather the facts necessary to make plans and take action toward making improvements.*

Total quality includes the control principle as part of the set of philosophies directed toward the efficient achievement of the objectives of the organization. Many of the individual components of total quality are practiced by American companies, but few practice total quality as a whole.

TOTAL QUALITY AS A SYSTEM

Introduction

Total quality begins with the redefinition of management, inspired by W. Edwards Deming:

> *The people work in a system. The job of the manager is to work on the system, to improve it continuously, with their help.*

One of the most frequent reasons for failed total quality efforts is that many managers are unable to carry out their responsibilities because they have not been trained in how to improve the quality system. They do not have a well-defined process to follow—a process founded on the principles of customer satisfaction, respect for people, continuous improvement, and speaking with facts. Deming's teachings, as amplified by Tribus,[3] focus on the following ten management actions:

1. Recognize quality improvement as a system.
2. Define it so that others can recognize it too.
3. Analyze its behavior.
4. Work with subordinates in improving the system.
5. Measure the quality of the system.
6. Develop improvements in the quality of the system.
7. Measure the gains in quality, if any, and link them to customer delight and quality improvement.
8. Take steps to guarantee holding the gains.
9. Attempt to replicate the improvements inother areas of the system.
10. Tell others about the lessons learned.

Discussions with Tribus to cross-examine these points have revealed that the manager must deal with total quality as *three* separate systems: a social system, a technical system, and a management system. These systems are depicted as three interlocking circles of a ballantine,[4] as shown in Figure 2.2.

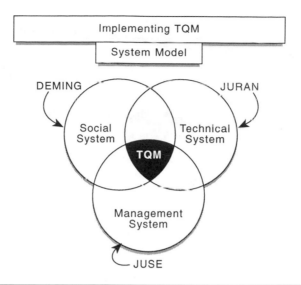

Figure 2.2 Implementing TQM—System Model.

Overview of the Social System

Management is solely responsible for the transformation of the social system, which is basically the culture of the organization. It is the social system that has the greatest impact on teamwork, motivation, creativity, and risk taking. How people react to one another and to the work depends on how they are managed. If they enter the organization with poor attitudes, managers have to re-educate, redirect, or remove them. The social system includes the reward structure, the symbols of power, the relationships between people and among groups, the privileges, the skills and style, the politics, the power structure, the shaping of the norms and values, and the "human side of enterprise," as defined by Douglas McGregor.

If a lasting culture is to be achieved, where continuous improvement and customer focus are a natural pattern, the social system must be redesigned so as to be consistent with the vision and values of the organization. Unfortunately, the social system is always in a state of flux due to pressure from ever-changing influences from the external political and technological environments. The situation in most orga-

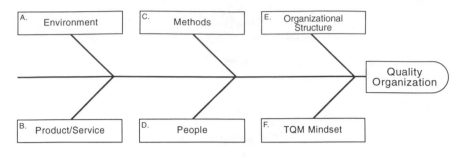

Figure 2.3 Strategic Areas for Cultural Transformation.

nizations is that the impact of total quality is not thought through in any organized manner. Change occurs when the pain of remaining as the same dysfunctional unit becomes too great and a remedy for relief is sought.

As shown in Figure 2.3, six areas of strategy must be addressed in order to change and transform the culture to that of a quality organization:

- Environment
- Product/service
- Methods
- People
- Organizational structure
- Total quality management mindset

Each of these areas will be covered in some detail in the chapters in this book. (See Figure 3.3 in Chapter 3 for an expanded version of this diagram, indicating the social system characteristics applicable to each strategic area.) Of the six, however, structure is key in that total quality is about empowerment and making decisions at lower levels in the organization. Self-managing teams are a way to bring this about quickly.

The Technical System

According to Tribus,[5] "The technical system includes all the tools and machinery, the practice of quality science and the quantitative aspects of quality. If you can measure it, you can probably describe and perhaps improve it using the technical systems approach." The technical system thus is concerned with the flow of work through the organization to the ultimate customer. Included are all the work steps performed, whether by equipment, computers, or people; whether manual labor or decision making; or whether factory worker or office worker.

The technical system in most organizations contains the following core elements:

- Scientific accumulation of technology
- Pursuit of standardization
- Workflow, materials, and specifications
- Job definitions and responsibility
- Machine/person interface
- Number and type of work steps
- Availability and use of information
- Decision-making processes
- Problem-solving tools and process
- Physical arrangement of equipment, tools, and people

The expected benefits from analyzing and improving the technical system are to (1) improve customer satisfaction, (2) eliminate waste and rework, (3) eliminate variation, (4) increase learning, (5) save time and money, (6) increase employee control, (7) reduce bottlenecks and frustration, (8) eliminate interruptions and idle time, (9) increase speed and responsiveness, and (10) improve safety and quality of work life.

The three basic elements of every system are (1) suppliers who input, (2) work processes which add value, and (3) output to the customer. High-performing units and teams eliminate the barriers and walls between these three elements. A standard problem-solving process is often used by teams, such as the Quality Control Story, Business Process Analysis, etc.[6]

The Management System

The third system is the managerial system, which becomes the integrator. Only senior managers can authorize changes to this system. This is the system by which the other two systems are influenced. It is the way that practices, procedures, protocols, and policies are established and maintained. It is the leadership system of the organization, and it is the measurement system of indicators that tell management and the employees how things are going.

The actual deployment of the management system can be visualized in the shape of a pyramid. As shown in Figure 2.4, there are four aspects or intervention points of deployment: strategy management, process management, project management, and individual activity management. A brief overview of these four aspects is as follows.

- **Strategy Management:** Purpose is to establish the mission, vision, and guiding principles and deployment infrastructure which encourage all employees to focus on and move in a common direction. Objectives, strategies, and actions are considered on a three- to five-year time line.
- **Process Management:** Purpose is to assure that all key processes are working in harmony to guarantee customer satisfaction and maximize operational effectiveness. Continuous improvement/ problem-solving efforts are often cross-functional, so that process owners and indicator owners need to be assigned.
- **Project Management:** Purpose is to establish a system to effectively plan, organize, implement, and control all the resources and activities needed for successful completion of the project. Various types of project teams are often formed to solve and implement both process-related as well as policy-related initiatives. Team activities should be linked to business objectives and improvement targets.
- **Individual Activity Management:** Purpose is to provide all employees with a method of implementing continuous improvement of processes and systems within each employee's work function and control. Flowcharting key processes and individual mission statements are important linkages with which all employees can identify. A quality journal is often used to identify and document improvements.

Various types of assessment surveys are used to "audit" the quality management system. Examples include the Malcolm Baldrige assessment, the Deming Prize audit, and the ISO 9000 audit, among others. Basic core elements are common to all of these assessments. Their usefulness is as a yardstick and benchmark by which to measure

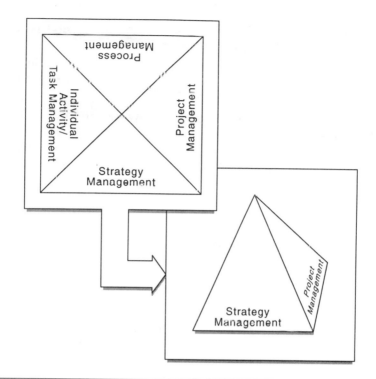

Figure 2.4 Management System Pyramid.

improvement and focus the problem-solving effort. Recent efforts using integrated quality and productivity systems have met with some success.[7]

The House of Total Quality

The House of Total Quality is a model which depicts the integration of all of these concepts in a logical fashion. Supporting the three systems of total quality described in the preceding section are the four principles of total quality: customer satisfaction, continuous improvement, speaking with facts, and respect for people. These four principles are interrelated, with customer satisfaction at the core or the hub (see Figure 1.1 in Chapter 1).

As with any house, the model and plans must first be drawn, usually with some outside help. Once the design has been approved, construction can begin. It usually begins with the mission, vision, values, and objectives which form the cornerstones upon which to build for the future. The pillars representing the four principles must be carefully constructed, well-positioned, and thoroughly understood, because the success of the total quality system is in the balance. As previously mentioned, many of the individual components of total quality are practiced by American companies, but few practice total quality as a whole.

HISTORY OF TOTAL QUALITY

In the Beginning

About the year one million B.C., give or take a few centuries, man first began to fashion stone tools for hunting and survival.[8] Up until 8000 B.C., however, very little progress was made in the quality control of these tools. It was at this time that man began assembling instruments with fitting holes, which suggests the use of interchangeable parts on a very limited basis. Throughout this long period, each man made his own tools. The evidence of quality control was measured to some extent by how long he stayed alive. If the tools were well made, his chances of survival increased. A broken axe handle usually spelled doom.

Introduction of Interchangeable Parts and Division of Labor

A little over 200 years ago, in 1787, the concepts of interchangeable parts and division of labor were first introduced in the United States. Eli Whitney, inventor of the cotton gin, applied these concepts to the production of 10,000 flintlock rifles for the U.S. military arsenal. However, Whitney had considerable difficulty in making all the parts exactly the same. It took him ten years to complete the 10,000 muskets that he promised to deliver in two years.

Three factors impacted Whitney's inability to deliver the 10,000 muskets in two years as promised. First, there was a dramatic shortage of qualified craftsmen needed to build the muskets. Consequently, Whitney correctly identified the solution to the problem—machines must do what men previously did. If individual machines were assembled to create each individual part needed, then men could be taught to operate these machines. Thus, Whitney's application of division of labor to a highly technical process was born. Whitney called this a *manufactory*.

Next, it took almost one full year to build the manufactory, rather than two months as Whitney originally thought. Not only did the weather inflict havoc on the schedule, but epidemics of yellow fever slowed progress considerably.

Third, obtaining the raw materials in a timely, usable manner was a hit-or-miss proposition. The metal ore used was often defective, flawed, and pitted. In addition, training the workers to perform the actual assembly took much longer than Whitney imagined and required a considerable amount of his personal attention, often fifteen to twenty hours a day. Also, once the men were trained, some left to work for competing armories.[9]

To compound these factors, his ongoing cotton gin patent lawsuits consumed a considerable amount of his highly leveraged attention and time. Fortunately for Whitney, his credibility in Washington granted him considerable laxity in letting target dates slip. War with France was no longer imminent. Thus, a quality product and the associated manufacturing expertise were deemed more important than schedule. What was promised in 28 months took almost 120 months to deliver.

Luckily for Whitney, the requirement of "on time and within budget" was not yet in vogue. What happened to Whitney was a classic study in the problems of trying to achieve a real breakthrough in operations. Out of this experience, Whitney and others realized that creating parts exactly the same was not possible and, if tried, would prove to be very expensive. This concept of interchangeable parts would eventually lead to statistical methods of control, while division of labor would lead to the factory assembly line.

The First Control Limits

The experiences of Whitney and others who followed led to a relaxation of the requirements for exactness and the use of tolerances. This allowed for a less-than-perfect fit between two (or more) parts, and the concept of the "go–no-go" tolerance was introduced between 1840 and 1870.[10]

This idea was a major advancement in that it created the concept of upper and lower tolerance limits, thus allowing the production worker more freedom to do his job with an accompanying lowering of cost. All he had to do was stay within the tolerance limits, instead of trying to achieve unnecessary or unattainable perfection.

Defective Parts Inspection

The next advancement centered around expanding the notion of tolerance and using specifications, where variation is classified as either meeting or not meeting requirements. For those pieces of product that every now and then fell outside the specified tolerance range (or limits), the question arose as to what to do with them. To discard or modify these pieces added significantly to the cost of production. However, to search for the unknown causes of defects and then eliminate them also cost money. The heart of the problem was as follows: how to reduce the percentage of defects to the point where (1) the rate of increase in the *cost of control* equals the rate of *increase* in *savings,* which is (2) brought about by *decreasing the number of parts rejected.*

In other words, inspection/prevention had to be cost effective. Minimizing the percent of defects in a cost-effective manner was not the only problem to be solved. Tests for many quality characteristics require destructive testing, such as tests for strength, chemical composition, fuse blowing time, etc. Because not every piece can be tested, use of the statistical sample was initiated around the turn of the century.

Statistical Theory

During the early part of the twentieth century, a tremendous increase in quality consciousness occurred. What were the forces at work that caused this sudden acceleration of interest in the application of statistical quality control? There were at least three key factors.

The first was a rapid growth in standardization, beginning in 1900. Until 1915, Great Britain was the only country in the world with some type of national standardization movement. The rate of growth in the number of industrial standardization organizations throughout the world, especially between 1916 and 1932, rose dramatically.[11] During that fifteen-year period, the movement grew from one country (Great Britain) to twenty-five, with the United States coming on line about 1917, just at the time of World War I.

The second major factor ushering in the new era was a radical shift in ideology which occurred in about 1900. This ideological shift was away from the notion of exactness of science (which existed in 1787 when interchangeability of parts was introduced) to probability and statistical concepts, which developed in almost every field of science around 1900.

The third factor was the evolution of division of labor into the factory system and the first assembly line systems of the early twentieth century. These systems proved to be ideal for employing an immigrant workforce quickly.

Scientific Management and Taylorism

Frederick Winslow Taylor was born in 1856 and entered industry as an apprentice in the Enterprise Hydraulics Shop in 1874. According to popular legend, the old-timers in the shop told him: "Now young man, here's about how much work you should do each morning and each afternoon. Don't do any more than that—that's the limit."[12]

It was obvious to Taylor that the men were producing below their capacity, and he soon found out why. The short-sighted management of that day would set standards, often paying per piece rates for the work. Then, when a worker discovered how to produce more, management cut the rate. In turn, management realized that the workers were deliberately restricting output but could not do anything about it.

It was Taylor's viewpoint that the whole system was wrong. Having studied the writings and innovations of Whitney, he came to realize that the concept of division of labor had to be revamped if greater productivity and efficiency were to be realized. His vision included a super-efficient assembly line as part of a management system of operations. He, more than anyone at the time, understood the inability of management to increase individual productivity, and he understood the reluctance of the workers to produce at a high rate. Because he had been a working man, it was apparent to him that there was a tremendous difference between *actual* output and *potential* output. Taylor thought that if such practices applied throughout the world and throughout all industry, the potential production capacity was at least three or four times what was actually being produced. When he became a foreman, Taylor set out to find ways to eliminate this waste and increase production.

For more than twenty-five years, Taylor and his associates explored ways to increase productivity and build the model factory of the future. The techniques they developed were finally formalized in writing and communicated to other people. During the early years of this experimentation, most who knew about it were associated with Taylor at the Midvale Steel Company and Bethlehem Steel.

Other famous names began to enter the picture and contribute to the body of science of the new management thinking. Among them were Carl G. L. Barth, a mathematician and statistician who assisted Taylor in analytical work, and Henry L. Gantt (famous for the Gantt chart), who invented the slide rule. Another associate of Taylor's, Sanford E. Thompson, developed the first decimal stopwatch.[12] Finally, there was young Walter Shewhart, who was to transform industry with his statistical concepts and thinking and his ability to bridge technical tools with a management system.

At the turn of the century, Taylor wrote a collection of reports and papers that were published by the American Society of Mechanical Engineers. One of the most famous was *On the Art of Cutting Metals*, which had worldwide impact. With Maunsel White, Taylor developed the first high-speed steel. Taylor was also instrumental in the development of one of the first industrial cost accounting systems, even though, according to legend, he previously knew nothing about accounting.

Frank G. and Lillian Gilbreth, aware of Taylor's work in measurement and analysis, turned their attention to mechanizing and commercializing Taylorism. For their experimental model, they chose the ancient craft of bricklaying. It had been assumed that production in bricklaying certainly should have reached its zenith thousands of years ago, with nothing more to be done to increase production. Yet Frank Gilbreth was able to show that, by following his techniques and with proper management planning, production could be raised from an average of 120 bricks per hour to 350 bricks per hour, and the worker would be less tired than he had been under the old system.

The Gilbreths refined some of the studies and techniques developed by Taylor. They used the motion picture camera to record work steps for analyses and broke them down into minute elements called "therbligs" (Gilbreth spelled backwards). Their results were eventually codified into the use of predetermined motion–time measures which were used by industrial engineers and efficiency experts of the day.

By 1912, the efficiency movement was gaining momentum. Taylor was called before a special committee of the House of Representatives which was investigating scientific management and its impact on the railroad industry. He tried to explain scientific management to the somewhat hostile railroad hearings committee, whose members regarded it as "speeding up" work. He said:

> Scientific management involves a complete mental revolution on the part of the *working man* engaged in any particular establishment or industry...a complete mental revolution on the part of these men as to their duties toward their work, toward their fellowman, and toward their employers.

> And scientific management involves an equally complete mental revolution on the part of those on *management's side*...the foreman, the superintendent, the owner of the business, and the board of directors. Here we must have a mental revolution on their part as to their duties toward their fellow workers in management, toward their workmen, and toward all of their daily problems. Without this complete mental revolution on both sides, scientific management does not exist!

> I want to sweep the deck, sweep away a good deal of the rubbish first by pointing out what scientific management is not—it is not an efficiency device, nor is it any bunch or group of efficiency devices. It is not a new system of figuring costs. It is not a new scheme of paying men. It is not holding a stopwatch on a man and writing things down about him. It is not time study. It is not motion study, nor an analysis of the movements of a man. Nor is scientific management the printing and ruling and unloading of a ton or two of blank forms on a set of men and saying, "Here's your system—go to it."

> It is not divided foremanship, nor functional foreman-
> ship. It is not any of these devices which the average man
> calls to mind when he hears the words "scientific manage-
> ment." I am not sneering at cost-keeping systems—at time-
> study, at functional foremanship, nor at any of the new and
> improved schemes of paying men. Nor am I sneering at
> efficiency devices, if they are really devices which make for
> efficiency. I believe in them. What I am emphasizing is that
> these devices in whole or part are *not* scientific management;
> they are useful adjuncts to scientific management, but they
> are also useful adjuncts to other systems of management.[12]

Taylor found out, the hard way, the importance of the cooperative spirit. He was strictly the engineer at first. Only after painful experiences did he realize that the human factor, the social system, and mental attitude of people in both management and labor had to be adjusted and changed completely before greater productivity could result.

Referring to his early experiences in seeking greater output, Taylor described the strained feelings between himself and his workmen as "miserable." Yet he was determined to improve production. He continued his experiments until three years before his death in 1915, when he found that human motivation, not just engineered improvements, could alone increase output.

Unfortunately, the human factor was ignored by many. Shortly after the railroad hearings, self-proclaimed "efficiency experts" did untold damage to scientific management. Time studies and the new efficiency techniques were used by incompetent "consultants" who sold managers on the idea of increasing profit by "speeding up" employees. Consequently, many labor unions, just beginning to feel their strength, worked against the new science and all efficiency approaches. With the passing of Taylor in 1915, the scientific management movement lost, for the moment, any chance of reaching its true potential as the catalyst for the future total quality management system. Still, the foundation was laid for the management system that was soon to become a key ingredient of organizations of the future.

Walter Shewhart—The Founding Father

Walter Shewhart was an engineer, scientist, and philosopher. He was a very deep thinker, and his ideas, although profound and technically perfect, were difficult to fathom. His style of writing followed his style of thinking—very obtuse. Still, he was brilliant, and his works on variation and sampling, coupled with his teachings on the need for documentation, influenced forever the course of industrial history.

Shewhart was familiar with the scientific management movement and its evolution from Whitney's innovation of division of labor. Although he was concerned about its evolution into sweatshop factory environments, his major focus was on the other of Whitney's great innovations—interchangeable parts—for this encompassed variation, rejects, and waste.

To deal with the issue of variation, Shewhart developed the control chart in 1924. He realized that the traditional use of tolerance limits was short-sighted, because they only provided a method for judging the quality of a product that had already been made.[13]

The control limits on Shewhart's control charts, however, provided a ready guide for acting on the process in order to eliminate what he called *assignable causes*[8] of variation, thus preventing inferior products from being produced in the future. This allowed management to focus on the future, through the use of statistical probability—a prediction of future production based upon historical data. Thus, the emphasis shifted from costly correction of problems to prevention of problems and improvement of processes.[14]

Like Taylor, Shewhart's focus shifted from individual parts to a systems approach. The notion of zero defects of individual parts was replaced with zero variability of system operations.

Shewhart's Control System

Shewhart identified the traditional act of control as consisting of three elements: the act of specifying what is required, the act of producing what is specified, and the act of judging whether the requirements have been met. This simple picture of the control of quality would work well if production could be viewed in the context of an exact science, where all products are made exactly the same. Shewhart knew, however, that because variation is pervasive, the control of quality characteristics must be a matter of probability. He envisioned a statistician helping an engineer to understanding variation and arriving at the economic control of quality.[15]

Shewhart's Concept of Variation

Determining the *state of statistical control* in terms of degree of variation is the first step in the Shewhart control system. Rather than specifying what is required in terms of tolerance requirements, Shewhart viewed variation as being present in everything and identified two types of variation: *controlled* and *uncontrolled.*

This is fundamentally different from the traditional way of classifying variation as either acceptable or unacceptable (go–no-go tolerance). Viewing variation as controlled or uncontrolled enables one to focus on the causes of variation in order to improve a process (before the fact) as opposed to focusing on the output of a process in order to judge whether or not the product is acceptable (after the fact).

Shewhart taught that controlled variation is a consistent pattern of variation over time that is due to random or *chance causes.* He recognized that there may be many chance causes of variation, but the effect of any one of these is relatively small; therefore, which cause or causes are responsible for observed variation is a matter of chance. Shewhart stated that a process that is being affected only by *chance* causes of variation is said to be *in a state of statistical control.*

All processes contain chance causes of variation, and Shewhart taught that it is possible to reduce the chance causes of variation, but it is not realistic or cost effective to try to remove them all. The control limits on Shewhart's control charts represent the boundaries of the occurrence of chance causes of variation operating within the system.

The second type of variation—uncontrolled variation—is an inconsistent or changing pattern of variation that occurs over time and is due to what Shewhart classified as *assignable causes.* Because the effects of assignable causes of variation are relatively major compared to chance causes, they can and must be identified and removed.[16] According to Shewhart, a process is *out of statistical control* when it is being affected by assignable causes.

One of Shewhart's main problems was how to communicate this newfound theory without overwhelming the average businessman or engineer. The answer came in the form of staged experiments using models which demonstrated variation. His *ideal bowl experiment*[17] with poker chips was modeled by his protege, W. Edwards Deming, some twenty years later with his famous *red bead experiment*.

Another major contribution of Shewhart's first principle of control was recognition of the need for operational definitions that can be communicated to operators, inspectors, and scientists alike. He was fond of asking, "How can an operator carry out his job tasks if he does not understand what the job is? And how can he know what the job is if what was produced yesterday was O.K., but today the same product is wrong?" He believed that inspection, whether the operator inspects his own work or relies on someone else to do it for him, must have operational definitions. Extending specifications beyond product and into the realm of operator performance was the first attempt to define the "extended system of operations" which would greatly facilitate the production process.

The Shewhart System of Production

Shewhart's second principle—the act of producing what is specified—consists of five important steps (Shewhart's teachings are in italics):

1. Outline the data collection framework: *Specify in a general way how an observed sequence of data is to be examined for clues as to the existence of assignable causes of variability.*
2. Develop the sampling plan: *Specify how the original data are to be taken and how they are to be broken up into subsamples upon the basis of human judgments about whether the conditions under which the data were taken were essentially the same or not.*
3. Identify the formulas and control limits for each sample: *Specify the criterion of control that is to be used, indicating what statistics are to be computed for each subsample and how these are to be used in computing action or control limits for each statistic for which the control criterion is to be constructed.*
4. Outline the corrective actions/improvement thesis: *Specify the action that is to be taken when an observed statistic falls outside its control limits.*

5. Determine the size of the database: *Specify the quantity of data that must be available and found to satisfy the criterion of control before the engineer is to act as though he had attained a state of statistical control.*[8]

The Shewhart system became a key component of the technical system of total quality. The works of Deming, Juran, Feigenbaum, Sarasohn, Ishikawa, and others who followed would amplify Shewhart's concept of quality as a *technical system* into its many dimensions, which eventually led to the body of knowledge known as total quality.

The Shewhart Cycle: When Control Meets Scientific Management

From the "exact science" days of the 1800s to the 1920s, *specification, production,* and *inspection* were considered to be independent of each other when viewed in a straight line manner. They take on an entirely different picture in an inexact science. When the production process is viewed from the standpoint of the control of quality as a matter of probability, then specification, production, and inspection are linked together as represented in a circular diagram or wheel. *Specification and production* are linked because it is important to know how well the tolerance limits are being satisfied by the existing process and what improvements are necessary. Shewhart compared this process (which he called the Scientific Method) to the dynamic process of acquiring knowledge, which is similar to an experiment. Step 1 was formulating the hypothesis. Step 2 was conducting the experiment. Step 3 was testing the hypothesis.[18] In the Shewhart wheel, the successful completion of each interlocking component led to a cycle of continuous improvement. (Years later Deming was to popularize this cycle of improvement in his famous Deming wheel.)

Shewhart Meets Deming

It was at the Bell Laboratories in New Jersey where Shewhart, who was leading the telephone reliability efforts during the 1930s, first met Deming. Shewhart, as discussed earlier, was developing his system for improving worker performance and productivity by measuring variation using control charts and statistical methods. Deming was impressed and liked what he saw, especially Shewhart's intellect and the *wheel* the Shewhart cycle of control. He realized that with training, workers could retain control over their work processes by monitoring the quality of the items produced. Deming also believed that once workers were trained and educated and were empowered to manage their work processes, quality would be increased and costly inspections could once and for all be eliminated. He presented the idea that higher quality would cost less, not more. Deming studied Shewhart's teachings and techniques and learned well, even if at times he was lost and said that his genius was in knowing when to act and when to leave a process alone. At times he was frustrated by Shewhart's obtuse style of thinking and writing.[19]

In 1938, Shewhart delivered four lectures to the U.S. Department of Agriculture (USDA) Graduate School at the invitation of Deming. In addition to being in charge of the mathematics and statistics courses at the USDA Graduate School, Deming was responsible for inviting guest lecturers. He invited Shewhart to present a series of lectures on how statistical methods of control were being used in industry to economically control the quality of manufactured products. Shewhart spent an entire year developing the lectures, titled them *Statistical Method from the Viewpoint of Quality Control*, and delivered them in March of 1938. They were subsequently edited into book format by Deming and published in 1939.

In a couple of years both Deming and Shewhart were called upon by the U.S. government to aid the war effort. As David Halberstam recounted, the War Department, impressed by Shewhart's theories and work, brought together a small group of experts on statistical process control (SPC) to establish better quality guidelines for defense contractors.[20] Deming was a member of that group and he came to love the work.

Origins of Deming

Who was Dr. W. Edwards Deming, the man who was to take Shewhart's teachings, popularize them, and even go beyond? He was born on October 14, 1900 and earned his Ph.D. in physics at Yale University in the summer of 1927, which is where he learned to use statistical theory. As a graduate student in the late 1920s, he did part-time summer work at the famous Western Electric Hawthorne plant in Chicago. It was at this plant that Elton Mayo some ten years later would perform his experiments later known as the Hawthorne Experiments. While working at Hawthorne, Deming could not help noticing the poor working conditions of this sweatshop environment, which employed predominantly female laborers to produce telephones. Deming was both fascinated and appalled by what he saw and learned. It was at Hawthorne where he saw the full effects of the abuses of the Taylor system of scientific management. He also saw the full effect of Whitney's second great innovation—division of labor—when carried to extreme by ivory tower management uncaring about the state of the social system of the organization. So what if the work environment was a sweatshop—the workers were paid well enough! "The women should be happy just to have a job" seemed to be the unspoken attitude.

When Deming Met Taylor(ism)

A couple of years before meeting Shewhart, when Deming encountered Taylorism at Hawthorne, he found a scientific management system with the following objectives:

- Develop a science for each element of work.
- Scientifically select a workman and train and develop him.
- Secure whole-hearted cooperation between management and labor to ensure that all work is done in accordance with the principles developed.
- Divide the work between management and labor. The manager takes over all work for which he is better suited than the workman.

It was the fourth point, which evolved out of the division of labor concept, that Deming found to be the real villain. In practice, this meant removing from the worker basic responsibility for the quality of the work. What Deming disliked was that workers should not be hired to think about their work. That was management's job. Errors will occur, but the worker need not worry—the inspector will catch any mistakes *before* they leave the plant. In addition, management could always reduce the per-piece pay to reflect scrap and rework. Any worker who produced too many inferior quality pieces would be fired.

The problem with Taylorism is that it views the production process mechanistically, instead of holistically, as a system which includes the human elements of motivation and respect. Taylorism taught American industry to view the worker as "a cog in the giant industrial machine, whose job could be defined and directed by educated managers administering a set of rules."[21] Work on the assembly lines of America and at Hawthorne was simple, repetitive, and boring. Management was top-down. Pay per piece meant that higher output equals higher take-home pay. Quality of work for the most part was not a factor for the average, everyday worker.

This system found a friend in the assembly line process developed by Henry Ford and was widely incorporated into America's private and public sectors. Taylor's management system made it possible for waves of immigrants, many of whom could not read, write, or speak English (and at times not even communicate with one another), to find employment in American factories. Taylor's ideas were even introduced into the nation's schools.[22]

Edwards Deming had various colleagues at the time, one of whom was Joseph Juran, another famous quality "guru." They rebelled at the scientific management movement. They felt that the authoritarian Taylorism method of management was degrading to the human spirit and counterproductive to the interests of employees, management, the company, and society as a whole.[23] Mayo and his Hawthorne research team confirmed these feelings with their findings: good leadership leads to high morale and motivation, which in turn leads to higher production. Good leadership was defined as democratic, rather than autocratic, and people centered, as opposed to production centered. Thus began the human relations era.

Post-World War II

When the war ended, American industry converted to peacetime production of goods and services. People were hungry for possessions and an appetite developed worldwide for products "made in the U.S.A." The focus in the United States returned to quantity over quality, and a gradual deterioration of market share occurred, with billions of dollars in international business lost to Japanese and European competitors. These were the modern-day phoenixes rising from the ashes of war. America became preoccupied with the mechanics of mass production and its role as world provider to a hungry people. What followed was an imbalance between satisfying the needs of the worker and a lack of appreciation for and recognition of the external customer. America moved away from what had made it great!

The Japanese Resurrection

Japan first began to apply statistical control concepts in the early 1920s, but moved away from them when the war began.[24] In 1946, under General Douglas MacArthur's leadership, the Supreme Command for the Allied Powers (SCAP) established quality control tools and techniques as the approach to affect the turnaround of Japanese industry. Japan had sacrificed its industry, and eventually its food supply, to support its war effort. Subsequently, there was little left in post-war Japan to occupy. The country was a shambles. Only one major city, Kyoto, had escaped wide-scale destruction; food was scarce and industry was negligible.[24]

Against a backdrop of devastation and military defeat, a group of Japanese scientists and engineers—organized appropriately as the Union of Japanese Scientists and Engineers (JUSE)—dedicated themselves to working with American and Allied experts to help rebuild the country. Reconstruction was a daunting and monumental task. With few natural resources available or any immediate means of producing them, export of manufactured goods was essential. However, Japanese industry—or what was left of it—was producing inferior goods, a fact which was recognized worldwide. JUSE was faced with the task of drastically improving the quality of Japan's industrial output as an essential exchange commodity for survival.

W. S. Magill and Homer Sarasohn, among others, assisted with the dramatic transformation of the electronics industry and telecommunications. Magill is regarded by some as the father of statistical quality control in Japan. He was the first to advocate its use in a 1945 lecture series and successfully applied SPC techniques to vacuum tube production in 1946 at NEC.[25]

Sarasohn worked with supervisors and managers to improve reliability and yields in the electronics field from 40 percent in 1946 to 80–90 percent in 1949; he documented his findings for SCAP, and MacArthur took notice. He ordered Sarasohn to instruct Japanese businessmen how to get things done. The Japanese listened, but the

Americans forgot. In 1950, Sarasohn's attention was directed toward Korea, and Walter Shewhart was asked to come to Japan. He was unable to at the time, and Deming was eventually tapped to direct the transformation.

In July 1950, Deming began a series of day-long lectures to Japanese management in which he taught the basic "Elementary Principles of Statistical Control of Quality." The Japanese embraced the man and his principles and named their most prestigious award for quality The Deming Prize. During the 1970s, Deming turned his attention back to the United States and at 93 years old (at the time of this writing) is still going strong. His Fourteen Points go far beyond statistical methods and address the management system as well as the social system or culture of the organization. In many ways, he began to sound more and more like Frederick Taylor, whose major emphasis in later years was on the need for a *mental revolution*—a transformation. Deming's Theory of Profound Knowledge brings together all three systems of total quality.

The Other "Gurus" Arrive

What began in Japan in the 1950s became a worldwide quality movement, albeit on a limited basis, within twenty years. During this period the era of the "gurus" evolved (Deming, Juran, Ishikawa, Feigenbaum, and Crosby). Beginning with Deming in 1948 and Juran in 1954, the movement was eventually carried back to the United States by Feigenbaum in the 1960s and Crosby in the 1970s. Meanwhile, Ishikawa and his associates at JUSE kept the movement alive in Japan. By 1980, the bell began to toll loud and clear in the West with the NBC White Paper entitled "If Japan Can Do It, Why Can't We?" The following are thumbnail sketches of the teachings of the other gurus.

Joseph Juran

Joseph Juran was the son of an immigrant shoemaker from Romania and began his industrial career at Western Electric's Hawthorne plant before World War II. He later worked at Bell Laboratories in the area of quality assurance. He worked as a government administrator, university professor, labor arbitrator, and corporate director before establishing his own consulting firm, the Juran Institute, in Wilton, Connecticut. In the 1950s, he was invited to Japan by JUSE to help rebuilding Japanese corporations develop management concepts. Juran based some of his principles on the work of Walter Shewhart and, like Deming and the other quality gurus, believed that management and the system are responsible for quality. Juran is the creator of statistical quality control and the author of a book entitled *The Quality Control Handbook*. This book has become an international standard reference for the quality movement.

Juran's definition of quality is described as "fitness for use as perceived by the customer." If a product is produced and the customer perceives it as fit for use, then the quality mission has been accomplished. Juran also believed that every person in the organization must be involved in the effort to make products or services that are fit for use.

Juran described a perpetual spiral of progress or continuous striving toward quality. Steps on this spiral are, in ascending order, research, development, design, specification, planning, purchasing, instrumentation, production, process control, inspection, testing, sale, service, and then back to research again. The idea behind the spiral is that each time the steps are completed, products or services would increase in quality. Juran explained that chronic problems should be solved by following this spiral; he formulated a breakthrough sequence to increase the standard of performance so that problems are eliminated. To alleviate sporadic problems, which he finds are often solved with temporary solutions, he suggests carefully examining the system causing the problem and adjusting it to solve the difficulty. Once operating at this improved standard of performance, with the sporadic problem solved, the process of analyzing chronic and sporadic problems should start over again.

Juran pointed out that companies often overlook the cost of producing low-quality products. He suggested that by implementing his theories of quality improvement, not only would higher quality products be produced, but the actual costs would be lower. His Cost of Quality principle was known as "Gold in the Mine."

Juran is known for his work with statistics, and he relied on the quantification of standards and statistical quality control techniques. He is credited with implementing use of the Pareto diagram to improve business systems as well.

Juran's concept of quality included the managerial dimensions of planning, organizing, and controlling (known as the Juran Trilogy) and focused on the responsibility of management to achieve quality and the need to set goals. His ten steps to quality are as follows:

1. Build awareness of opportunities to improve.
2. Set goals for improvement.
3. Organize to reach goals.
4. Provide training.
5. Carry out projects to solve problems.
6. Report progress.
7. Give recognition.
8. Communicate results.
9. Keep score.
10. Maintain momentum by making annual improvement part of the regular systems and processes of the company.

Ishikawa and the Japanese Experts

Kaoru Ishikawa studied under both Homer Sarasohn and Edwards Deming during the late 1940s and early 1950s. As President of JUSE, he was instrumental in developing a unique Japanese strategy for total quality: the broad involvement of the entire organization in its *total* sense—every worker, every process, and every job. This also included the complete life cycle of the product, from start to finish.

Some of his accomplishments include the success of the quality circle in Japan, in part due to innovative tools such as the cause-and-effect diagram (often called the Ishikawa fishbone diagram because it resembles a fish skeleton). His approach was to provide easy-to-use analytical tools that could be used by all workers, including those on the line, to analyze and solve problems.

Ishikawa identified seven critical success factors that were essential for the success of total quality control in Japan:

1. Company-wide total quality control (CWTQC) and participation by *all* members of the organization
2. Education and training in all aspects of total quality, which often amounts to thirty days per year per employee

3. Use of quality circles to update standards and regulations, which are in constant need of improvement
4. Quality audits by the president and quality council members (senior executives) twice a year
5. Widespread use of statistical methods and a focus on problem prevention
6. Nationwide quality control promotion activities, with the national imperative of keeping Japanese quality number one in the world
7. Revolutionary *mental* attitude on the part of both management and workers toward one another and toward the customer, including welcoming complaints, encouraging risk, and a wider span of control

Ishikawa believed that Japanese management practices should be democratic, with management providing the guidelines. Mission statements were used extensively and operating policies derived from them. Top management, he taught, must assume a leadership position to implement the policies so that they are followed by all.

The impact on Japanese industry was startling. In seven to ten years, the electronics and telecommunications industries were transformed, with the entire nation revitalized by the end of the 1960s.

Armand Feigenbaum

Unlike Deming and Juran, Feigenbaum did not work with the Japanese. He was Vice President of Worldwide Quality for General Electric until the last 1960s, when he set up his own consulting firm, General Systems, Inc. He is best known for coining the term *total quality control* and for his 850-page book on the subject. His teachings center around the integration of people–machine–information structures in order to economically and effectively control quality and achieve full customer satisfaction.

Feigenbaum taught that there are two requirements to establishing quality as a business strategy: establishing customer satisfaction must be central and quality/cost objectives must drive the total quality system. His systems theory of total quality control includes four fundamental principles:

- Total quality is a continuous work process, starting with customer requirements and ending with customer satisfaction.
- Documentation allows visualization and communication of work assignments.
- The quality system provides for greater flexibility because of a greater use of alternatives provided.
- Systematic re-engineering of major quality activities leads to greater levels of continuous improvement.

Like Juran and Deming, Feigenbaum used a visual concept to capture the idea of waste and rework—the so-called Hidden Plant. Based upon studies, he taught that this "Hidden Plant" can account for between 15 and 40 percent of the production capacity of a company. In his book, he used the concept of the "9 M's" to describe the factors which affect quality: (1) markets, (2) money, (3) management, (4) men, (5) motivation, (6) materials, (7) machines and mechanization, (8) modern information methods, and (9) mounting product requirements.

According to Andrea Gabor in "The Man Who Discovered Quality," Feigenbaum took a nut-and-bolts approach to quality, while Deming is often viewed as a visionary. Nuts and bolts led him to focus on the benefits and outcomes of total quality, rather than only the process to follow. His methods led to increased quantification of total quality program improvements during the 1970s and 1980s.

Philip Crosby

Unlike the other quality gurus, who were scientists, engineers, and statisticians, Philip Crosby is known for his motivational talks and style of presentation. His emergence began in 1961, when he first developed the concept of zero defects while working as a quality manager at Martin Marietta Corporation in Orlando, Florida. He believed that "zero defects" motivated line workers to turn out perfect products. He soon joined ITT, where he quickly moved up the ranks to Vice President of Quality Control Operations, covering 192 manufacturing facilities in 46 countries. He held the position until 1979, when he opened his own consulting company, which became one of the largest of its kind with over 250 people worldwide.

He established the Quality College in 1980 and used that concept to promote his teachings and writings in eighteen languages. It has been estimated that over five million people have attended its courses, and his trilogy of books are popular and easy to read. It is in these works where he introduces the four absolutes of his total quality management philosophy:

1. The definition of quality is conformance to requirements.
2. The system of quality is prevention of problems.
3. The performance standard of quality is zero defects.
4. The measurement of quality is the price of nonconformance, or the cost of quality.

The fourth principle, the Cost of Quality, is similar to Feigenbaum's Hidden Plant and Juran's Gold in the Mine. Like Deming, he has fourteen steps to quality improvement. Also like Deming, he has been very critical of the Malcolm Baldrige National Quality Award, although his influence (like Deming's) can be seen in virtually all seven categories.

He departs from the other gurus in his emphasis on performance standards instead of statistical data to achieve zero defects. He believes that identifying goals to be achieved, setting standards for the final product, removing all error-causing situations, and complete organizational commitment comprise the foundation for excellence.

ISO 9000 and the Quality Movement

At the turn of the century, England was the most advanced nation in the world in terms of quality standards. During World War I, England led the charge and during World War II was at least the equal of the United States—with one exception. England did not have Shewhart, Deming, and the other American quality gurus. It was not until the Common Market accepted the firm touch of Prime Minister Margaret Thatcher that the European movement was galvanized in 1979 with the forerunner of ISO 9000. It was Thatcher who orchestrated the transformance of the British ISO 9000 series for the European community. In less than 20 years, it has become the worldwide quality standard.

ENDNOTES

1. During the course of the Deming Prize examination at Florida Power & Light in 1988 and 1989, Dr. Kano consistently emphasized this point during site visits to various power plants and district customer service operations The concept of worker self-inspection, while new in the United States, has been a practiced art in Japan over the past twenty years.

2. Whethan, C. D. (1980). *A History of Science*. 4th edition, New York: Macmillan.

3. Tribus, Myron (1990). *The Systems of Total Quality*. published by the author.

4. The total quality ballantine was developed by Frank Voehl to illustrate the three-dimensional and interlocking aspects of the quality system. It is loosely based on the military concept of three interlocking bullet holes representing a perfect hit.

5. Tribus, Myron (1990). *The Three Systems of Total Quality*. published by the author; referenced in Voehl, Frank (1992). *Total Quality: Principles and Practices within Organizations*. Coral Springs, Fla.: Strategy Associates, pp. IV, 20.

6. The use of a storyboard to document the various phases of project development was introduced by Dr. Kume in his work on total quality control and was pioneered in the United States by Disney Studios, where it was used to bring new movies to production sooner.

7. For details, see Voehl, F. W. (1992). *The Integrated Quality System*. Coral Springs, Fla.: Strategy Associates.

8. Shewhart, W. A. (1931). *Economic Control of Quality of Manufactured Product*. New York: Van Nostrand.

9. Olmstead, Denison (1972). *Memoir of Eli Whitney, Esq*. New York: Arno Press.

10. Walter Shewhart on the "go–no-go" concept: If, for example, a design involving the use of a cylindrical shaft in a bearing is examined, interchangeability might be ensured simply by using a suitable "go" plug gauge on the bearing and a suitable "go" ring gauge on the shaft. In this case, the difference between the dimensions of the two "go" gauges gives the minimum clearance. Such a method of gauging, however, does not fix the maximum clearance. The production worker soon realized that a slack fit between a part and its "go" gauge might result in enough play between the shaft and its bearing to cause the product to be rejected; therefore, he tried to keep the fit between the part and its "go" gauge as close as possible, thus encountering some of the difficulties that had been experienced in trying to make the parts exactly alike.

11. Walter Shewhart was the first to realize that, with the development of the atomic structure of matter and electricity, it became necessary to

regard laws as being statistical in nature. According to Shewhart, the importance of the law of large numbers in the interpretation of physical phenomena will become apparent to anyone who even hastily surveys any one or more of the following works: Darrow, K. K. (1929). "Statistical Theories of Matter, Radiation, and Electricity." *The Physical Review Supplement*, Vol. I, No. I, July 1929 (also published in the series of Bell Telephone Laboratories reprints, No. 435); Rice, J. (1930). *Introduction to Statistical Mechanics for Students of Physics and Physical Chemistry*. London: Constable & Company; Tolman, R. E. (1927). *Statistical Mechanics with Applications to Physics and Chemistry*. New York: Chemical Catalog Company; Loeb, L. B. (1927). *Kinetic Theory of Gases*. New York: McGraw-Hill; Bloch, E. (1924). *The Kinetic Theory of Bases*. London: Methuen & Company; Richtmeyer, F. K. (1928). *Introduction to Modern Physics*. New York: McGraw-Hill; Wilson, H. A. (1928). *Modern Physics*. London: Blackie & Son; Darrow, K. K. (1926). *Introduction to Contemporary Physics*. New York: D. Van Nostrand; Ruark, A. E. and Urey, H. C. (1930). *Atoms, Molecules and Quanta*. New York: McGraw-Hill.

12. Matthies, Leslie (1960). "The Beginning of Modern Scientific Management." *The Office*, April 1960.

13. Walter Shewhart on the use of the control chart: Whereas the concept of mass production of 1787 was born of an *exact* science, the concept underlying the quality control chart technique of 1924 was born of a *probable* science, which has empirically derived control limits. These limits are to be set so that when the observed quality of a piece of product falls outside of them, even though the observation is still within the limits L_1 and L_2 (tolerance limits), it is desirable to look at the manufacturing process in order to discover and remove, if possible, one or more causes of variation that need not be left to chance.

14. Shewhart noted that it is essential, however, in industry and in science to understand the distinction between a stable system and an unstable system and how to plot points and conclude by rational methods whether they indicate a stable system. To quote Shewhart, "This conclusion is consistent with that so admirably presented in a recent paper by S. L. Andrew in the *Bell Telephone Quarterly*, Jan., 1931, and also with conclusions set forth in the recent book *Business Adrift*, by W. B. Donham, Dean of the Harvard Business School. Such reading cannot do other than strengthen our belief in the fact that control of quality will come only through the weeding out of assignable causes of variation—particularly those that introduce lack of constancy in the chance cause system."

15. As the statistician enters the scene, the three traditional elements of control take on a new meaning, as Shewhart summarized: "Corresponding to these three steps there are three senses in which statistical control may play an important part in attaining uniformity in the

quality of a manufactured product: (a) as a concept of a statistical state constituting a limit to which one may hope to go in improving the uniformity of quality; (b) as an operation or technique of attaining uniformity; and (c) as a judgment."

16.   Deming refers to assignable causes as being "specific to some ephemeral (brief) event that can usually be discovered to the satisfaction of the expert on the job, and removed."

17.   Shewhart used what he called the *Ideal Bowl Experiment* to physically characterize a state of statistical control. A number of physically similar poker chips with numbers written on them are placed in a bowl. Successive samples (Shewhart seems to prefer a sample size of four) are taken from the bowl, each time mixing the remaining chips. The chips removed from the bowl are drawn by chance—there are only chance causes of variation. In speaking of chance causes of variation, Shewhart proves, contrary to popular belief, that the statistician can have a sense of humor. "If someone were shooting at a mark and failed to hit the bull's-eye and was then asked why, the answer would likely be *chance*. Had someone asked the same question of one of man's earliest known ancestors, he might have attributed his lack of success to the dictates of fate or to the will of the gods. I am inclined to think that in many ways one of these excuses is about as good as another. The Ideal Bowl Experiment is an abstract means of characterizing the physical state of statistical control." A sequence of samples of any process can be compared mathematically to the bowl experiment and, if found similar, the process can be said to be affected only by random or chance causes of variation or can be characterized as being in a *state of statistical control*. Shewhart states: "It seems to me that it is far safer to take some one physical operation such as drawing from a bowl as a physical model for an act that may be repeated at random, and then to require that any other repetitive operation believed to be random shall in addition produce results similar in certain respects to the results of drawing from a bowl before we act as though the operation in question were random."

18.   It may be helpful to think of the three steps in the mass production process as steps in the scientific method. In this sense, specification, production, and inspection correspond, respectively, to formulating a hypothesis, conducting an experiment, and testing the hypothesis. The three steps constitute the dynamic scientific process of acquiring knowledge.

19.   The following story was related at one of Deming's now-famous four-day quality seminars: I remember him (Shewhart) pacing the floor in his room at the Hotel Washington before the third lecture. He was explaining something to me. I remarked that these great thoughts should be in his lectures. He said that they were already written up in his third and fourth lectures. I remarked that if he wrote up these

lectures in the same way that he had just explained them to me, they would be clearer. He said that his writing had to be foolproof. I thereupon remarked that he had written his thoughts to be so darn foolproof that no one could understand them.

20. Halberstam, David (1960). The War Effort during WWII, Lectures, Articles and Interview Notes.

21. This is a general consensus feeling among many historians and writers as to the inherent "evil" of Taylorism—machine over man. Walter Shewhart, to his credit and genius, tries to marry quality control and scientific management. In the foreword to his 1931 master work referred to in Endnote 8, he writes, "Broadly speaking, the object of industry is to set up economic ways and means of satisfying human wants and in so doing to reduce everything possible to routines requiring a minimum amount of human effort. Through the use of the scientific method, extended to take account of modern statistical concepts, it has been found possible to set up limits within which the results of routine efforts must lie if they are to be economical. Deviations in the results of a routine process outside such limits indicate that the routine has broken down and will no longer be economical until the cause of trouble is removed."

22. Bonstingal, John Jay (1992). *Schools of Quality*. New York: Free Press.

23. The Hawthorne Experiments, Elton Mayo, 1938.

24. Voehl, F. W. (1990). "The Deming Prize." *South Carolina Business Journal*, 1990 edition, pp. 33–38.

25. This was first pointed out by Robert Chadman Wood in an article about Homer Sarasohn, published in *Forbes* in 1990.

26. Figure 2.2 ©1991 F. W. Voehl. Figure 2.3 ©1992 Strategy Associates, Inc.

ABSTRACTS

ABSTRACT 2.1
TOTAL QUALITY MANAGEMENT IN HIGHER EDUCATION

Edwards, David
Management Services (MNS), Vol. 35, Issue 12, Dec. 1991, pp. 18–20

This is a useful article in that it is a concise presentation of the benefits of total quality management (TQM) in terms of three components of the total quality system: teamwork, statistical process control, and a documented measurement/management system. The author points out that TQM is typically directed toward manufacturers in order to convince them that they need to introduce it. However, the technique is equally applicable to service industries and, therefore, can be applied to education. Higher education could benefit from TQM because of the increased emphasis on quality and consumer satisfaction and interest. Being driven in the U.K. by the Education Reform Act, the author argues that during 1993 all universities will be audited as to "fitness of purpose." TQM can help higher education: (a) focus on the proper needs of the market, (b) achieve top-quality performance in all areas, (c) produce systems for achieving quality performance, (d) develop measures of achievement, (e) help institutions to become competitive, (f) develop team approaches, (g) improve communication, (h) reward outstanding achievement, and (i) facilitate a continual review process. The major components of TQM—a documentable quality management system, statistical process control, and teamwork—can be applied to higher education with initiative from the management team (both academic and nonacademic) and input from staff support areas. Limited references are included. An implementation framework is provided by Edwards.

ARTICLES

QUALITY IMPROVEMENT IN TEACHING*

Sushil K. Gupta

INTRODUCTION

Improving quality of teaching is (or should be) an important goal of any professor in an educational institution. Total Quality Management (TQM), which is a widely accepted concept in business organizations, could be used as a means to achieve this goal. TQM is a management philosophy that solicits participation and commitment from all levels of employees to improve quality of goods and services that the customer of the organization needs. TQM is not a one time activity; rather, it endeavors to continuously improve quality. "Employee participation and commitment" and "customer focus" form the foundation of the TQM concept. Based on this foundation are built the key themes of TQM which include the quality of "design," the quality of "output" and the quality of "process" to meet customer needs. In this paper we would discuss design, output and process as they relate to the goal of "teaching" in higher education.

THE EDUCATIONAL SYSTEM

An educational system is similar to any other operating system consisting of a set of input resources which go through a transformation process to produce a set of outputs. However, the following important characteristics of an educational system distinguish it from any other system:

- There are inadequacies in the current measurement system of inputs and outputs.
- The interrelationships among different activities in the transformation process are not clearly understood.

* Reprinted from *Explorations in Teaching & Learning*, Vol. 3, No. 3, pp. 4-5, January 1993. From the Academy for the Art of Teaching, Florida International University, Miami.

- Incentives and reward structures are not clearly defined.
- The decision making process is diffused and limits managerial control.
- There are no industry standards and norms.

Briefly, the outputs, input resources and the transformation process of an educational institution include the following:

Outputs. The outputs are the educated people, research findings and service to the community.

Input Resources. The resources of an educational institution include, but are not limited to, students, faculty, staff, administrators and other personnel; financial support; library, computing and laboratory facilities; recreational facilities; student housing; buildings and other physical facilities.

Transformation Process. The transformation process in an educational institution consists of activities performed to disseminate knowledge, to conduct research and to provide community service. The transformation process also specifies the "interactions" among the input resources.

The educational system could be viewed as consisting of several administrative and academic subsystems. These include admissions, registration and records, financial aid, purchasing, teaching and research, etc.

Teaching as a subsystem, within the larger system of higher education, consists of its own sets of input resources, outputs and the process. To put it in the context of TQM, we have to identify "customers" of teaching and the "quality" of teaching desired by these customers. Once this is done, an appropriate transformation process could be designed.

CUSTOMERS AND THEIR EXPECTATIONS OF QUALITY FROM TEACHING

Students are generally considered to be the customers of "teaching." The expectations of students from teaching include more knowledge in their chosen field of study, good grades, and acquisition of diplomas and degrees. However, there are several other customers of "teaching" who include the employers of graduating students, graduate schools, professors, and the society at large. From the view point of these customers, students could be viewed as "input" to the educational system. The expectations of these customers from an educational system are as follows:

Employers. Employers want our universities to produce well qualified and trained graduates who could work efficiently and effectively in the jobs for which they have been hired.

Graduate Schools. Graduate schools require that students who are admitted into their programs possess enough knowledge, skills and preparation to take up higher studies.

Professors. A professor teaching a particular class requires that students have acquired appropriate background in the prerequisite courses.

Society. Society wants our universities to produce educated and responsible citizens.

INPUT RESOURCES REQUIRED FOR TEACHING

The resources required for teaching include the professor, the physical environment in which the classes are conducted (including the size and layout of the classroom, sound and light system), availability of the audio-visual equipment, availability of tutors and student assistants to the professors, computer support and library facilities. Students could also be viewed as an input resource.

DESIGN OF THE SYSTEM FOR TEACHING

The resources described influence the design of the system of teaching. An important component of the system design is the specification of "interactions" among resources. In the teaching subsystem one of the important interactions is the "delivery" of the course material to the students. A professor may choose from many of the available methods to deliver knowledge. These include, but are not limited to, lecture, case study, group discussion, management game, simulation exercise, reading assignment, term paper, quiz, and examination. Obviously, the best method depends on the course objective and the resources available. For example, a well designed case study room would facilitate the case study approach of teaching. The size of the class might influence the number of quizzes, assignments and examinations that a professor gives. The level of students, graduate vs. undergraduate, would influence the decision to choose a particular style of teaching.

Measurement of the output is also an important consideration in system design. In addition to being the means for disseminating knowledge examinations, quizzes and assignments are also a means to measure the quality of output. An important consideration is the frequency with which these measures are administered. Evaluation of the professor and the course at the end of the term also serves to evaluate the effectiveness of the system. Other means for evaluating the quality of teaching include surveys of students, alumni, parents and employers. Pass rates on professional examinations and success rates in getting admission in graduate schools are additional indicators of the quality of educational programs of a university.

The quality of teaching would change with a change in the mix of input resources. A different teacher, a different mix of students, a different classroom, the availability of computers would make a difference in the quality of output. In this paper, we are not establishing quality objectives of any individual course or a program of study or passing judgment on different approaches for teaching. Rather, the objective is to propose that the systems approach is one of the effective ways to analyze and improve the quality of teaching.

THE DEMING PRIZE VS. THE BALDRIGE AWARD*

Joseph F. Duffy

The Deming Prize and the Baldrige Award. They're both named after Americans, both very prestigious to win, both standing for a cry for quality in business, both engaged by their share of critics. One is 40 years old; the other a mere four. One resides in an alluring, foreign land; the other on American soil. One is awarded to the paradigm of Japanese business, individuals and international companies; the other to the best of U.S. business. One has grown in what a psychologist might call a mostly safe, nurturing environment; the other amongst a sometimes sour, some-times sweet, bipolar parental image of government officials, academia and business gurus who seem to critically tug every way possible. One represents a country hailed as the world leader in quality; the other is trying to catch up—trying very hard.

A battle between Japan's Deming Prize and the Malcolm Baldrige National Quality Award would be as good a making for a movie as *Rocky* ever was: You have the older, wiser Japanese, who emanates a wisdom that withstands time, against the younger, quickly maturing American who has an outstanding reputation for being a victorious underdog. Who would win? We took the two awards to center ring, made them don their gloves and have a go.

ROUND 1: HISTORY

Although residing almost half a world apart, the Deming Prize and the Malcolm Baldrige National Quality Award are bonded by influence. After the ravages unleashed during World War II took a ruinous toll on Japan, W. Edwards Deming came to aid this seemingly hopeless land. With his expertise in statistical quality control (SQC), Deming helped lift Japan out of the rubble and into the limelight by having Japanese businesses apply SQC techniques.

*This article is reproduced from *Quality Digest*, pp. 33–53, August 1991. In it, the author interviewed four individuals representing organizations with a reputation for being involved in the formation of the Baldrige Award. While no conclusions are drawn, the topics are central to total quality and worthy of debate.

In 1951, the Union of Japanese Scientists and Engineers (JUSE) created an accolade to award companies that successfully apply companywide quality control (CWQC) based on statistical quality control. In honor of their American quality champion, JUSE named the award the Deming Prize.

Not until 31 years later did a similar prize take root in the United States, mainly due to the efforts of Frank C. Collins, who served as executive director of quality assurance for the Defense Logistics Agency and has formed Frank Collins Associates, Survival Twenty-One—a quality consulting firm; he also serves on the board of directors of the Malcolm Baldrige National Quality Award Consortium.

Collins, after many trips to Japan, based his U.S. quality award idea on the Deming Prize. "That's where I got the idea for the Malcolm Baldrige Award," he explains, "although I never in my wildest dreams expected it to be connected to Malcolm Baldrige."

Malcolm Baldrige, Secretary of Commerce in the Reagan administration, was killed in a rodeo accident in 1987. Reagan chose to honor Baldrige by naming the newly created award after him.

"The original concept was that it would be the National Quality Award," says Collins. "It would be strictly a private sector affair. The government would have no part in it other than the president being the awarder of the recognition."

ROUND 2: PROCESS

The Deming Prize has several categories: the Deming Prize for Individual Person, the Deming Application Prize and the Quality Control Award for Factory. Under the Deming Application Prize and the Deming Application Prize for Small Enterprise and the Deming Application Prize for Division. In 1984, another category was added: The Deming Application Prize to Oversea Companies, which is awarded to non-Japanese companies.

The Deming Application Prize has 10 examination items and is based on CWQC—the Prize's main objective.

A company or division begins the Deming Prize process by submitting an application form to the Deming Prize Committee, along with other pertinent information. Prospective applicants are advised to hold preliminary consultations with the secretariat of the Deming Prize Committee before completing and submitting the application.

After acceptance and notification, applicants must submit a description of quality control practices and a company business prospectus, *in Japanese*. If successful, the applicant will then be subject to a site visit. If the applicant passes, the Deming Prize is awarded.

Sound easy? Sometimes the applicant's information can fill up to 1,000 pages, and the examination process for U.S. companies is expensive.

The Baldrige Award applicant must first submit an Eligibility Determination Form, supporting documents and $50. Upon approval, the applicant must then submit an application package—running up to 50 pages for small business, 75 pages for a manufacturing or service company—and another fee. Among seven categories, 1,000 points are awarded. No particular score guarantees a site visit.

Each of the three categories—manufacturing, service and small company—are allowed up to two winners only.

ROUND 3: PURPOSE

The American obsession for winning is enormous. From Watergate to Iran-Contra, the American Revolution to Desert Storm, Americans have shown that they love to win no matter what the cost. So it's no wonder that as soon as quality awards and prizes have an impact, they fall under scrutiny. But most critics of these two world-class quality awards think these coveted prizes are mostly pristine in purpose.

Frank Voehl, *Quality Digest* columnist and corporate vice president and general manager of Qualtec Inc., a Florida Power & Light Group company, oversees the implementation of the total quality management programs within Qualtec's client companies. In 1987, Florida Power & Light (FPL) became the first and only U.S. company to win the Deming Prize. Through his work with hundreds of Japanese and U.S. companies, Voehl feels that there are seven reasons why companies quest for the Deming Prize or the Baldrige Award.

"The first general comment that a number of companies that I've talked to in Japan that have applied for the Deming Prize said was, 'We did not apply for the Deming Prize to win but to drive us toward better quality control,' says Voehl. "Second is applying for and receiving the examination had more meaning than did winning the Prize." Voehl's other five reasons are:

- The audit or the exam itself helped point out many areas of deficiencies and continuous improvement activities that they hadn't noticed.
- Since the Deming Prize dictates a clear goal and time limit, quality control advanced at an extremely rapid rate.
- The company going for the quality award was able to accomplish in one or two years what would normally have taken five or 10 years.
- There was a unification of a majority of the employees.
- They were able to communicate with a common language to the whole company. This is where the cultural change takes place.

Robert Peach, who was project manager of the Malcolm Baldrige National Quality Award Consortium for three years and now serves as a senior technical advisor to the administrator, feels the Baldrige Award "is not an award for the sake of the award—it is the 200,000 guidelines and applications that go out that matter, not the handful that actually apply."

And the companies that experiment with and implement the Baldrige criteria, as well as the Deming criteria, can only learn from their endeavor. However, for the companies taking it a step further and committing to win the prize, it isn't Little League, where the profits extracted from learning and having fun are supposed to outweigh the benefits of scoring more points than the other team. The Deming and the Baldrige are the Majors, where going for the award may mean 80-hour work weeks, quick hellos and goodbyes to spouses and missing your child's Little League games.

ROUND 4: GOING TO WAR

So your boss comes up to you and says, "Get ready—we're going for it." How you react may depend on the attitude of your senior-level management and the present quality state of your company. Ken Leach, a senior examiner for the Baldrige Award and founder of Leach Quality Inc., implemented the quality system at Globe Metallurgical—1988 winner of the Baldrige Award's small company category. He says winning the Baldrige was easy because its quality system was in place well before the birth of the Baldrige Award criteria.

"We got into it before Baldrige was even heard of, and we got into it at the impetus of our customers—Ford and General Motors in particular," explains Leach. "So we implemented a number of specific things to satisfy the customer, and you don't have a choice with them—you have to go through their audit system. We did that and did it very well. So that gave us the base to apply for the Baldrige and win it the very first year without trying to redo what we were already doing."

Leach says that because Globe was in such a readied state before the inception of the Baldrige Award, the company did not add any people or spend large sums of money on the implementation of a quality system. In fact, Globe was so advanced in its quality system that Leach claims he took the Baldrige Award application home after work on a Friday and returned it complete by the following Monday.

But even Leach agrees that Globe was exceptional and that not all companies can implement the Baldrige criteria as smoothly as Globe did.

Yokogawa-Hewlett-Packard (YHP) won the Deming Prize in 1982. Unlike Globe and its easy conquest of the Baldrige, YHP claims the quest for the Deming was no Sunday stroll. The company released the following statement in *Measure* magazine:

"Japanese companies compete fiercely to win a Deming Prize. Members of a management team typically work several hundred extra hours each month to organize the statistical charts, reports and exhibits for judging."[1] YHP also says that "audits had all the tension of a championship sports event."[2]

Voehl calls these extra hours and added stresses "pain levels and downside effects" and found that they were typical of most companies going for the Deming Prize. And because the Baldrige Award is a "second generation" of the Deming Prize, Voehl says the Baldrige Award is no exception to possible disruption. He explains that the quest for winning becoming greater than the quest for quality is a "natural thing that occurs within these organizations that you can't really prevent. Senior management focuses in on the journey and the overall effects that will happen as a result of going for the examination and the prize."

Voehl adds, "Getting ready for the examination and the site exams brings a tremendous amount of pressure upon the organizations, whether it's the Deming or the Baldrige, because of the implications that you should be the one department that results in the prize not being brought home."

William Golomski, who is the American Society for Quality Control's representative to JUSE, says deadline time for the award may be a time of pressure.

In the case of the Baldrige, there have been a few companies that hired consultants to help them get ready for a site visit after they've gone through an evaluation by examiners and senior examiners," recalls Golomski. "So I can understand that people who are still being asked to go through role playing for a site visit might get to the point where they'll say, 'Gosh, I don't know if I'm interested as I once was.' "

Collins looks at customers in a dual sense: your internal customers—employees or associates—and your external customers—the people who pay the freight to keep you in business.

"To me," Collins says forcefully, "when you *squeeze* your internal customer to win an award, you're really making a mockery of the whole thing."

But for the companies that take the Baldrige application guidelines and implement them without competing, Peach says the quality goal remains the biggest motivator.

"In my exposure both to applicants and other companies that are using the practice and guidelines independent of applying, I feel that they have the right perspective, that companies identify this as a pretty good practice of what quality practice should be," expounds Peach. "And they're using it that way. That's healthy; that's good."

Deming says it best: "I never said it would be easy; I only said it would work." And this piece of wisdom can pertain to the implementation and competing processes of both the Baldrige Award and the Deming Prize. But although sometimes not easy to pursue, these awards spark many companies to the awareness and benefits of a quality system. But as more companies win the Baldrige, more critics are discussing which accolade—the Baldrige or the Deming—holds more advantages over the other.

ROUND 5: ADVANTAGES VS. DISADVANTAGES

With a U.S. company capturing the Deming Prize, U.S. businesses are no longer without a choice of which world-class quality award to pursue. Motorola, before it went for the Baldrige Award, contemplated which award would improve Motorola's quality best, according to Stewart Clifford, president of Enterprise Media, a documentary film company that specializes in management topics. In a recent interview with Motorola's quality staff, Clifford asked if Motorola was interested in questing for the Deming Prize.

"I asked them the question about if they were looking at applying and going for the Deming," remembers Clifford. "And they said that they felt frankly that while the Deming Prize had some valuable points for them, the reason why they liked the Baldrige Award better was because of its much more intense focus on the customer."

But Voehl claims this is a misconception and that both approaches focus heavily on the customer. "Florida Power & Light really got a lot of negatives from our counselors that we weren't zeroing in on the external and internal customers enough," recalls Voehl. "We had to demonstrate how our quality improvement process was a means of planning and achieving customer satisfaction through TQC."

Section Seven of the Baldrige Award covers total customer satisfaction, and it's worth more points than any other section. In the Deming criteria, total customer satisfaction may seem lost among the need for applicants to document, document, document and use statistical approaches.

One reason Collins says he would compete for the Baldrige instead of the Deming is the Deming's unbending demand to have everything documented. "If you say something, you have to have a piece of paper that covers it," he jokes. "Having worked for the government for 33 years, I see that as a bureaucratic way of doing things. And the Japanese are extremely bureaucratic."

And in an open letter to employees from James L. Broadhead, FPL's chairman and CEO, printed in *Training* magazine, his employees confirm Collins' beliefs: "At the same time, however, the vast majority of the employees with whom I spoke expressed the belief that the mechanics of the QI [quality improvement] process have been overemphasized. They felt that we place too great an emphasis on indicators, charts, graphs, reports and meetings in which documents are presented and indicators reviewed."[3]

However, Collins says that what he likes about the Deming Prize criteria that's missing in the Baldrige Award criteria is the first two examination items of the Deming Prize: policy organization and its operation.

If you want people to understand what you mean by quality, you have to spell it out, you have to define it as policy, explains Collins. As far as objectives go, he remembers asking a Japanese firm what their objectives were. The president of this company said, "First to provide jobs to our company." "How many American firms would say that?" asks Collins. Organization and understanding its operation is extremely important. He says, "Those two criteria are the bedrock foundation of the Deming Prize that makes it somewhat stronger and of greater value than the Malcolm Baldrige National Quality Award."

Another point that may persuade a U.S. company to compete for one of the two awards is cost. All things considered, U.S. companies going for the Deming Application Prize to Oversea Companies seems more costly than U.S. companies competing for the Baldrige Award. Leach describes Globe's venture as very inexpensive: "It doesn't have to cost an arm and a leg for the Baldrige. You don't have to reinvent the wheel of what you're already doing." Peach worked with a small-category company that spent $6,000 on its Baldrige Award venture, and that included the application fee and retaining a technical writer for $1,000.

But these are small companies with 500 employees or fewer. FPL, on the other hand, with about 15,000 employees, spent $1.5 million on its quest for the Deming Prize, according to Neil DeCarlo of FPL's corporate communications. And there are some Baldrige applicants that have spent hundreds of thousands or even millions of dollars on their quality quest, according to *Fortune* magazine.[4]

But no matter how much the Baldrige applicant pays, whether it be $6,000 or millions, it still receives a feedback report as part of the application cost. In comparison, those companies not making it past the first level of the Deming Prize criteria may pay JUSE for counselors, who will come into the company and do a diagnostic evaluation.

Because FPL was a pioneer in the oversea competition, many of the costs that would have otherwise been associated with this award for an overseas company had been waived by JUSE, according to Voehl. But still, FPL dished out $850,000 of that million-and-a-half for counselor fees, says DeCarlo—an amount Voehl claims would be three or four times more if FPL had to hire a U.S. consulting firm.

One of FPL's reasons to go for the Deming award was because in 1986 when it decided to go for a quality award, the Baldrige Award did not yet exist. In fact, what many people, including some FPL critics, don't now is that the company heavily funded the activities leading to the Baldrige Award. FPL agreed not to try for the Baldrige Award for five years to deter any conflict of interest, says Voehl. Also, FPL had an excellent benchmarking company in Japan's Kansai Electric, which had already won the Deming Prize.

The Deming Prize puts no cap on the number of winners; the Baldrige allows a maximum of two winners for each of the three categories. Leach contests that by putting a limit on the winners, you make the Baldrige Award a more precious thing to win. Peach agrees. "I think there should be a limit," he says. "You just don't want scores of winners to dilute this."

Voehl disagrees. "We should take the caps off," he argues. "I think we'd do a lot more for the award, for the process if we didn't have a win-lose mentality toward it."

ROUND 6: CONTROVERSY

"The Baldrige is having such an impact," asserts Peach, "that now people will take a look at it and challenge. That will always happen—that's our American way." And at four years old, the Baldrige Award has already received a fair share of controversy. One of the most disturbing criticisms aimed at the Baldrige Award comes from Deming himself. Deming called the Baldrige Award "a terrible thing, a waste of industry" in a recent issue of *Automotive News*. The article states: "Among the reasons Deming denounces the award is its measurement of performance and the effects of training with numerical goals, which he cites as 'horrible things.'

" 'It's a lot of nonsense,' he said. 'The guidelines for 1991 (make that) very obvious.' "[5]

Golomski says that Deming is unhappy with two parts of the Baldrige guidelines. One is the concept of numerical goals, which Deming believes can cause aberrations within companies. "I don't take quite as strong a stand as Deming does," Golomski explains. "He makes another statement about goals and that far too often, goals are set in the absence of any way of knowing how you're going to achieve these goals."

Leach does not know what to think of "Deming's non-supportive or active disregard for the Baldrige Award." He finds it ironic that "a company could very much have a Deming-type philosophy or a Deming-oriented kind of company and could do quite well in the Baldrige application. I'm sure that Cadillac [1990 Baldrige Award winner] must have had a number of Deming philosophies in place."

Deming Prize Application Checklist: Items and Their Particulars

1. Policy

- Policies pursued for management, quality and quality control
- Methods of establishing policies
- Justifiability and consistency of policies
- Utilization of statistical methods
- Transmission and diffusion of policies
- Review of policies and the results achieved
- Relationship between policies and long- and short-term planning

2. Organization and Its Management

- Explicitness of the scopes of authority and responsibility
- Appropriateness of delegations of authority
- Interdivisional cooperation
- Committees and their activities
- Utilization of staff
- Utilization of quality circle activities
- Quality control diagnosis

3. Education and Dissemination

- Education programs and results
- Quality-and-control consciousness, degrees of understanding of quality control
- Teaching of statistical concepts and methods and the extent of their dissemination
- Grasp of the effectiveness of quality control
- Education of related company (particularly those in the same group, subcontractors, consignees and distributors)
- Quality circle activities
- System of suggesting ways of improvements and its actual conditions

4. Collection, Dissemination and Use of Information on Quality

- Collection of external information
- Transmission of information between divisions
- Speed of information transmission (use of computers)
- Data processing, statistical analysis of information and utilization of the results

5. Analysis

- Selection of key problems and themes
- Propriety of the analytical approach
- Utilization of statistical methods
- Linkage with proper technology
- Quality analysis, process analysis
- Utilization of analytical results
- Assertiveness of improvement suggestions

6. Standardization

- Systematization of standards
- Method of establishing, revising and abolishing standards
- Outcome of the establishment, revision or abolition of standards
- Contents of the standards
- Utilization of the statistical methods
- Accumulation of technology
- Utilization of standards

7. Control

- Systems for the control of quality and such related matters as cost and quantity
- Control items and control points
- Utilization of such statistical control methods as control charts and other statistical concepts
- Contribution to performance of quality circle activity
- Actual conditions of control activities
- State of matters under control

8. Quality Assurance

- Procedure for the development of new products and services (analysis and upgrading of quality, checking of design, reliability and other properties)
- Safety and immunity from product liability
- Process design, process analysis and process control and improvement
- Process capability
- Instrumentation, gauging, testing and inspecting
- Equipment maintenance and control of subcontracting, purchasing and services
- Quality assurance system and its audit
- Utilization of statistical methods
- Evaluation and audit of quality
- Actual state of quality assurance

9. Results

- Measurement of results
- Substantive results in quality, services, delivery, time, cost, profits, safety, environment, etc.
- Intangible results
- Measuring for overcoming defects

10. Planning for the Future

- Grasp of the present state of affairs and the concreteness of the plan
- Measures for overcoming defects
- Plans for further advances
- Linkage with long-term plans

Even if Deming is trying to be the burr under the saddle and spark U.S. companies into a quality quest, Leach doesn't think that Deming's "serving the pursuit of quality in general or himself very well by making public statements like that."

But Voehl agrees with some of Deming's points. "Cadillac got severely criticized by the board of trustees of the Baldrige because Cadillac took the Baldrige Award and General Motors tried to use it as a marketing tool," he says. "And that's not the intention. Those sort of things do not do the Baldrige Award any good because it seems like all you're interested in is public relations.

Cadillac has fallen under scrutiny from many critics for taking home the Baldrige Award.

After returning from consulting in Israel, Collins heard that Cadillac had won the Baldrige Award. "I couldn't believe my eyes," Collins exclaims. "Cadillac has gotten so much bad press over the last decade—transmission problems, difficulty with their diesel engines, their service record—a whole number of things that to me when they said Cadillac won it, I said, 'Impossible. They couldn't win it. Somebody's pulling a cruel joke.' "

Deming is not the only quality guru criticizing the Baldrige Award. Philip Crosby says in *Quality Digest* (February 1991) that customers should nominate the companies that compete for the Baldrige, not the companies themselves.

It is difficult to come by harsh criticism about the Deming Prize since few Americans are familiar with it. However, Collins questions FPL's quest for winning as superseding their quest for quality.

"There's no question in my mind that Florida Power & Light's John Hudiburg was intent on leading Florida Power & Light in a blaze of glory," insists Collins. "And money was absolutely no consideration as far as winning the Deming Prize. I don't know what the final tab on it was, but he bought the prize—there's no question about it."

Collins' comments do not go without backing. A number of articles on FPL's quest contain complaints from disgruntled employees who worked long hours to win the Deming Prize.

"If the goal is to win an award then the cost of winning the award is not worth the award itself," Voehl admits. "The focus needs to be on the outcomes for the organization." And Voehl feels that FPL's quality outcomes very much outweigh the cost put forth.

ROUND 7: CONSULTANTS

With the two awards, there's a big difference in the use of consultants or counselors, as they're called in Japan. In the case of the Deming Prize, a successful applicant uses counselors trained by JUSE throughout the examination, explains Golomski. "For the Baldrige, you're on your own or you use whomever you wish to help you—if you think it's worth it."

"Considering the tremendous number of brochures I get every day," says Collins, "it appears that everybody and his brother is an expert on the Malcolm Baldrige National Quality Award. And my experience tells me that there *ain't* that many experts on the Malcolm Baldrige National Quality Award."

So, are some consultants or counselors using the Baldrige Award to prey on aspiring companies? Voehl says he sees it happening all over and calls it "absolutely preposterous and absurd and unethical."

Voehl compares it to just like everybody jumping on the TQC bandwagon. "Everybody from a one-man or two-man mom-and-pop consulting company to a 1,000-employee consulting arm of the Big 8 seems to be an expert in TQM," he says. "It's like a dog with a rag: They're shaking it and shaking it, and they won't let it go because they see it can mean money to their bottom line. It's giving the consulting field a terrible black eye. It's giving the people who bring in these consultants the expectations clearly that they are going to win the award. These are false expectations, false hopes and false starts. They shouldn't even be looking at winning the award; they should be looking at implementing a quality system that can ensure customer satisfaction."

But there are good reasons to have consultants help you through the Baldrige quest. Leach points out that if a CEO of a company needs to change his or her approach on something, an employee will probably be intimidated to approach the CEO; instead, a consultant can do this. Also a consultant may carry in an objective view that brings different ideas to the company.

Deming Prize counselors, however, have a reputation to guard. That's why Golomski feels FPL had no chance to "buy the Prize."

"The counselor simply wouldn't agree with them that they [FPL] were ready," Golomski argues. "The counselors help an organization improve itself, but if they don't think the company is ready for the big leagues, they simply won't recommend it."

ROUND 8: MODIFICATIONS

The Baldrige Award criteria are constantly modified to meet changing expectations. This is how it grows stronger, becomes more mature. When awarded the Baldrige Award, recipients must share their knowledge of total quality, but Golomski wants to see better ways of technology transfer.

Collins thinks we will probably have a follow-up award similar to the Japan Quality Control Prize—which is awarded to Deming Prize winners if they have improved their quality standards five years after winning the Deming Prize and pass rigorous examination—but not until the Baldrige Award can be further improved.

Peach feels the Baldrige criteria are at a position where modifications will be in smaller increments. He says cycle time might become important enough to be emphasized more.

The possible modifications of the Deming Prize are hard to predict. However, modifications of the Baldrige Award may be based on the Deming Prize's influence.

ROUND 9: SAVING FACE

Junji Noguchi, executive director of JUSE, was contacted for an interview for this article. When he learned of the subject matter—comparing the two world-class quality awards—he declined to answer. He said, "I am sorry I have to reply that I cannot answer your interviews. That is because the contents were not preferable and that they are not what I was expecting."

Noguchi continued, "Awards or prizes in the country have been established under the most suitable standards and methods considering their own background of industries, societies and cultures. We do not understand the meaning of comparing awards in different countries that have different backgrounds."

Noguchi is displaying some of that ancient wisdom and showing a difference in our cultures that even Americans find difficult to explain. Is this why their award has been going strong for 40 years and why the Baldrige Award is a 4-year-old child growing much too fast thanks to our intrinsic desire to slice it up, examine it and try to put it back together more completely than before? Maybe. But as a result, our U.S. quality award will always remain provocative and exciting and keep the people talking. And this is good.

REFERENCES

1. "YHP Teamwork Takes the Prize," Measure (January-February 1983), 3000 Hanover St., Palo Alto, CA 94304, pg. 6.
2. Measures, pg. 6.
3. James L. Broadhead, "The Post-Deming Diet: Dismantling a Quality Bureaucracy," Training, Lakewood Building, 50 S. Ninth St., Minneapolis, MN 55402, pg. 41.
4. Jeremy Main, "Is the Baldrige Overblown?" Fortune (July 1, 1991), Time & Life Building, Rockefeller Center, New York, NY 10020-1393, pg. 62.
5. Karen Passino, "Deming Calls Baldrige Prize 'Nonsense,' " Automotive News (April 1, 1991), 1400 E. Woodbridge, Detroit, MI, 48207.

CHAPTER 3

The HOUSE of QUALITY

The metaphor used here to present the basic concepts and principles associated with total quality is the House of Quality (Figure 3.1). As in a well-built house, the major components of the House of Quality are (1) the *roof*, or superstructure, consisting of the social, technical, and management systems; (2) the *four pillars* of customer satisfaction, continuous improvement, speaking with facts, and respect for people; (3) the *foundation* of four managerial levels—strategy, process, project, and task management; and (4) the *four cornerstones* of mission, vision, values, and goals and objectives.

As in building any house, the plans must be developed first, usually by experienced individuals working together—a team. Once the plans are approved, construction (implementation) can begin.

Total quality efforts frequently fail because the individuals responsible for the efforts (i.e., management) are unable to carry out their responsibilities. They do not recognize the importance of systems thinking and do not have a well-defined purpose and process to follow. As discussed in Chapters 1 and 2, Deming's work and the Baldrige Award focus on the following ten management guidelines as part of the implementation process (from Tribus[1]):

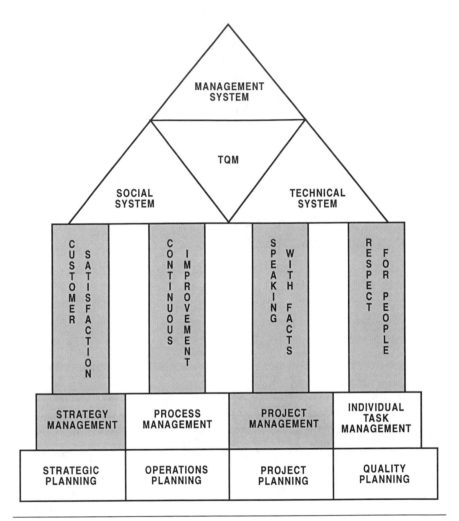

Figure 3.1 House of Total Quality.

- Recognize quality improvement as a system.
- Define it so others can recognize it, too.
- Analyze its behavior.
- Work with subordinates in improving the system.
- Measure the quality of the system.
- Develop improvements in the quality of the system.
- Measure the gains in the quality, if any, and link these to customer delight and quality improvement.

- Take steps to guarantee holding the gains.
- Attempt to replicate the improvements into other areas of the organization.
- Tell others about the lessons learned.

These guidelines, when implemented, will assure success because of their impact on all aspects of the college or university. They are also reflected in the House of Quality, which illustrates the universality of the basic principles and procedures for carrying out total quality. Use of the House of Quality does not negate, but rather supports, the works of Deming and Baldrige. Throughout this chapter the fourteen principles of Deming and the seven categories of the Baldrige Award are presented within the context of the House of Quality. The principles and categories have been modified to emphasize their application to higher education.[2] Collectively, this provides a functional guide for understanding and implementing quality within a college or university.

SYSTEMS AND TOTAL QUALITY

The superstructure for the House of Total Quality involves a system composed of three subsystems held together by total quality (Figure 3.2). The three subsystems are managerial, social, and technical. Their interdependencies are depicted in the three interlocking circles of a ballantine,[3] as shown in Figure 3.2. The successful implementation of total quality and continuous improvement efforts requires the redefinition of management to recognize the importance of the systems. Deming[4] states, "The people work in a system. The job of the manager is to work on the system, to improve it continuously, with their help." Within the House of Quality the manager must work on the three systems.

The Social System

The social system includes factors associated with the formal and informal characteristics of the organization: (1) organizational culture (the values, norms, attitudes, role expectations, and differentiation that exist in each organization); (2) quality of social relationships between

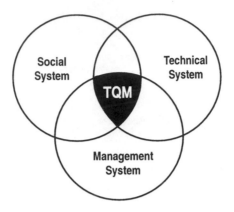

Figure 3.2 Total Quality as a Management System.

individual members and among groups, including reward structures and symbols of power; and (3) behavioral patterns between members, including roles and communication. It is the social system that has the greatest impact on such factors as motivation, creativity, innovative behavior, and teamwork. Managers have a major responsibility for the nature and character of the social system.

The social system may or may not have a planned function within the organization. Many managers would like to deny, or at least ignore, the existence of cultures, roles, or organizational values. However, social systems exist, and they exert influence, both positive and negative, on the activities of an organization.

To achieve total quality, a social system must be developed in which constituent or customer satisfaction, continuous improvement, management based on facts, and a genuine respect for people are accepted practices of the college or university. Frequently this requires a substantial change in the social system, and change does not come easily for most colleges and universities. Change usually occurs when the cost (disadvantages, lost opportunities) of remaining the same becomes greater than the benefit of an alternative condition. As indicated in Chapter 1, several characteristics of higher education encourage resistance to change, many of which are both intellectually correct and philosophically appropriate.

Figure 3.3 presents a fishbone diagram (also known as a cause-and-effect or causal analysis diagram) of social system characteristics that help create a total quality organization. As shown in Figure 3.3, six areas of strategy must be addressed in order to change and transform the culture of an organization to a quality-driven organization: (1) the environment, (2) product or service, (3) methods, (4) people, (5) organizational structure, and (6) mindset of total quality improvement. Thus, in a college or university driven by total quality, people feel they belong, feel pride in their work, learn continuously, and work to their potential. Each of these major areas will be covered in some detail in the following sections. (For additional information, see Abstract 3.1 at the end of this chapter.)

The Technical System

According to Tribus,[5] "The technical system includes all the tools and machinery, the practice of quality and the quantitative aspects of quality. If you can measure it, you can probably describe and perhaps improve it using the technical systems approach." The technical system is concerned with the flow of work through the organization. It is driven by two primary guides: fulfillment of its mission and service to the customer. In most organizations the technical system contains the following core elements:

- Accumulation of technology
- Pursuit of standardization
- Workflow, materials, and specifications
- Job definitions and responsibility
- Machine/person interface
- Number and type of work steps
- Availability and use of information
- Decision-making processes
- Problem-solving tools and processes
- Physical arrangements of equipment, tools, and people

The expected benefits from analyzing and improving the technical system(s) are to:

- Reduce (eliminate) waste and rework
- Reduce (eliminate) negative variation
- Increase learning

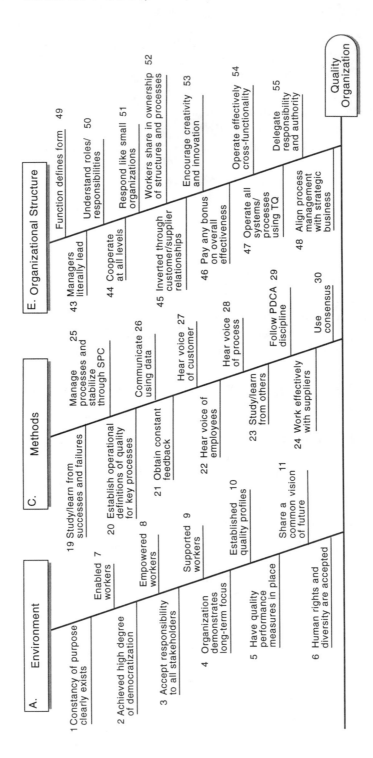

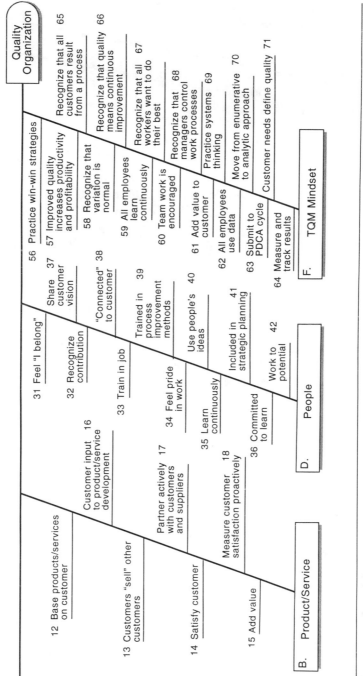

Figure 3.3 Social System Characteristics of a Total Quality Organization (Fishbone Diagram).

- Reduce (eliminate) interruptions and idle time
- Save time and money
- Increase employee control over the work process
- Reduce bottlenecks and frustration
- Improve safety and quality of work life
- Increase speed and responsiveness
- Improve customer satisfaction

In higher education, the technical system primarily involves the transformation process described in Figure 1.2 (see Chapter 1). The specific core elements, in addition to the above, include students, curriculum, courses, schedules, faculty, administrative staff, classrooms, library holdings, and instructional equipment. The benefits are (as listed in Figure 1.2) academic achievement, competency, and personal development. (For additional information, see Abstract 3.2 at the end of this chapter.)

The Managerial System

The managerial system includes factors associated with (1) the organizational structure (formal design, policies, division of responsibilities, and patterns of power and authority); (2) the mission, vision, and goals of the institution; and (3) administrative activities (planning, organizing, directing, coordinating, and controlling organizational activities). Management provides the framework for the policies, procedures, practices, and leadership of the organization. The management system is deployed at four levels: strategy, process, project, and personal management. These comprise the foundation of the House of Quality and will be briefly discussed later in this chapter and more thoroughly in Chapters 4 through 7.

As stated at the beginning of this chapter, the Deming principles and Baldrige categories are an integral part of the House of Quality. Deming's first two principles and the third category of the Baldrige Award address the superstructure and the three systems described above.

Deming Principle 1. Create a constancy of purpose toward the improvement of academic programs and administrative services. Aim to create quality students capable of entering meaningful positions in society and improving all forms of practices and processes.

Deming Principle 2. Adopt the new philosophy. Management in higher education must awaken to the challenge, learn their responsibilities, and take on leadership for change.

Baldrige Category 3. *Strategic quality planning* examines the planning process of the college or university and how all key quality requirements are integrated into an overall plan. Also examined are short and longer term plans, as well as how quality and performance requirements are deployed to all work units, both academic and administrative.

The roof or superstructure consists of the three critical systems necessary for any organization to function. The effectiveness of the organization is governed by the strength of four pillars.

THE PILLARS OF QUALITY

Total quality management in any organization is supported by four driving forces, or pillars, that move the organization toward the full application of quality service. The four pillars of the House of Quality (see Figure 3.1) are customer service, continuous improvement, processes and facts, and respect for people. All are distinct, but equal in potential strength. All four must be addressed; minimizing one weakens the others. By not addressing one, the entire House of Quality will fall.

Serving the Customer (The First Pillar)

College and university enrollments have not diminished substantially over the past three decades; then why be concerned about who is served? According to Voehl, Schmidt and Finnigan (1992), and others, the two most basic questions for all organizations, public and private, are *what is our mission* and *who are our customers?* Every college and university has (and many can readily state their own) a mission (discussed in Chapter 4), but very few fully identify who they serve. Even fewer acknowledge that they serve *customers.*

The very notion of having customers is alien to most campuses. Considering students as customers is perceived by many faculty as relegating themselves to the position of being employees. The traditional role of faculty is threatened when defining the academic role within the framework of its impact upon the end user. Within this framework, the student (the customer) is seen as a partner in developing and delivering quality education (the product or service). To many faculty, this is anathema to the historic, traditional academic role as the purveyor of knowledge.

This traditional academic perspective is reinforced by administrative actions (i.e., administrative convenience too often supersedes customer orientation). Schedules are developed, courses and classes offered, and facilities designed for the benefit of the institution first and students second.

While viewing the campus as a customer-driven entity may be anathema to many, one truth has been proven repeatedly: customer-driven organizations are effective because they focus on a full commitment to satisfying, even anticipating, the needs of the customer. While colleges and universities have been successful, their future success will increasingly be determined by customer satisfaction. Those campuses that are successful will be those that most clearly identify their mission and the customers they serve. (For additional information, see Abstract 3.3 at the end of this chapter.)

Who is the customer of higher education or, more accurately, who are its customers? Like most complex organizations, colleges and universities must be sensitive to multiple constituencies. One framework for identifying the customers of higher education is to view them from three perspectives: internal customers, direct external customers, and indirect external customers (Table 3.1). *Internal customers* are the students, faculty, programs, and departments within the academic programs of a campus that influence a specific program. The internal customers for administration are students as well, but also include employees and units, departments, or divisions that influence a service or activity. *Direct external customers* include employers of the students, other colleges and universities that are recipients of the students and services of the college or university, and suppliers (i.e., those from whom the college or university receives students, products, or services, such as high schools, product suppliers, service suppliers). *Indirect external customers* are legislative bodies, communities served, accrediting agencies, alumni, and donors (i.e., those that impact the decisions and operation of the college or university).

Attention to these customers should be prioritized in this order, as the internal and direct external customers are the direct recipients of the quality academic programs, services, and research of the college or

Table 3.1   The Customers of Higher Education

Customers	Needs
Internal customers—academic	
Students	Knowledge, skills, and abilities to pursue personal and professional goals; joy in learning
Faculty	Continuous personal growth, security, joy in work, information, and input
Programs/departments	Continuous improvement, information exchange (input/output), cooperation, and collaboration
Internal customers—administrative	
Students	Service provided when requested, questions answered when asked
Employees	Continuous personal growth, security, joy in work, information, and input
Units/departments, divisions	Continuous improvement, information exchange (input/output), cooperation, and collaboration
External customers—direct	
Employers	Competent employees, productive performance
Other colleges, universities	Students capable of advanced learning and research
External customers—indirect	
Legislature (state, federal)	Be elected or re-appointed, compliance, make a contribution
Community	Competent workforce, leaders and followers, volunteers in community services, politically active citizens
Accrediting agencies	Compliance with established criteria and standards
Alumni	Pride in having attended, continuing education
Donors	Awareness of both the quality and needs of the college/university, appropriate acknowledgment of a donation

university. However, because of their financial and accreditation controls, a proportionately larger amount of time is spent serving the indirect external customers. Many quality measures used by accrediting agencies and legislative bodies mean very little to students, yet students ultimately are the *raison d'être*.

Colleges and universities must hold onto a simple truth: customer-driven organizations are successful because they have a unified focus on what they do and who they serve. As stated by Roger Enrico,[7] president of PepsiCo, "If you are totally customer-focused and you deliver the services your customers want, everything else will follow." Seymour[8] brings this emphasis into the halls of higher education in stating, "Developing a lot of happy, satisfied customers—whether they are students, parents of students, alumni, professors, or industry employers—should be a primary goal of causing quality in higher education."

Which of the Deming principles and Baldrige categories address customer service? When asked what a quality school is, Deming replied that one need only ask whether a person is "better off having gone to that school."[9] Deming clearly demonstrates his strong commitment to the customer. He discusses at length one internal customer: the recognition and development of *all* employees. This is discussed as part of the fourth pillar, respect for people. Principle 4 addresses the external customer—those organizations providing the college or university with students and the suppliers of goods and services.

Deming Principle 4 (Students). Work with the educational institutions from which the students come. Improve the relationship with student sources, and help improve the quality of students coming into the system. When effective, this will provide an opportunity to build long-term relationships based on loyalty and trust for the benefit of the students.

Deming Principle 4 (Suppliers). End the practice of awarding business based on price. Instead, minimize total cost. Move toward a single supplier for any one item, building a long-term relationship based on loyalty and trust.

The seventh Baldrige category addresses customer focus and satisfaction. For higher education, three customers need to be identified: the student, the employers of the students, and the colleges and universities accepting the graduates of the college or university.

Baldrige Category 7: *Focus on satisfaction of the student.* Relationships with students must be based on knowledge of their requirements and the key quality factors that determine their success upon leaving the college or university. This includes methods to determine student satisfaction, current trends and levels of satisfaction, and how other competing colleges and universities relate with and satisfy their students.

Baldrige Category 7: *Focus on satisfaction of the recipients of the students.* Build relationships with the employers that hire and the colleges and universities that accept the students based on knowledge of their requirements, the key quality factors of their success, and how the students will contribute to their success.

Continuous Improvement (The Second Pillar)

Continuous improvement is both a commitment (continuous quality improvement or CQI) and a process (continuous process improvement or CPI). The Japanese word for this second pillar is *kaizen* and is, according to Imai,[10] the single most important concept in Japanese management. The commitment to quality is initiated with a statement of dedication to a shared mission and vision and the empowerment of all participants to incrementally move toward the vision. The process of improvement is accomplished through the initiation of small, short-term projects and tasks throughout the organization which collectively are driven by the achievement of the long-term vision and mission. Both are necessary; one cannot be done without the other.

Continuous improvement is dependent on two elements: learning the appropriate processes, tools, and skills and practicing these newfound skills on small achievable projects. The process for continuous improvement, first advanced many years ago by Shewhart and implemented by Deming,[11] is *Plan, Do, Check, and Act* (PDCA), a never-ending cycle of improvement that occurs in all phases of the organization (e.g., admissions, registration, student affairs, academic programming, maintenance, etc.) (Figure 3.4). While no rigid rules are required to carry out the process, the general framework of each step can be described.

The first step, *Plan*, asks such key questions as what changes are needed, what are the needed results, what obstacles need to be overcome, are data available, and what new information is needed. *Do* is the implementation of a small-scale change or pilot test to provide data for answers. *Check* is the assessment and measurement of the effects of the change or test. *Act*, the final step, first asks whether the data confirm the intended plan, whether other variables are influencing the plan, and whether the risks in proceeding are necessary and worthwhile. Then, based on these answers, the project or task is modified and moves into the *Plan* stage again, where the iteration continues, expanding knowledge and implementing further improvement. Ideally, this process would continue indefinitely.

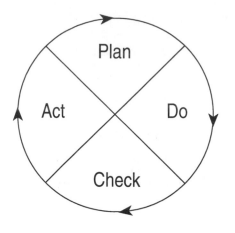

Figure 3.4 Plan, Do, Check, Act.

Two of Deming's principles and two Baldrige categories address this important aspect of total quality.

Deming Principle 3. Cease dependence on inspection and testing to achieve quality. Eliminate the need for inspection by building quality into the programs and services in the first place. Within academic programs, cease dependence on testing to achieve quality. Provide learning experiences that create quality performance. Work to abolish grading and the harmful effects of rating people.

Deming Principle 5. Improve constantly and forever the system of program quality and service in order to improve quality performance.

Baldrige Category 5. *Management of process quality* is the key element of how the college or university develops and realizes the full potential of the workforce to pursue its quality and performance objectives. Also examined are the efforts required to build and maintain an environment for quality excellence that is conducive to full participation and personal organizational growth.

Baldrige Category 6. *Quality and operational results* examines quality levels and improvement trends in operational performance of administrative and academic programs and supplier quality, as well as the current quality and performance levels of competitors.

For additional information, see Abstract 3.4 at the end of this chapter.

Managing with Facts (The Third Pillar)

Deming, paraphrasing the axiom "In God we trust, all others bring cash," noted the central tenet of this third pillar: *In God we trust. All others bring facts.* Too often, the management of a program is based on intuition, influence, hunches, or organizational politics. External and internal forces require the elimination of this precarious managerial approach. Stable or diminished funding; the increasing cost of salaries, supplies, and services; the increased number of women and minorities at all levels of the organization; and continuous competition for students, grants, and financial support will force *all* colleges and universities to be driven by decisions and actions based on facts, rather than only partial awareness of the issues, reliance on traditional networks, and/or just doing what has always been done. Tom Peters, paraphrasing the axiom, "If it isn't broke, don't fix it," repeatedly states, *"If it isn't broke, break it!"*

This requires a substantial shift in many areas of higher education to a process of carrying out continuous improvement (the second pillar—plan, do, check, act) and effective process management through the extensive use of a variety of tools designed to gather and analyze data and make decisions based on facts (the third pillar). Seven basic, highly effective tools were identified early in the history of the total quality movement: fishbone diagram (cause-and-effect diagram), checksheet, control chart, histogram, Pareto diagram, run chart, and scatter diagram; the control chart, cause-and-effect diagram, and Pareto diagram are the three tools most commonly used in the total quality process. A description of 21 tools now being used follows.[12] The seven original tools are denoted by an asterisk (*). Also identified are tools for planning and development, denoted by a plus (+).

1. *Affinity diagram/KJ method.*[+] Organizes pieces of information into groupings based on the natural relationships that exist among them. Used when large numbers, issues, and other items are being collected.
2. *Block diagram.* Traces the paths that materials and/or information take between the point of input and final output.
3. *Brainstorming.* Used to stimulate a group to generate as many ideas as possible in a short period of time and to promote group participation.

4. *Cause-and-effect or fishbone diagram.** Shows all possible causes of a specific problem or condition. Helps identify the root causes and cause-and-effect relationships.
5. *Cause-and-effect or force-field analysis.* Used to identify problems, their causes, and the driving and retraining forces that affect the problem.
6. *Checksheet.** A form used to record data on an ongoing basis over a period of time, for the purpose of collecting data for further analysis.
7. *Competitive benchmarking.\+* Measures processes, product, and/ or service against those of recognized leaders. Helps establish priorities and targets, which leads to a competitive advantage.
8. *Control chart.** Monitors the ongoing performance of a process, showing variances from a standard or objective.
9. *Customer/supplier relations checklist.* Used to assess the relationship with customers and suppliers.
10. *Flowchart.\+* A pictorial diagram of the steps in a process, useful for finding out how a process works.
11. *Histogram.** Used to measure frequency of occurrence and displayed as a frequency distribution.
12. *Interview.* An information-gathering technique which encourages direct input into quality improvement efforts and fosters cooperative working relationships.
13. *Nominal group technique.\+* A structured group decision-making process used to assign priorities or rank order a group of ideas.
14. *Pareto diagram.** A graphical technique for rank ordering causes or issues from the most to least significant.
15. *Run chart.** Shows the results of a process plotted over time. Useful to see the dynamic aspects of a process and identify cyclical patterns.
16. *Scatter diagram.** Shows the relationship or association between any two variables.
17. *Survey.\+* Written questionnaire in which specific questions addressing a problem or issue are posed.
18. *Tree diagram.* A systematic approach to defining a hierarchy of needs, objectives, characteristics, or goals.
19. *Trend chart.\+* Used to monitor shifts in long-range averages and graph results of a process such as enrollment, admissions, machine downtime, or phone calls.
20. *Excelerator.* A personal computer software tool for systems

analysis, design, and documentation. Available from Index Tech. Corp., 1 Main Street, Cambridge, MA 02142.

21. *Q-Map (Quality Map)*. A personal software program for developing measures of process performance. Available from Pacesetter Software, P.O. Box 5270, Princeton, NJ 08540.

The last two tools are computer-based programs that aid in the application of the other tools.

None of the Deming principles or Baldrige categories directly apply to this pillar. Managing with facts requires two actions. First, collect objective data so that the information is valid. Second, whenever possible, manage according to this information, not according to instinct, preconceptions, or other nonobjective factors. Managing with facts is important because *people* collect and use the facts, providing a common framework for communication in order to understanding what is being done and what needs to be done. Thus, not only does it provide a solid base of objective data upon which reliable decisions can be made, but it also contributes to empowerment of and respect for the people within the organization (the fourth pillar of the House of Quality).

Respect for People (The Fourth Pillar)

For whom does one work? No one works just for the customers and the college or university (in that order, preferably). In the end, each individual works for himself or herself, trying to create a meaningful and satisfying life in the best way possible. The output of colleges and universities is not only teaching, service, and research. It also encompasses the quality of life of everyone who works in, or is affected by, the college or university. Fortunately, quality of output goes hand-in-hand with quality of work. The only way total quality will be attained is through total commitment and participation.

Every employee must be fully developed and involved. The result will be an empowered individual—a value-added resource, with loyalty to the program, the team, and the entire college or university. Respect for people often boils down to such simple things as:

• Creating a sense of purpose in the workplace so that people are motivated to do their best.

- Keeping people informed and involved, and showing them how they are a part of the bigger picture.
- Educating and developing people so that each individual is the best that he or she can be at what they do.
- Helping people communicate well so that they can perform their jobs with peak effectiveness.
- Delegating responsibility and authority downward so that people are not just doing what they are told, but are taking the initiative to try to make things work better.

It is not enough just to go through the motions. These behaviors work well when they are part of a genuine attitude of respect and caring for other people. Managers who do not have this attitude of respect and caring cannot pretend for very long that they do.

It is to this fourth pillar that Deming directed eight of his fourteen principles. It reinforces the reason he retains the opinion that most organizations are unable to truly implement total quality because of their pervasive attitude that people are an expense to be controlled rather than an asset to be developed.

Deming Principle 6. Institute education and training for everyone: faculty, administration, staff, and students.

Deming Principle 7. The goal of supervision should be to help people use procedures, techniques, machines, and materials to do a better job. Leadership of faculty, management, staff, and students is in need of a general overhaul.

Deming Principle 8. Drive out fear, so that everyone can work effectively for the college or university. Create an environment in which people are encouraged to speak freely.

Deming Principle 9. Break down barriers between departments and programs and between faculty, administration, staff, and students. Those involved in teaching, research (faculty and institutional), student services, food service, accounting, academic affairs, etc. must work as a team (work teams and cross teams). Develop strategies for increasing the cooperation among groups and individuals.

Deming Principle 10. Eliminate slogans, exhortations, and targets that promote perfect performance and new levels of productivity (e.g., increased enrollments/reduce expenses by $X\%$). Exhortations create adversarial relationships. The bulk of the causes of low quality and low productivity belong to the system and thus lie beyond the control of faculty, administration, staff, and students.

Deming Principle 11. Eliminate performance standards (quotas) for faculty, administration, staff, and students (e.g., raise test scores by 10%, lower dropout rate by 15%). Eliminate management by numbers and numerical goals. Substitute leadership.

Deming Principle 12. Remove barriers that rob faculty, administration, staff, and students of the right to take pride in and enjoy the satisfaction of personal performance and productivity. This means, among other things, abolishing annual or merit ratings and management by objectives. The focus of responsibility for all managers, academic and administrative, must be changed from quantity to quality.

Deming Principle 13. Institute a vigorous program of education and self-improvement for everyone.

For additional information, see Abstract 3.5 at the end of this chapter.

Two of the seven Baldrige categories also address leadership and the development of people.

Baldrige Category 1. *Leadership* examines the personal involvement of senior executives in creating and sustaining customer focus and clear and visible quality values. Also examined is how the quality values are integrated into the management system of the college or university, which is reflected in the manner in which public responsibilities are addressed.

Baldrige Category 4. *Human resource development and management* examines the key elements of how colleges and universities develop and realize the full potential of their workforce in pursuing their quality and performance objectives. Also examined are the efforts to build and maintain an environment for quality excellence in which full participation and personal organizational growth are encouraged.

THE FOUNDATION AND CORNERSTONES

The roof and four pillars rest upon a foundation and cornerstone consisting of four managerial and planning processes. This discussion has evolved from a broad systemic framework, i.e., the three total quality management systems (social, technical, and managerial), to the four principles that guide these systems (customer satisfaction, continuous improvement, managing with facts, and respect for people), and now to the procedural functions that make the systems and principles operational. The roof (the systems) is the most theoretical, with the principles providing guides for actualizing the system, but still not making it operational. It remains for the managerial and planning processes to be put into action in order to actualize the quality improvement process. Therefore, with the metaphor of the House of Quality, it is appropriate that these functions are the foundation and cornerstones of the entire house. It is here where the construction begins. It is also here where you get your hands dirty! These functions are so important that the guidelines and strategies for their implementation are provided in Chapters 4 through 7. What follows is a brief summary.

Strategy Management. *Quality planning* is the broadest of the managerial levels. It establishes the organization-wide total quality management strategy and framework. It is a top-down strategy, initiated by senior management but developed with everyone involved through a variety of consensus, team-building, and brainstorming activities. The outcome is a three- to five-year plan containing the mission, vision, guiding principles or values, and goals and objectives for the organization. "Ownership" of the plan is achieved when everyone acknowledges the focus of the plan and accepts its potential to help the organization move in a common direction.

Process Management. *Operations planning* assures that all key processes work in harmony with the mission and meet the needs and expectations of the constituents or customers by maximizing operational effectiveness. Its key components are continuous improvement problem-solving methods. Efforts at this managerial stage are often cross-functional, as many functions cross departmental boundaries (e.g., student services, maintenance, degree requirements, course programs, and schedules). This requires interdepartmental collaboration, with process and indicator functions appropriately assigned. The outcomes are a common process and language for documenting and communicating activities and decisions and for realizing success in eliminating waste, redundancy, and bottlenecks.

Project Management. *Project planning* establishes a system to effectively plan, organize, implement, and control all the resources and activities needed for successful completion of the quality program. It is at this stage that teams are formed to solve and carry out both process- and policy-related initiatives. Team activities are linked to operational objectives and improvement targets. They develop the critical success factors: control systems, schedules, tracking mechanisms, performance indicators, and skill analysis. The outcome of each is a vision of the project that is linked with the organizational objectives, a work plan with designated milestones, a communication process for documenting key decisions and improvements, and a project completed on time and within budget.

Personal Management. *Personal quality planning* provides all employees with the means to implement continuous improvement of the above processes and systems through development of individual work functions and control. Each individual is guided through the development of a personal mission and vision and an analysis of how his or her work responsibilities complement this mission and vision. Key objectives, with quality indicators and personal controls, are developed. The outcome of personal management is a shared organizational vision, people empowered to make decisions and solve problems, a greater sense of job satisfaction, improved communication, and better work systems.

The implementation of a total quality program can begin at any of these managerial points (i.e., a team of workers can develop a quality-centered project management plan and facilitate personal growth and management). However, as will be shown, an organization-wide total quality process is best initiated through strategy management, which begins with process management and is followed by project and personal management.

To summarize, the House of Quality, which consists of a roof or superstructure (social, technical, and managerial systems), four pillars supporting the roof (customer satisfaction, continuous improvement, managing with facts, and respect for people), the four foundational supports (strategy, process, project, and personal management), and four cornerstones (total quality, operations, project, and personal quality planning), provides the basis for the systemic achievement of total quality. The impact upon the college or university, if fully adopted and implemented, can best be represented by two illustrative statements. The first is the final Deming principle.

Deming Principle 14. Put everyone in the college or university to work to accomplish the transformation. The transformation is everyone's job.

This principle, in turn, is best represented in the following statement by Thomas Plough (as stated in Seymour[9]), which emphasizes that quality will not be understood through massive change, but through the thousand-and-one acts done every day.

The professor who takes time out to explain criticism of student work in a constructive way, the health service nurse who visits the hospitalized students, the president who sits down at a table in the cafeteria with a group of students, the computer services department that responds, in writing, in its newsletter to every comment and suggestion made to them by students for improving the service, the dean who writes a short note to students who appear in the campus paper as sponsors of a community service project, the professor of television production and the residence hall advisor who sponsor a group of students to develop a documentary on residential life, the ombudsperson, dean of undergraduate students, or director of student life research who clearly presents valid data that supports improvement in the lives of students, the student leaders who initiate a process to shadow incoming students for several weeks as they become acquainted with the college as an organization, and the secretary who takes the time to smile and track down the answer to a question of importance for a student— these are the agents of the university responsible for the quality of student life.

These are the realistic results of full implementation of the House of Quality. (For additional information, see Abstract 3.6 at the end of this chapter.)

ENDNOTES

1. Tribus, Myron (1992). "Ten Management Practices." In: Voehl, Frank (1992). *Total Quality: Principles and Practices within Organizations.* Coral Springs, Fla.: Strategy Associates, pp. IV, 20.
2. While both the principles and categories have been referred to extensively, the source of the Baldrige criteria is Ross, J. E. (1993). *Total Quality Management.* Delray Beach, Fla.: St. Lucie Press. In developing the modification of the Deming principles for higher education, reference was made to a modification by Langford Quality Education.
3. The total quality ballantine was developed by Frank Voehl to illustrate the three-dimensional and interlocking aspects of the quality system. It is loosely based on the military concept of three interlocking bullet holes representing a perfect hit.

4. Deming, W. Edwards (1986). *Out of Crisis*. Cambridge: MIT Center for Advanced Engineering Study.

5. Tribus, Myron (1992). "Ten Management Practices." In: Voehl, Frank (1992). *Total Quality: Principles and Practices within Organizations*. Coral Springs, Fla.: Strategy Associates, pp. IV, 19.

6. Voehl, Frank (1992). *Strategy Management*. Coral Springs, Fla.: Strategy Associates, p. 3.

7. Cited in "King Customer." *Business Week*, March 12, 1990, p. 88.

8. Seymour, Daniel (1992). *On Q: Causing Quality in Higher Education*. New York: Macmillan, p. 24.

9. Seymour, Daniel (1992). *On Q: Causing Quality in Higher Education*. New York: Macmillan, pp. 43, 44.

10. Imai, Masaaki (1986). *Kaizen: The Key to Japan's Competitive Success*. New York: Random House. He also states, "The message of the kaizen strategy is that not a day should go by without some kind of improvement being made somewhere in the company" (p. 5).

11. Shewhart, W. A. (1931). *Economic Control of Quality of Manufactured Product*. New York: Van Nostrand (republished in 1980 as a fiftieth anniversary commemorative publication by ASQL Quality Press, Milwaukee).

12. From Voehl, Frank (1993). *TQM Toolkit #1: Tools, Techniques, and Timesavers*. Coral Springs, Fla.: Strategy Associates.

13. Figures 3.1 to 3.3 ©1992 Strategy Associates, Inc.

ABSTRACTS

ABSTRACT 3.1
ON THE ROAD TO QUALITY

Rhodes, Lewis A.
Educational Leadership (GEDL), Vol. 49, Issue 6, March 1992, pp. 76–80

The underlying theme of the article is that total quality can provide the continuing information and management support all school personnel need in order to improve teaching and learning. This applies equally well to grades 16 and above as it does to pre-K.

The central theme deals with why total quality is proving so attractive to educational practitioners at all levels. Of particular interest is the "student's eye view" of total quality management with a look at the "two systems" view of schooling. It ends with a provocative definition of total quality as a "value-based, information-driven management process through which the minds and talents of people at all levels are applied fully and creatively to the organization's continuous improvement." Limited references are provided. The article is short, but informative.

ABSTRACT 3.2
LESSONS FROM ENLIGHTENED CORPORATIONS

Blankstein, Alan M.
Educational Leadership (GEDL), Vol. 49, Issue 6, Mar. 1992, pp. 71–75

The formula for improving schools in the United States can be adapted from the philosophies of W. Edwards Deming, Homer Sarasohn, and the others who helped transform Japanese industry and from the principles that guide many forward-looking American corporations. Deming's Fourteen Principles and his argument against setting quotas or numerical goals are outlined and encapsulated in his incisive 1989 statement: "The same evils that have brought our economy to destruction also afflict and affect education. Our system of rewards has ruined both." Beginning with a wake-up call from David Kearns, Deputy Secretary of Education, the author goes on to both expand upon the Deming method for (higher) education and provide a good lead-in for "On the Road to Quality," by Lewis Rhodes, which appears in the same magazine (see Abstract 3.1). References and author's notes are provided.

ABSTRACT 3.3
MEETING CUSTOMER NEEDS

Foggin, James H.
Survey of Business (SOU), Vol. 28, Issue 1, Summer 1992, pp. 6–9

The University of Tennessee has been a "pioneer university" in the total quality management movement, and the College of Business Administration has applied the tools and much of the philosophy of total quality management to its MBA program. A task force established in April 1990 reviewed the business education literature available on the shortfalls of the MBA education and encouraged the university to treat the student as a customer. The team concluded that many of the criticisms were accurate. Based on the information gathered, a vision of the ideal MBA student was defined, along with eight dimensions in which the student should be proficient: (1) an integrated framework with a cross-functional emphasis, (2) experiential learning and current issues, (3) analytical skills, (4) global (international) perspective, (5) managing technology, (6) social responsibility, (7) organizational reality, and (8) interpersonal skills and persuasive leadership. The task force recommended that the college establish a core of faculty that would have primary responsibility for the MBA program. A team of ten senior faculty was set up to develop the new MBA core curriculum. The program began in August 1991, and results thus far have been positive. In addition, some 6500 executives from over 500 companies have attended the Management Development Center's total quality programs since 1981, making this one of the largest institutions in the United States offering executive education. References are provided.

ABSTRACT 3.4
THE QUALITY REVOLUTION IN EDUCATION

Bonstingl, John Jay
Educational Leadership (GEDL), Nov. 1992, pp. 4–9

In this introductory article to total quality management (TQM) in an educational setting, some interesting analogies are provided between industrial and educational aspects of TQM. Given the fact that in a TQM organization everyone is both a customer and a supplier, in the university instructor/student teams are the equivalent of industry's frontline workers. The student must be recognized as the university's *primary customer* and also as a worker whose product is his or her own continuous improvement.

Schools also must adjust their focus away from student limitations and toward their inner strengths. W. Edwards Deming suggests that we "abolish grades (A, B, C, D) in school, from toddlers up through the university," for when they are graded, students tend to put emphasis on the grade, with little thought for what they have learned. In the Total Quality University, continual improvement of education and learning processes will replace the outdated "teach and test" mode of instruction and focus on the *processes* that are necessary to bring out the best in *all* students. This article contains several brief yet poignant case studies, a good analysis of barriers toward total quality in the university, notes from the author, and several references.

ABSTRACT 3.5
THE TOPIC OF QUALITY IN BUSINESS SCHOOL EDUCATION AND RESEARCH

Kaplan, Robert S.
Selections (SEL), Autumn 1991, pp. 13–21

The author starts out by describing his search for literature on the teaching of quality in business schools. Finding none, he approached Jack Evans, former dean at North Carolina University, who in 1991 performed an extensive survey on the subject which resulted in responses from 89 schools. His conclusion was that there was virtually no coverage on how total quality management changes the way organizations are managed. Therefore, Kaplan decided to conduct his own case study of 20 major universities. Of the 19 that responded, the author was most impressed with the University of Chicago. Other schools included Columbia, Duke, NYU, Penn, Northwestern, Virginia, and Yale, among others.

The results of Kaplan's survey showed that leading business practice in quality management is well ahead of current academic research and teaching. Teaching programs in business schools are adjusting to contemporary developments with lags that are long (ten years or more) and variable; also, there is no evidence to indicate that an adjustment has been made in faculty research programs. For example, fifteen of the schools had three or fewer sessions on quality in their introductory operations management course. Even more damaging is that what is taught in the quality segment is not material that has emerged from academic research. Kaplan notes that of the more than 1500 possible papers on productivity and global competition, *far fewer than one percent* were produced by business school research on total quality. The study of total quality management in business schools will require individuals with multidisciplinary skills. Changes must be made in journals, doctoral programs, and the types of research and educational innovation that are rewarded by promotion committees. Business schools must be prepared to face competition from company-sponsored MBA and executive programs and European business schools. Compare Kaplan's analysis with the comments of William Glavin, who left Rank Xerox in London to become President of Babson College in Boston. Unlike Kaplan, Glavin finds that in many areas academia is thinking further ahead than corporations, who he feels "manage today's problems today." Limited references are given.

ABSTRACT 3.6
RESTORING THE PILLARS OF HIGHER EDUCATION

Bemowski, Karen
Quality Progress (QPR), Vol. 24, Issue 10, Oct. 1991, pp. 37–42

In 1988, Dr. Peter Kolesar of Columbia University (New York) began a total quality management (TQM) journey (with Kaiser Aluminum as a partner) which has had a profound impact not only at Columbia, but at other universities as well. The author shows how the Columbia University experience can be a benchmark for other universities to follow. Bemowski points out that although U.S. colleges and universities are recognized worldwide for education and research, a number of problems threaten their strength and stability, including (1) increasing costs and decreasing funds, (2) a decreasing number of high school graduates, and (3) competition. One source of competition is Europe, Japan, and other countries, where world-class schools are being built. The second source of competition is major companies such as Motorola and General Electric, which are educating their executives internally. Several colleges and universities have recognized their precarious state and have begun using the principles and practices of TQM to improve how they educate and generate knowledge. As previously mentioned, Columbia University has incorporated TQM into its curriculum with education modules, courses on TQM, and a TQM master's degree program. To be successful, U.S. colleges and universities need to re-evaluate their curricula, research, and operations. An interesting side panel is included on the ASQC committee work of Bill Golomski of the Chicago Graduate School of Business.

CHAPTER 4

STRATEGY MANAGEMENT

Strategy is the great work of the organization. In situations of life or death, it is the tao of survival or extinction. Its study cannot be neglected.[1]

As indicated at the close of Chapter 3, total quality can be initiated at four managerial levels: strategic, process, project, and task. This chapter describes the issues and provides guided activities for the first level, the central or strategic level of the organization. This is the first pillar and first foundation of the House of Quality, as highlighted in Figure 4.1. Efforts to introduce principles of quality improvement at this level offer both the greatest potential of success and the greatest threat of failure. The potential for success is high because intervention at the strategy management level involves the very purpose of the organization, the role of its leadership, the culture in which it operates, and the constituents or customers which it serves. Success at this level clearly increases the chances for success at all of the other three levels. The risk of failure is high because of the complexity of the issues involved and the potential for an orientation toward the status quo, inertia, and even atrophy.

Figure 4.1 House of Quality.

What is strategy? *Webster's New World Dictionary* defines strategy as the science of planning and directing large-scale military operations, skill in managing or planning, especially by using stratagem.[2] The term stratagem is derived from two Greek words for leading an army, *straos* (army), and *agein* (to lead). The term was used to describe a plan or trick to deceive an enemy.

The concept of strategy was not confined to Western civilization. In China, during the period of the Warring States (480 to 221 B.C.), the philosopher Sun Tzu wrote a manual on *The Art of Strategy*.[3] Over time, the concept of strategy was applied to nonmilitary settings, first to private businesses and then to public and nonprofit organizations. Used in this context, the term organizational strategy has come to refer to actions taken to establish and to achieve the goals and objectives of an organization. Tregoe and Zimmerman[4] define organizational strategy as, "The framework which guides those choices that determine the nature and direction of an organization." Ultimately, the essence of organizational strategy is determining the right thing to do.

STRATEGY MANAGEMENT: SETTING AND MAINTAINING DIRECTION

The purpose of strategy management as it relates to continuous quality improvement is to establish an organization-wide continuous quality improvement strategy and a deployment infrastructure which encourage all employees to focus on quality and move in a common direction. The major components of strategy management efforts include: mission, vision, goals and objectives, and culture (values, norms, attitudes, and behavior). In this chapter, strategy management and quality improvement efforts are discussed in terms of the *total* organization—the entire college or university. However, these concepts, activities, and techniques are also applicable to major divisions (such as academic affairs, business and finance, and students affairs) and smaller units (such as the registrar's office and specific colleges, schools, centers, and even academic departments).

Five functions are critical for setting and maintaining a direction driven by the principles of total quality management and continuous improvement: (1) implement leadership for quality, (2) develop an organizational mission for quality improvement, (3) create a vision that inspires everyone to seek quality in all aspects of their work, (4) generate a culture that encourages quality improvement efforts at all levels, and (5) establish overarching goals and objectives consistent with the principles of total quality and continuous improvement. Each function will be described and exercises presented (at the end of the chapter) for reflection and implementation. The final section of this chapter introduces the application of these functions at Oregon State University, the single institution the authors found to have effectively documented its total quality implementation process.

Leadership (The First Function for Quality Implementation)

In discussing leadership, two important beliefs must be emphasized. First, the concept of leadership is a central principle of quality improvement. Leadership is a catalyst for positive change, and quality management efforts require positive change. While Deming's seventh principle, *adopt and institute leadership*, stresses the importance of leadership, a review of all fourteen principles shows that success in the total implementation of quality requires leadership. Can a new philosophy be adopted without leadership? Can the barriers to pride of workmanship be achieved without leadership? Can fear be eliminated without leadership? (For additional information, see Abstract 4.1 at the end of this chapter.)

Second, there is a difference between leadership and management (often still referred to as administration in higher education). Bart Giamatti, former president of Yale and former baseball commissioner, made it clear that he believes that this distinction applies to universities:[5]

> Management is the capacity to handle multiple problems, neutralize various constituencies, motivate personnel; in a college or a university it means hitting, as well, the actual budget at break-even. Leadership, on the other hand, is essentially a moral act, not—as in most management—an essentially protective act. It is the assertion of a vision, not simply the exercise of style: the moral courage to assert a vision of the institution in the future and the intellectual energy to persuade the community or the culture of the wisdom and validity of the vision. It is to make the vision practical, and compelling.

Bennis[6] summarized the differences between management and leadership:

Manager	Leader
1. Administers	1. Innovates
2. Is a copy	2. Is an original
3. Maintains	3. Develops
4. Focuses on systems and structure	4. Focuses on people
5. Relies on control	5. Inspires trust
6. Has short-range view	6. Has long-range perspective
7. Asks how and when	7. Asks what and why
8. Has eye on bottom line	8. Has eye on the horizon
9. Imitates	9. Originates
10. Accepts status quo	10. Challenges status quo
11. Classic good soldier	11. Own person
12. Does things right	12. Does the right thing

Both management and leadership are necessary to produce an effective, efficient organization. Most *managers* have at least some leadership skills, and most *leaders* have some management skills. The focus in this chapter is on leadership, because it takes leadership to introduce the principles of quality and sustain the practice of quality management in an organization.

Put more directly, leadership is the enabling catalyst for a successful intervention at the strategic management level. Leadership must be provided by the individuals who occupy the central management positions of the college or university and who have the broad authority associated with these positions.

Does the need to adopt and institute leadership apply to colleges and universities? There certainly are individuals who believe it does. As Giamatti[7] states, "American institutions in general and those of higher education in particular have been coping, but have not adapted to changing times, and they are no longer perceived as leading. They are not perceived as leading because, in fact the institutions themselves, while being competently managed in most cases, are not necessarily themselves being led." (For additional information, see Abstract 4.2 at the end of this chapter.)

The clarion call, then, is to provide a framework for actualizing leadership at the central or executive level. In terms of the introduction of quality improvement at the strategy management level, college or university leaders should first assess where they are in terms of the basic principles and underlying management assumptions associated with continuous quality improvement efforts. The Baldrige Award[8] criteria describe the leadership category as examining: "senior executives' personal leadership and involvement in creating and sustaining a customer focus and clear and visible quality values. Also examined is how the quality values are integrated into the company's management system and reflected in the manner in which the company addresses its public responsibilities and corporate citizenship."

Exercises for Evaluating Leadership

Exercise 4.1 (all exercises appear at the end of this chapter) is a self-assessment leadership questionnaire focused on issues related to the implementation of total quality improvement efforts. It is designed to provide insight concerning the degree to which an individual holds views consistent, or inconsistent, with the principles of total quality improvement. It may be used for self-diagnosis, or the results may be used to stimulate group discussions when the possibility of total quality improvement efforts is being explored. Other assessment instruments that include sections on leadership are available from the (1) U.S. Office of Personnel Management (*Federal Total Quality Management Handbook*), (2) U.S. Department of Defense (*Quality and Productivity Self-Assessment Guide for Defense Organizations*), and (3) U.S. Department of Commerce (*Malcolm Baldrige National Quality Award Criteria*).

A second action that leaders can initiate is an assessment of current conditions relative to quality. This assessment is necessary for two reasons. First, it provides insight into the institution which can be used to establish priorities for quality improvement efforts. Second, it provides baseline data by which to later assess the quality improvement accomplishments of the institution.

Exercise 4.2 provides an example of the type of questions that should be asked about the institution at this stage of activity. One approach would be for all key managers to answer the Quality Readiness questions.

The Quality Council

One of the most important actions a college or university president can take at the organizational level is to create and support the activities of a Quality Council, composed of the top leaders in the organization. They are responsible for initiating and coordinating the strategy of quality improvement efforts. The importance of the council is emphasized in the *Federal Total Quality Management Handbook*:[9]

> By establishing a Quality Council, top management provides identity, structure and legitimacy to the quality improvement effort. It is the first concrete indication that top management has recognized the need to improve and has begun to change the way the organization conducts business. The direction this change will take becomes clear when the Council publishes its vision, guiding principles and mission statement.

Voehl[10] provides some specific guidelines for the operation of Quality Councils (Exhibit 4.1). He contends that the primary role of the Quality Council[10] is the development a total quality mindset in the organization by:

- Creating a sense of urgency among organizational members concerning the need to adopt a total quality improvement approach
- Establishing a clear sense of direction shared by all members of the organization
- Engaging, encouraging, and empowering members of the organization
- Demonstrating personal commitment to the principles and practices of total quality improvement
- Sponsoring teams and providing resources for total quality improvement efforts throughout the organization
- Implementing a measurement system(s) to help ensure the development of a feedback system for fact-driven decisions
- Conducting management reviews of quality improvement efforts and team activities
- Coaching and communicating with organizational members to provide feedback concerning quality improvement efforts
- Recognizing and rewarding members of the organization for their quality improvement efforts and achievements

Identifying the Mission (The Second Function for Quality Implementation)

Create a constancy of purpose toward the improvement of academic programs and administrative services. Aim to create quality students capable of entering meaningful positions in society, and improving all forms of practices and processes. (Deming Principle 1)[11]

The mission of an organization is the basic purpose it seeks to accomplish—the reasons why the organization exists. The first critical step in setting and maintaining the direction of the college or university is the collaborative development of an institutional mission statement. A mission statement is the formal expression of the institutional

Exhibit 4.1 Guidelines for Quality Councils

General Mission Statement

- The mission of the Quality Council is to provide ongoing leadership toward establishing and maintaining a Total Quality Management (TQM) process.

Organizing and Reporting Structure

- The Quality Council is the governing body of the TQM process.
- The initial members are the top managers in the organization and of organizations representing major stakeholders.
- The Quality Council meets on a regular basis to perform its mission.

Responsibilities

- Participate in Quality Council activities.
- Establish a Design Team for the implementation of the TQM process.
- Approve the design for implementation of the TQM process.
- The role of the Quality Council is to support the development a total quality mindset in the organization by:
  1. Creating a sense of urgency among organizational members concerning the need to adopt a total quality improvement approach.
  2. Establishing a clear sense of direction that is shared by all members of the organization.
  3. Engaging, encouraging, and empowering members of the organization.
  4. Demonstrating personal commitment to the total quality improvement process and its principles.
  5. Sponsoring teams and providing resources for total quality improvement efforts throughout the organization.
  6. Implementing a measurement system(s) to help ensure the development of a feedback system for fact-driven decisions.
  7. Conducting management reviews of quality improvement efforts and team activities.
  8. Coaching and communicating with organizational members, both from them and to them, to provide feedback concerning quality improvement efforts.
  9. Recognizing and rewarding members of the organization for their quality improvement efforts and achievements.

purpose for members of the college or university, its constituents, and the public at large. One of the contributions the quality improvement effort makes to the vitality of a college or university is to focus attention on the institutional mission and its development.

Successful strategy development is driven by a clear sense of organizational mission. However, many individuals believe that colleges and universities are not particularly good at developing clear and specific mission statements. Sherr and Lozier emphasize this point:[12] "Most college and university mission statements identify the services performed, such as teaching, research and scholarship, and community service. However, these statements seldom assist in determining which services are or are not appropriate in light of its customers. We are often more clear about what we do than for whom we do it, and we attend better to our needs or to their needs as we see them than to their needs as they see them."

During the mission identification process, colleges and universities must distinguish between mandates and mission. This is important because many institutions (both private and public) have a formal mandate written into their charters stipulating the expectations of various external constituents. It is important for all schools to review their charters and other documents in order to identify the general framework upon which the institutional mission will be developed.

Once the mandated expectations have been clarified, the focus can turn to the organizational mission. Questions to ask concerning the status of the institutional mission statement include:

- Is there a clear statement of the mission of the college/university?
- Has this statement been shared with all members of the institution?
- Do members of the institution know about the mission statement? (Could they describe it if asked?)
- Is there a consensus on the institutional mission?
- Is the behavior of institutional members influenced by the mission?

Exercises for Developing a Mission Statement

To facilitate answering these questions, Exercise 4.3 provides some questions to be answered in any attempt to develop a mission statement. These questions are used in the strategic planning process and are designed to identify explicit and implicit assumptions about the college or university. They should be answered by the leaders of the college or university and by critical external constituents, such as members of the board of trustees or other types of supervisory bodies or funding sources. The actual drafting of the mission statement should be done in a group setting involving all these key members. Exercise 4.4 provides a three-part guideline for developing and drafting the mission statement.

In the final section of this chapter, which describes the total quality implementation process at Oregon State University, their mission statement is presented. It is both brief and comprehensive and illustrates the need for a statement that people can own and can identify with in order to develop related processes, projects, and tasks.

Creating a Vision (The Third Function for Quality Implementation)

Where there is no vision, the people perish. (Proverbs 29:18)

The third critical step in establishing direction is the development of a vision, or common belief, of what the college or university should be like at some point in the future. An institutional vision is a shared mental image of a desired future—what the college or university wants to be seven to ten years in the future. A vision statement should be a clear, positive, credible, engaging, challenging, and shared image, a collective "video" of the desired future.

The concept of creating an organizational vision has become popular in recent years in the higher education community for three reasons. First, a number of organizational studies have reported greater success in vision-directed organizations.[13] The concepts of vision and the visionary leader have taken hold in society in general, and in colleges and universities. Second, accrediting bodies have begun to emphasize the need for strategic planning, with the criteria usually including the development of an institutional vision statement. Third, to the degree that they have been adopted by colleges and universities, total quality improvement guidelines place a major emphasis on institutional vision and thus have encouraged this development. (For additional information, see Abstract 4.3 at the end of this chapter.)

The concept of vision is difficult for many individuals to deal with because it defies conventional approaches to organizational management and/or because they are not clear about the concept. To clarify this issue, Nanus[14] identified six things that a vision is *not*:

- While a vision is about the future, it is not a prophecy (although after the fact it may seem so).
- A vision is not a mission. To state that an organization has a mission is to state its purpose, not its direction.

- A vision is not factual. It does not exist and may never be realized as originally imagined. It deals not with reality but with possible and desirable futures.
- A vision cannot be true or false. It can be evaluated only relative to other possible directions for the organization
- A vision is not—or at least should not be—static, enunciated once for all time.
- A vision is not a constraint on actions, except for those inconsistent with the vision.

The benefits associated with a clear, positive, and engaging vision for a college or university include:

- Greater clarity of direction, which provides a framework for organizational decision-making concerning desirable outcomes and actions, and identification of institutional opportunities and threats.
- Greater unity of purpose and action.
- Enhanced expectational guidance, which provides guideposts for determining appropriate behavior and assessing how individuals fit into the larger organizational picture.
- Increased emphasis on anticipatory management and innovation because of the orientation toward the future provided by the vision.
- Increased motivation and commitment. The creation of dynamic tensions between the present and the desired future helps provide meaning and challenges for members of the organization.
- Greater potential for decentralized decision-making. When units and teams are aware of the vision and the related mission, goals, and objectives, they are able to incorporate these factors into their decision-making.

A vision defines what is to be created as opposed to what is to be accomplished. It is not derived from an analysis of existing conditions and trends. A vision is a creative leap of faith that transcends, but does not ignore, facts. Experience in strategic planning has shown that derived visions ignore too many potentials to be creative. The creation of a vision involves hindsight, foresight, and insight.

The vision statement of Oregon State University (presented in the concluding section of this chapter) represents a process of shared creativity. It identifies the desired development of the students and the commitment of the faculty. The vision also addresses a commitment to meeting the needs of the clients and empowering the employees toward continuous improvement within teams consisting of "the most appropriate people, regardless of their level or jobs in the university."

Exercises for Creating a Vision

Exercise 4.5 is a questionnaire for assessing an organizational vision statement. It can also be used to compare the vitality of alternative visions. The results should be shared and discussed with a broad spectrum of individuals with the college or university. Exercise 4.6 provides a summary of activities that can be carried out in a group session to revise or develop a new vision statement.

Achieving Acceptance of the Vision

Having a vision statement—even a good one—is not sufficient. Once the vision has been completed, awareness and acceptance of the vision is initiated. Commitment to the reality of the vision must be achieved at all levels of the college or university. Voehl[15] identifies four processes for gaining an organizational commitment to a vision: communication, boundary testing, sign-on, and celebration. Responsibility for implementing these processes clearly lies with the leaders of the college or university.

Communicating the Vision.[16]   This first process is the most basic. It is done in an iterative manner, i.e., active participation in developing the vision is followed by awareness, sensitivity, and signing-on. It requires the leader of the quality process to create a responsive, open environment that encourages participation, understanding, acceptance, and ownership of the vision. Exercise 4.7 provides an action plan for designing activities to communicate the vision. The specific issues addressed in Exercise 4.7 are presented in Exhibit 4.2.

Boundary Testing the Vision.   The second process is boundary testing. This is the process of identifying those characteristics (policies, practices, attitudes, and norms) within the culture of the college or university that must be modified if the vision is to be achieved. The question to be asked consistently is, "What are the expected impacts of achieving the vision?" If existing organizational boundaries are not challenged, then the vision clearly is inadequate. It is the role of the leader of the quality process to anticipate and even encourage these challenges. Exercise 4.8 provides an action plan for boundary testing, focusing on the specific areas listed in Exhibit 4.2.

Signing onto the Vision. The third process is achieving the commitment of everyone to the vision. Ultimately, this is a personal act, where an individual asks, "What will I receive from this vision?" If the answer is positive, then the next question is, "What can I do to make the vision happen?" The leader of the quality process can initiate activities to help facilitate commitment to the vision. These are described in Exhibit 4.2. Exercise 4.9 provides an action plan for initiating these activities.

Celebrating the Effort toward and Achievement of the Vision. The fourth and final process is the celebration of actions that support the achievement of the vision. The term celebration is used because it connotes ceremony, acclaim, festivity, and collective involvement. Celebration is important for two reasons. First, the effort and ultimate success should be acknowledged. This is important because in many cases the existing values and norms of the college or university system may actually impede behavior to achieve the vision. Second, celebration sends a clear message throughout the college or university community concerning the types of action that support the vision. In this sense, celebration is a continual communication of the vision. Exercise 4.10 provides an action framework for developing the celebration process. The specific issues that the action plan should address are described in Exhibit 4.2.

Organizational Culture (The Fourth Function for Quality Implementation)

If the vision sets the direction for the organizational ship, then it is upon the sea of organizational culture that quality improvement efforts must sail if they are to be successful. Organizational culture refers to the patterned ways of feeling, thinking, and acting that are shared by members of the organization. The specific dimensions of culture include systems and structures, actions, roles, behaviors, attitudes, norms, and values. These dimensions provide the basic assumptions and attitudes on which members operate. They are often so well internalized that they are taken for granted. (For additional information, see Abstract 4.4 at the end of this chapter.)

Exhibit 4.2 Achieving Acceptance of the Vision

Communicating the Vision

- *Education on the Vision and Visionary Leadership.* Most people will either be unfamiliar with or suspicious of any new effort. It is important that members understand the visionary process, including the emphasis on the future, human values, and the involvement of the entire organization.
- *Creating the Environment.* People will test management's commitment to the vision. The leader must be prepared to spend time with people so that they can learn about the vision.
- *Producing Signs.* People will want early concrete signs of the commitment to the vision. It is the responsibility of the leaders to help provide these signs.
- *Dealing with Uncertainty and Ambiguity.* The uncertainty and ambiguity will involve both details about the vision and concerns of individuals about their future in the institution. The leaders must help assure organizational members that not knowing all the answers in okay. In fact, it is expected.
- *Consistency.* The process of sharing the vision must be consistent with the vision.
- *Accepting and Responding to Criticism.* The communication process must allow people to criticize the vision and be given appropriate responses to their criticisms.
- *Focusing on the Future.* Discussions about the vision should focus on the desired future (not the past) and how to get there.
- *Recognizing that Visions Create Problems.* Any effort toward change is likely to create as many problems as it solves, at least in the beginning. Leaders must recognize this fact and, wherever possible, anticipate problems.
- *Networking.* After the initial publicity and promotion about the vision, the major communications problem becomes the building of ongoing communications networks among groups and individuals to operationalize the strategic plan and accomplish the vision.

Boundary Testing the Vision

- *Challenging Organizational Values and Norms.* Organizational values represent conceptions (standards) of the desirable that are shared by many members of an organization. Norms are shared expectations (informal rules) for behavior. An engaging vision will challenge existing values and norms, and quality must anticipate these challenges.
- *Existing and Emerging Leadership.* The quality leader must encourage existing leadership to be engaged by the vision. At the same time, however, she/he must also encourage the emergence of new leadership inspired by the vision. Ultimately, encouraging boundary by institutional leaders may be the most significant leadership challenge after the creation of the vision.
- *Flexibility.* Detailed steps to implement a vision cannot always be planned, and where detailed plans exist, changes in the environment may make them inappropriate. The leader of the quality process must help provide a setting in which the potential for and the means to achieve change exist.
- *Risk and Risk Taking.* The achievement of a vision will require changes in how things are done, with ensuing risks for both the college or university and its

people. The leader must try to anticipate the areas of risk and provide support, even rewards, for those willing to explore nontraditional paths.

- *Training.* Formal training sessions focused on issues related to the vision should be conducted in order to encourage people to test the boundaries of the vision.
- *Meetings and Stories.* Formal meetings and shared stories can and should be used to encourage boundary testing by group members.
- *Experimentation.* Experiments (pilot projects) are a good method for exploring the value of ideas and for testing the implications of doing things in a new way.
- *Task Groups and Simulations.* Task groups can be organized and asked to explore (simulate) the institutional impacts of the vision.
- *Developing and Maintaining Momentum.* The leader cannot take success for granted. Even successful efforts to communicate the vision will need attention and nurturing if a vision-driven institution is to emerge.

Signing onto the Vision

- *Action Environment.* The leader must help provide an environment in which the vision and actions related to the vision impact the ongoing activities of the college or university and its people. Everyone should have the opportunity to become familiar with the vision and to be challenged to share it.
- *Mini Visions.* The environment of the college or university must provide opportunities for units (divisions, departments, etc.) to adopt their own vision within the framework of the organizational vision.
- *Personal Visioning.* Assist individuals to develop their personal visions of what they want to be like in the future (discussed in Chapter 7). The leader must provide opportunities for each individual to develop a personal vision.
- *Symbols and Ceremonies.* A personalized symbol or logo that reflects a person's commitment to the vision can be a powerful aid to the sign-on. The leader needs to provide a symbol and have an appropriate ceremony when it is awarded.

Celebrating the Effort toward and Achievement of the Vision

- *Positive Reinforcement.* Celebrations are positive reinforcements. They help encourage people to continue their commitment to the vision.
- *Accentuating the Positive.* Whenever a vision is published, part of the organization will sign on quickly, part (probably the majority) will adopt a wait-and-see attitude, and part will resist. Too much time and energy is often devoted to getting the resisters on board. Celebrations are effective ways to focus energy and attention on those who have signed on and to give those who "wait and see" something positive to see.
- *Variety.* Celebration commemorates an event with a ceremony. Celebrations can be large or small, planned or spontaneous. They can occur at formal or informal meetings, seminars, or training programs. Ways to celebrate include ovations, letters from top management, dinners, trips, etc. Hoopla is not always required. Often a handshake, smile, or congratulations for a job well done is enough. The important point is to do it and be creative.

Debate exists among academics as to whether organizations *have* or *are* cultures. This distinction is not critical for the discussion here because the authors strongly believe that the organizational culture must be addressed if total quality improvement efforts are to be successful. Many believe that the culture of most colleges and universities will have to be transformed if quality improvement efforts are to be successful. Chaffee and Sherr contend:[17]

> The implementation of total quality will call for a major transformation of organizational values, norms, structures and processes. This transformation does not mean that the essential values of academic freedom, intellectual creativity and the new wisdom must be sacrificed. Old habits based on outdated needs will have to be discarded. But the characteristics that have made U.S. higher education a world standard will be further guaranteed only when they become part of the articulated value and mission of an institution seeking the highest possible quality standards for its students, faculty, and society.

If cultural transformation is required, as it is in most cases, then there must be a plan to achieve the transformation. Carr and Littman[18] identified nine key steps in the cultural transformation process:

1. Planning for cultural change
2. Assessing the cultural "baseline"
3. Training managers and the workforce
4. Management adopting and modeling new behavior
5. Making organizational and regulation changes that support quality action
6. Redesigning individual performance appraisal and monetary reward systems to reflect the principles of total quality management
7. Changing budget practices
8. Rewarding positive change
9. Using communication tools to reinforce TQM principles

Several of these steps need to be emphasized. Assessing the culture "baseline" is critical because it provides the data needed to establish priorities for change. Figure 3.3 (see Chapter 3) presents a summary of the six factors associated with a quality-oriented organizational culture (the environment, product or service, methods, people, organizational structure, and the mindset of total quality improvement). This material was presented in the form of a fishbone diagram (one of the 21 total quality tools described in Chapter 3) to emphasize the causal relationship between the various factors and the achievement of a quality organization. Exercise 4.11 provides a questionnaire for assessing the current cultural status of a college or university.

Steps 3, 4, and 5 (training, modeling, and organizational changes) are essential elements in producing cultural change because they provide both the knowledge and the experiences upon which a quality culture is built. As shown in Figure 3.3, the factors involved in creating an organizational culture are part of a causal hierarchy that initiates and ultimately leads to changing the culture. Given this hierarchy, the best way to generate and maintain organizational change is to develop a transformation process that follows the basic flow of the hierarchy. Exercise 4.12 presents an action plan for addressing this hierarchy as part of the effort to transform the institutional culture. The specific items in the exercise are described in Exhibit 4.3.

Steps 8 and 9 (rewarding positive change and using communication tools to reinforce the principles of total quality management) are critical because they are the type of activities that encourage initial changes in behavior in order to produce changes in attitudes, norms, and values.

At Oregon State University, transformation of the culture was addressed in the total quality management process by the development of a one-page statement of the mission, values, and principles. These are presented and discussed in the final section of this chapter.

Establishing Goals and Objectives (The Fifth Function for Quality Implementation)

Establishing overarching goals and objectives of the college or university provides the linkage between the macro-level focus of mission, vision, and culture and the operational activities of the organiza-

Exhibit 4.3 Specific Issues to Address in Transforming the Culture

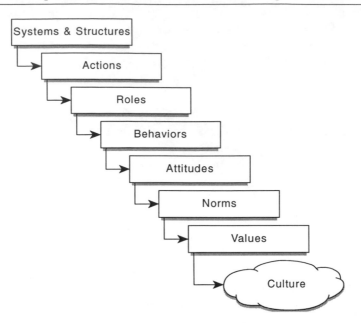

- *Change in Systems and Structures.* Modify or change systems and structures to be consistent with the principles of total quality improvement.

- *Change in Actions.* Actions should be based on both achieving the vision and mission of the college and university and on the principles of total quality improvement.

- *Change in Roles.* Management must assume new roles as facilitator, supporter, provider, creator, and promoter.

- *Change in Behaviors.* The changes in the roles of management must be evident in the daily behavior of the managers, i.e., they must facilitate, support, provide, create, and promote.

- *Change in Attitudes.* Behavioral change produces attitudinal change. If you want people to think differently, get them to behave differently first.

- *Change in Norms.* Over time, changes in roles, behaviors, and attitudes will be reflected in changes in personal and organizational norms.

- *Change in Values.* Ultimately, the collective change will affect the values of the organization and the people who are a part of the organization.

tion. The benefits derived from well-established goals and objectives include:

- *Operationalization.* Overarching goals and objectives provide a new level of specificity needed for the operationalization of the mission and vision of the college or university.
- *Define the desired future.* Goals and objectives define the desired direction and future (the *should be* and the *could be*) and help prepare everyone for change.
- *Goal-directed behavior.* Enhances organizational planning and encourages the assessment of resources needed to achieve the desired goal(s).
- *Engagement and motivation.* Well-articulated and well-communicated goals and objectives will engage and motivate people to achieve the vision of the college or university and fulfill its purpose.
- *Common (shared) framework.* Goals and objectives can provide a common framework, or larger picture, and can help unite everyone, focusing their efforts toward the institutional mission and vision.

Exercise 4.13 is a questionnaire that can be used to assess the statement of goals and objectives. These questions are based on the criteria described in Exhibit 4.4.

Efforts to develop overarching goals and objectives should follow the same type of processes used to develop the mission and vision statements. They should involve as many people as possible in personally meaningful activities. Exercise 4.14 provides an action plan for developing overarching goals in a college or university. The five basic steps of the plan are

1. *Affirm the vision.* People must clearly understand and be committed to the vision of the college or university.
2. *Identify strategic goals.* In general, organizations can only afford to focus attention on a limited number of goals at any one time. Therefore, the most important issues facing the organization must be identified. At least two approaches to this are possible. The simplest approach is gap analysis, by which the current state of the organization is compared with the desired future state and those issues for which the greatest gap exists are selected. The second approach is strategic issue analysis, which

Exhibit 4.4 Criteria for Assessing Goals and Objectives Statements

- *Specificity/Measurability.* Specific goals are more useful because they encourage people to consider the next steps in the process—the behaviors and skills that need to be developed, attitudes that need to be changed, and actions that need to be taken.
- *Significance of Issues.* Goals that have large, pervasive significance in the organization are needed to both encourage the involvement of everyone and to facilitate individual development of goals and objectives.
- *Consistency with Mission.* Overarching goals and objectives must be consistent with the core mission of the institution.
- *Attainability.* Effective goal setting involves establishing goals that are both challenging and attainable. This is not an easy criterion to meet, but failure to meet it leads to either underachievement or disillusionment and low morale.
- *Challenge.* Effective goals challenge individuals and the entire organization.
- *Feasibility.* Achieving the goal(s) must be feasible within the context of the human, economic, physical, and other resources.
- *Focus on Performance.* Well-articulated goals and objectives force people to think about performance (activities) needed to achieve the goals of the college or university.
- *Involvement.* People should be so engaged by the goals and objectives statement that they focus attention on their own involvement: "What will I be doing?"
- *Observability.* Progress toward the goals must be observable. Without the ability to observe progress, the motivation toward goal achievement will quickly disappear.
- *Verifiability.* The achievement of overarching institutional goals must be verifiable.

---

compares not only the current and desired future conditions, but also developments in the external and internal environments of the organization, selecting the goals that best reflect this collective analysis. Whichever approach is used, the issues must ultimately be turned into goals for effective organizational performance in the future.

3. *Determining objectives.* The means by which to achieve the goals of the college or university must be determined. Achieving organizational goals is part of a means–end process in which short-term operational objectives that lead to achieving the goal must be identified.

4. *Selecting activities, developing projects.* In turn, short-term objectives can only be achieved through a series of activities or actions that are arranged into projects and related tasks.

5. *Selecting inputs.* The human, financial, and physical resources must be identified and procured in a timely manner, which is determined through the development of a project-based schedule of activities.

Collectively, the goals, objectives, activities, and projects determine the quality and scope of the input resources needed to achieve the mission and vision of the college or university.

Exercise 4.15 is a questionnaire to be used in developing organizational goals. It must be stressed that merely identifying overarching goals and developing a plan to implement them is not sufficient. The factors previously discussed concerning vision also apply to overarching goals. That is, they must be communicated, boundaries must be tested, there must be sign-on, and ultimately celebration must occur. At this point, it may be helpful to review Exercises 4.5 through 4.8 to create an action plan for developing effective goals and objectives.

APPLICATION OF STRATEGY MANAGEMENT AT OREGON STATE UNIVERSITY

Beginning in this chapter, and continuing in Chapters 5 to 7, the total quality program at Oregon State University (OSU) is presented as an example of the application of the principles and practices advocated in this book. The selection of OSU is based on the extensive documentation prepared, which is perhaps the best record of the implementation of total quality in a still sparse area of attention in higher education. The activities at OSU have been identified within the framework of the four managerial levels (strategy, process, project, and task) in order to provide an actual case study of activities conducted at these levels. The authors were not involved in the implementation process, nor was OSU aware of the specific concepts (e.g., the House of Quality) presented in this book.

The applicability of the concepts presented in this book to the implementation of total quality at OSU (which was still in process at the time of this writing) emphasizes the universality of the total quality movement and its importance to higher education. The process goes beyond parochial author-based concepts and language. It can be grasped within a general principle and value—the desire to provide quality products or services and to continuously improve the process. It is within this framework that the application of strategy management at OSU is presented. (For additional information, see Abstract 4.5 at the end of this chapter.)

Vision

OSU's vision statement is presented as an example of an overarching vision with sufficient detail to draw the desired commitment from everyone and to guide the university and its members into the future:

> *It is OSU's vision to be recognized as a premier international university.* We want each student to have at least one additional language, to have at least one quarter's experience in a foreign country, and to be computer literate. We want our faculty to have international experiences, and to increase our international research programs by 100% (from 26 countries to 52). We want to increase foreign undergraduates from 10 to 15% of the student body.
>
> *We also want our university to be the best university in which to study and work.* We want to be a university that knows what its clients will want ten years from now and what it will do to exceed all expectations. We want to be a university whose employees understand not only how to do their jobs but also how to significantly improve their jobs on a regular basis; where problems and challenges are met by a team of the most appropriate people, regardless of their level or jobs in the university.

Mission, Values, Guiding Principles

The mission statement of OSU (Exhibit 4.5) consists of three sentences. It is a fine illustration of a mission statement that is both brief and comprehensive. It can be committed to memory or printed for easy distribution. It is a statement that people can adopt and for which supportive practices can be developed.

Related values and guiding principles were also developed (Exhibit 4.5). A single-page mission statement was developed by OSU as part of its quality improvement effort.

Exhibit 4.5 Oregon State University's Mission, Values, and Guiding Principles

Oregon State University is among the leading comprehensive teaching and research universities in the nation. Our mission on a land grant university is to serve the people of Oregon, the nation, and the world through education, research, and service. Through our dedicated teaching, through the pursuit of knowledge, and through our extended relationships to the broader society, we seek continually to improve our contributions to the general welfare.

Values

How we accomplish our mission is as important as the mission itself. The following values are fundamental to our success:

- *People.* Our people—students, faculty, staff, and alumni—are our strength. They are the source of our creativity, they determine our reputation, and they provide our vitality.
- *Respect.* All our people are important contributors. Respect, humanity, and integrity are required in our treatment of each other.
- *Openness.* In the classrooms, laboratories, studios, and field stations, our efforts are open to challenge and debate.
- *Truth and Truths.* We seek truths in our pursuit of knowledge. But we know that there is no such thing as "the truth." Understandings in the sciences, arts, and humanities change. We challenge dogma when we encounter it in our classrooms, in our laboratories and studios, and in our role of serving the broader society.

Guiding Principles

- Students are our most important clients. The quality and completeness of their education is our top priority.
- We have a responsibility to society to contribute to its social, aesthetic, and economic well-being.
- Our social responsibility extends to offering informed criticism even when that criticism may not be well received. We maintain an internal environment that will nurture this important contribution.
- Flexibility, change, and constant improvement are essential to our continued success.
- In instruction, research, and service activities, we honor and impart principles of academic honesty, freedom, and integrity.
- Diversity is a key to our success. Not only are our doors open to men and women alike without regard to race, ethnicity, personal belief, disability, age, or sexual preference, but we also have a moral obligation to open the doors wider for any groups that are under-represented or that have suffered from discrimination.

Source: Coate, L. Edwin (July 1990). *Implementing Total Quality Management in a University Setting.* Corvallis: Oregon State University, p. 23.

Cultural Transformation

The process of cultural transformation was acknowledged to take a long time; it is still going on, in fact. An initial step was the development of the declarative statement of the mission (presented earlier) and the supporting values and guiding principles of the university. It would be beneficial to review them and consider how the culture of the college or university is reflected by the stated values and principles.

Goals and Objectives

The overarching goals adopted by OSU are presented in Exhibit 4.6. Also included are two representative objectives for each goal. (The complete list contains five to nine objectives for each goal.) Collectively, they cut across numerous institutional boundaries and help set high and challenging expectations.

A collective review of these strategy statements should help anticipate and facilitate the degree of effort associated with goal setting activities and the implications they have for the future of a specific college or university.

Exhibit 4.6   Oregon State University's Strategic Plan Goals and Objectives

GOAL 1   Serve people through instruction, research, and extension
1.1   Promote and recognize good teaching.
1.2   Adequately staff and support academic programs essential to the university's mission.

GOAL 2   Help students to achieve their full potential
2.1   Improve recognition for teaching, academic advising, and student–faculty interaction.
2.2   Improve students' experiences in living groups, orientation, peer relationships, academic learning/assistance centers.

GOAL 3   Expand research and artistic creativity
3.1   Recruit and support faculty, staff, and students of high research, artistic capability.
3.2   Improve research facilities and equipment.

GOAL 4   Attract, develop, retain excellent faculty and staff
4.1   Bring faculty salaries to competitive levels.
4.2   Expand facilities and program supports as required for a major teaching and research university.

GOAL 5   Expand opportunities for minorities, females, disadvantaged, and disabled
5.1   Intensify recruitment of women and people of color to faculty positions in which they are under-represented.
5.2   Evaluate classified employment processes to increase personnel from under-represented groups; seek external policy change where necessary.

GOAL 6   Increase enrollments of outstanding students
6.1   Improve the quality and rigor of academic programs.
6.2   Raise undergraduate admission standards.

GOAL 7   Sharpen the university's international focus
7.1   Strengthen the international dimensions of the curriculum.
7.2   Expand the international perspective of faculty.

GOAL 8   Improve facilities and equipment
8.1   Give fund-raising priority first to library expansion, second to visual and performing arts instructional facilities, third to computer science facilities.
8.2   Upgrade instructional laboratory facilities and equipment.

GOAL 9   Improve library and computing services
9.1   Qualify for membership in the Association of Research Libraries.
9.2   Review information support services needs and fund a major library facilities expansion to meet them.

GOAL 10   Improve the university's relationships with its constituencies
10.1   Create and maintain a clear OSU image to emphasize quality of students, instruction, research, and service.
10.2   Motivate OSU's constituencies to increase their support.

Source: Coate, L. Edwin (July 1990). *Implementing Total Quality Management in a University Setting.* Corvallis: Oregon State University, pp. 24–26.

ENDNOTES

1. Wing, R. (1988). *The Art of Strategy.* New York: Dolphin Books, p. 21.
2. *Webster's New World Dictionary* (1982). Compact School and Office Edition, New York: Simon and Schuster.
3. Wing, R. (1988). *The Art of Strategy.* New York: Dolphin Books, p. 13.
4. Tregoe, Benjamin and Zimmerman, John (1980). *Top Management Strategy: What It Is and How It Works.* New York: Simon and Schuster, p. 17.
5. Giamatti, A. Bartlett (1988). *The Free and Ordered Space.* New York: W. W. Norton, p. 36.
6. Bennis, Warren (1989). *On Becoming A Leader.* New York: Addison Wesley, p. 45.
7. Giamatti, A. Bartlett (1988). *The Free and Ordered Space.* New York: W. W. Norton, p. 36.
8. *1993 Award Criteria, Malcolm Baldrige National Quality Award.* Milwaukee: American Society for Quality Control, p. 16.
9. *Federal Total Quality Management Handbook* (1989). Washington, D.C.: U.S. Government Printing Office, p. 18.
10. Voehl, Frank W. (1992). *TQM Implementation Models and Critical Success Factors.* Coral Springs, Fla.: Strategy Associates, pp. 1–2.
11. Deming's first principle, as revised in Chapter 3.
12. Sherr, Lawrence, and Lozier, Gregory (1992). "Total Quality Management in Higher Education." Chapter 1 In: Sherr, Lawrence and Teeter, Deborah. *New Directions for Institutional Research: Total Quality Management in Higher Education.* San Francisco: Jossey-Bass, p. 8.
13. Peters, Tom and Waterman, Robert (1982). *In Search of Excellence.* New York: Random House.
14. Nanus, Bert (1992). *Visionary Leadership.* San Francisco: Jossey-Bass, pp. 31–32.
15. Voehl, Frank W. (1992). *Total Quality: Principles and Practices within Organizations.* Coral Springs, Fla.: Strategy Associates.
16. The four processes for building organizational commitment to a vision have been discussed in various writings and periodicals. Of these, the work entitled *Transforming Leadership: Vision to Results* (edited by John D. Adams) is the most comprehensive. Excerpts from "The Leader as Creator" by Robert Fritz and "After the Vision: Suggestions to Corporate Visionaries and Vision Champions" by Richards and Engel are cited as being most useful in the visioning process for universities.
17. Chaffee, Ellen and Sherr, Lawrence (1992). *Quality: Transforming Postsecondary Education.* ASHE-ERIC Higher Education Report #3, pp. xix–xx.
18. Carr, David and Littman, Ian (1990). *Excellence in Government: Total Quality Management in the '90's.* Arlington, Va.: Coopers and Lybrand, pp. 190–203.
19. Figure 4.1, Exhibits 4.1 to 4.4, and Exercises 4.1 to 4.5 ©1992 Stragegy Associates, Inc.

EXERCISES

EXERCISE 4.1   LEADERSHIP SELF-ASSESSMENT

This instrument is designed to provide an individual with insight concerning the degree to which she or he holds views that are consistent, or inconsistent, with total quality improvement principles. It may be used entirely for self-diagnosis or the results may be used to stimulate group discussions when the possibility of total quality improvement efforts is being explored. Responses to the questionnaire may be yes or no or a rating system such as 1 = strong agreement, 2 = agreement, 3 = undecided, 4 = disagreement, 5 = strong disagreement.

Agreement with the statements indicates a belief system consistent with the general principles of total quality improvement. When you complete the exercise, if you have not answered yes to most of the questions, you probably should not attempt to implement quality improvement efforts at any level, let alone try to intervene in terms of strategy management.

Please indicate your agreement or disagreement with the following statements.

1. I recognize all work (activities) as processes that involve inputs, transforming activities, outputs, and outcomes.

2. I believe that quality improvement requires building quality in (the prevention of errors and defects, the avoidance of rework) rather than merely the detection of defects.

3. I believe in a problem-solving approach that emphasizes systematic problem identification based on data developed through the use of feedback systems, understanding the causes of problems (both common and special) and statistical thinking.

4. I believe in a problem-solving approach that emphasizes experimental efforts to find the right solution through the use of data and feedback systems. This ultimately is reflected in the use of the Shewhart model: Plan, Do, Check, Act (PDCA). (Academics may be more comfortable if the process is described as Analyze, Experiment, Study, Implement).

5. I believe that it is the primary function of management to facilitate quality performance, particularly the elimination of barriers that prevent individuals from achieving quality performance

6. I believe that most problems (errors, defects) are the result of existing processes (common causes), not special causes—including workers. Thus, I first look for ways to improve the process.

7. I believe that the people closest to the operational activities (the process) have substantial knowledge about the process and how to improve it.

8. I believe that most people are motivated toward quality performance.

9. I believe that the people closest to the process must be empowered to improve the quality of the process.

EXERCISE 4.2   QUALITY READINESS ASSESSMENT

This exercise provides examples of the type of questions that should be asked about the college or university during exploratory discussions concerning the possibility of becoming involved in a total quality improvement effort. One approach to its use would be for all key managers to answer the Quality Readiness Assessment questions.[a] If a Quality Council has already been established, its members should answer the questionnaire. In either case, the answers should be shared and discussed.

It is probably best if the synthesis of the results is done by a single individual and a written document provided to the entire group. The use of a written report is suggested because it allows individuals an opportunity to review all of the responses and to develop a holistic interpretation of the results before becoming involved in the discussion of details. Ultimately, the results should be used to make decisions concerning the need for becoming involved in a total quality improvement effort.

Please answer the following questions concerning current conditions in your organization relative to the status of your quality system.[b] Your answers may be brief but they should be specific enough to be understood when they are presented in the report on the responses of the group.

1. *Top Management:*   How (to what degree) does top management make planning an integrated part of the college or university culture?

2. *Customer Satisfaction:*   How (to what degree) does the college or university use customer feedback to identify problems and design and plan improvements?

3. *Design:*   How (to what degree) does the college or university attempt to improve operations by finding and solving potential problems while products and services are being designed?

4. *Purchasing/Recruitment:*   How (to what degree) do individuals responsible for purchasing (or recruitment) make suppliers an integral part of the planning process and team?

5. *Production:* How (to what degree) does the college or university strategic plan emphasize that productivity and quality have a common goal as partners in productivity?

6. *Education and Training:* How (to what degree) does the college or university provide every member with the knowledge and skills needed to do his or her job and to take part in the total quality improvement process?

7. *Speaking with Facts:* How (to what degree/how well) does the college or university use data as the basis for identifying problems and reaching decisions?

8. *Technology:* How (to what degree) does the college or university build quality into automated processes, rather than attempting to automate a mess?

9. *Teams, Teamwork, and Synergy:* How (to what degree) does the college or university develop and train teams and encourage teamwork?

10. *Quality Costs:* How (to what degree) does the college or university attempt to identify the costs of nonquality? How (to what degree) is this information used to identify targets for future quality improvement efforts?

11. *Internal Auditing:* How (to what degree) does the college or university conduct audits of major internal processes such as the Strategic Planning System?

12. *Continuous Improvement:* How (to what degree) does the college or university set planning teams that bridge departmental boundaries.

13. *People:* To what degree does the college or university demand good planning from everyone?

14. *Integrated Vision:* To what degree does the college or university have an integrated vision of a desired future?

a Voehl, Frank (1992). *Total Quality: Principles and Practices within Organizations.* Coral Springs, Fla.: Strategy Associates, pp. III, 25–31.

b The questions in this readiness survey are a loosely based adaptation of the general elements contained in the ASQC-based Quality System elements.

EXERCISE 4.3
DETERMINING THE MISSION OF THE COLLEGE OR UNIVERSITY

This exercise provides an example of the types of questions that should be answered in any attempt to develop a mission statement for your college or university. These questions are generally used in the strategic planning process and are designed to identify explicit and implicit assumptions about the institution.

This questionnaire should be answered by key members of the college or university and by critical external constituents such as members of the board of trustees or other types of supervisory bodies and funding sources. It is recommended that the questionnaire be distributed to individuals and a written summary of the responses developed. It is probably best if the synthesis of the results is done by a single individual and a written document provided to the entire group. The use of a written report is suggested because it allows individuals an opportunity to review all of the responses and to develop a holistic interpretation of the results before becoming involved in the discussion of details. It is also recommended that the results be discussed in a formal retreat in which members of the group have the opportunity to discuss issues and to develop a mission statement for the college or university.

Mission Statement Form: This form provides an example of the type of document to be given to participants when they are asked to initiate the development of a mission statement for the college or university.

Answer these questions concerning _____. Where you have data (or access to individuals with data), use it. Otherwise, provide the most realistic answers you can.

1.   _____ exists to do _____?
2.   What is distinctive (or even unique) about _____?
3.   What are the primary products and services provided by _____?
4.   Who are the primary customers (consumers) of the products and services provided by _____? Why have you identified these as the primary customers?
5.   What other types of individuals or groups (stakeholders) have a vested interest in _____ (its performance and success)? What is the nature of their interest?
6.   What core values (principles) are important to the operation and future of _____ ?
7.   What is different (if anything) about _____ and/ or its environment now from what it was five (5) years ago? Why is it different?
8.   What is likely to be different about _____ and/or its environment five (5) years from now. Why will it be different?
9.   What new (different) products and services could _____ provide in the future?
10. What must be done by _____ in order to provide these new products and services in the future?

EXERCISE 4.4 MISSION STATEMENT GUIDELINE FORM

1. Describe your beliefs concerning the mission (purpose) of
   _____ _____ ____. (Why does it exist and/or why should it exist in
   your opinion?)
2. Record points from other people's beliefs concerning the institutional mission of _____ that you want to include in your draft of
   a mission statement.
3. Develop your personal mission statement for _____.

EXERCISE 4.5 ASSESSING VISION STATEMENTS

Questions to be asked about your college or university vision include
1. Does the organization have a clearly stated vision?
2. Do the key people (stakeholders—internal and external) know and agree with the vision?
3. What are the boundaries to your vision? Are there time, geographical, or social constraints to the implementation of your vision?

Please rate your existing institutional vision statement on the following criteria. (1 = high, 2 = somewhat high, 3 = neutral, 4 = somewhat low, 5 = low). To what extent does/is your existing institutional vision statement:

1. Future oriented?   1 2 3 4 5

2. Express creativity and is not merely derived   1 2 3 4 5
   from current conditions and trends?

3. Based on value principles that reflect   1 2 3 4 5
   respect for people?

4. Recognize the history, culture, and values of   1 2 3 4 5
   the organization—even if change is envisioned?

5. Set high standards of excellence, ideals,   1 2 3 4 5
   and expectations for members of the organization?

6. Clarify institutional purpose and set   1 2 3 4 5
   direction?

7. Likely to inspire enthusiasm and encourage   1 2 3 4 5
   institutional commitment?

8. Reflect the uniqueness of the organization   1 2 3 4 5
   in its competency and image?

9. Ambitious, challenging organizational   1 2 3 4 5
   members?

It should be noted that this series of questions and criteria can be used to compare the vitality of alternative institutional visions.

EXERCISE 4.6   DEVELOPING VISION STATEMENTS

1. Describe your maximum vision for _____ ten years in the future. (What will _____ be like in ten years if it achieves your ideal vision for it? Be specific!) _____ will:

2. Describe your vision for _____ in five years if it is to achieve your maximum vision for the future. (What would _____ be like in five years if it is in the process of achieving your ideal vision? Again, be specific!) _____ will:

EXERCISE 4.7 ACTION PLAN FOR COMMUNICATING VISION

Key Success Factors	Action Steps	Persons	Target Dates
Educate			
Create environment			
Produce materials			
Reduce ambiguity			
Consistency			
Accept criticism			
Focus on the future			
Anticipate problems			
Networking			

EXERCISE 4.8 ACTION PLAN FOR BOUNDARY TESTING THE VISION

Key Success Factors	Action Steps	Persons	Target Dates
Challenging values and norms			
Leadership			
Flexibility			
Risk			
Momentum			
Training			
Meetings and stories			
Experimentation			
Task groups and simulations			
Momentum			

EXERCISE 4.9   ACTION PLAN FOR SIGNING-ON THE VISION

Key Success Factors	Action Steps	Persons	Target Dates
Action environment			
Mini-visions			
Personal visions			
Symbols and ceremonies			

EXERCISE 4.10 CELEBRATING THE VISION

Key Success Factors	Action Steps	Persons	Target Dates
Positive reinforcement			
Accentuate the positive			
Variety			

EXERCISE 4.11 TOTAL QUALITY CULTURE ASSESSMENT FORM

Please rate your organization on the following criteria. (1 = definitely applies, 2 = somewhat applies, 3 = neutral, 4 = does not apply, 5 = definitely does not apply.)

A. Environment

1. Constancy of purpose clearly exists	1	2	3	4	5
2. High degree of democratization achieved	1	2	3	4	5
3. Accepts responsibility to all stakeholders	1	2	3	4	5
4. Organization demonstrates long-term focus	1	2	3	4	5
5. Quality performance measures in place	1	2	3	4	5
6. Human rights and diversity accepted	1	2	3	4	5
7. Workers enabled to do their jobs	1	2	3	4	5
8. Workers empowered	1	2	3	4	5
9. Workers supported by management	1	2	3	4	5
10. Quality profiles established	1	2	3	4	5
11. A shared common vision exists	1	2	3	4	5

Environmental Total _____

B. Products and Services

12. Products and services based on customer need	1	2	3	4	5
13. Customers "sell" other customers	1	2	3	4	5
14. Satisfy customer needs and expectations	1	2	3	4	5
15. Reflect added value	1	2	3	4	5
16. Customer input to product and service development	1	2	3	4	5
17. Partnership with customers and suppliers	1	2	3	4	5
18. Measure customer satisfaction proactively	1	2	3	4	5

Products and Services Total _____

C. Methods

19. Study/learn from successes and failures	1	2	3	4	5
20. Establish operational definitions of quality for key processes	1	2	3	4	5
21. Obtain constant feedback	1	2	3	4	5
22. Hear voices of employees	1	2	3	4	5
23. Study/learn from others	1	2	3	4	5
24. Work effectively with suppliers	1	2	3	4	5

25. Manage processes and stabilize through   1 2 3 4 5
    Statistical Process Control
26. Communicate using data   1 2 3 4 5
27. Hear voice of customer   1 2 3 4 5
28. Hear voice of process   1 2 3 4 5
29. Follow PDCA discipline (Plan, Do, Check, Act)   1 2 3 4 5
30. Use consensus   1 2 3 4 5
Methods Total   _____

D. People

31. Feel "I belong"   1 2 3 4 5
32. Recognize contribution   1 2 3 4 5
33. Train in job   1 2 3 4 5
34. Feel pride in work   1 2 3 4 5
35. Learn continuously   1 2 3 4 5
36. Committed to team   1 2 3 4 5
37. Share customer vision   1 2 3 4 5
38. "Connected" to customer   1 2 3 4 5
39. Trained in process improvement methods   1 2 3 4 5
40. Use people's ideas   1 2 3 4 5
41. Included in strategic planning   1 2 3 4 5
42. Work to potential   1 2 3 4 5
People Total   _____

E. Organizational Structure

43. Managers literally lead   1 2 3 4 5
44. Cooperate at all levels   1 2 3 4 5
45. Inverted through customer/supplier   1 2 3 4 5
    relationships
46. Pay any bonus based on overall effectiveness   1 2 3 4 5
47. Operate all systems/processes using total quality 1 2 3 4 5
48. Align process management with strategic   1 2 3 4 5
    business
49. Function defines form   1 2 3 4 5
50. Understand roles/responsibilities   1 2 3 4 5
51. Respond like small organizations   1 2 3 4 5

52. Members share in ownership of structure and processes   1 2 3 4 5
53. Encourage creativity and innovation   1 2 3 4 5
54. Operate effectively cross-functionally   1 2 3 4 5
55. Delegate responsibility and authority   1 2 3 4 5

Organizational Structure Total   _____

F. Total Quality Mindset

56. Practice win–win strategies   1 2 3 4 5
57. Improved quality increases   1 2 3 4 5
58. Recognize that variation is normal   1 2 3 4 5
59. All members learn continuously   1 2 3 4 5
60. Teamwork is encouraged   1 2 3 4 5
61. Added value to customer   1 2 3 4 5
62. All employees use data   1 2 3 4 5
63. Employ the PDCA cycle   1 2 3 4 5
64. Measure and track results   1 2 3 4 5
65. Recognize that all outcomes result from a process   1 2 3 4 5
66. Recognize that all quality means continuous improvement   1 2 3 4 5
67. Recognize that all workers want to do their best   1 2 3 4 5
68. Recognize that managers control (are responsible for) the work process   1 2 3 4 5
69. Practice systems thinking   1 2 3 4 5
70. Move from enumerative to analytical approach   1 2 3 4 5
71. Customer needs define quality   1 2 3 4 5

Total Quality Mindset   _____

EXERCISE 4.12 ACTION PLAN FOR TRANSFORMING THE CULTURE OF THE COLLEGE OR UNIVERSITY

Key Success Factors	Action Steps	Persons	Target Dates
Systems and structure			
Actions			
Roles			
Behaviors			
Attitudes			
Norms			
Values			

EXERCISE 4.13 GOAL AND OBJECTIVE ASSESSMENT QUESTIONNAIRE

General questions to be asked about your college or university and overarching goals include:

1. Does the college or university have a clear statement of overarching goals?
2. Do the key people (stakeholders—internal and external) know and agree with the goals?
3. What are the boundaries to your goals? Are there time, geographical, or social constraints to the implementation of your goals?

Please rate your college or university goal and objective statements using the following criteria (1 = definitely meets the criteria, 2 = somewhat meets the criteria, 3 = neutral, 4 = does not meet the criteria, 5 = definitely does not meet the criteria).

Our college or university goal and objective statement:

1.	Identifies specific goals to be achieved	1	2	3	4	5
2.	Addresses significant issues in the life of the institution	1	2	3	4	5
3.	Is consistent with the institutional mission	1	2	3	4	5
4.	Is realistic	1	2	3	4	5
5.	Is challenging	1	2	3	4	5
6.	Is feasible	1	2	3	4	5
7.	Encourages a focus on performance	1	2	3	4	5
8.	Encourages individuals to ask the question, "What will I be doing?"	1	2	3	4	5
9.	Provides enough specificity that achievement measures could be developed	1	2	3	4	5
10.	Progress toward goals is verifiable	1	2	3	4	5
11.	Goal achievement is verifiable	1	2	3	4	5

EXERCISE 4.14   ACTION PLAN FOR DEVELOPING OVERARCHING COLLEGE OR UNIVERSITY GOALS

Institutional Vision

Overarching Goals

Operational Objectives

Specific Activities

Selection of Inputs

EXERCISE 4.15 OVERARCHING GOAL IDENTIFICATION

Based on your understanding of the college or university vision:

1. Identify the three most important issues facing _____ over the next five to ten years.

   1.

   2.

   3.

2. Please rank these issues based on the following criteria: (1) urgency—does the issue need immediate attention; (2) seriousness—significance of consequences if issue is not addressed; (3) growth potential—potential that situation will worsen if issue is not addressed; (4) overall negative impact on institution.

Urgency	Seriousness	Growth	Impact
1	1	1	1
2	2	2	2
3	3	3	3

3. Identify (in rank order) what you consider to be the three most important goals for the institution to adopt for the next five to ten years.

   1.

   2.

   3.

4. What are the benefits (positive aspects) of selecting your highest ranked goal as an overarching institutional goal?

5. What are the costs (negative aspects) of selecting your highest ranked goal as an overarching institutional goal?

6. What are the costs (negative aspects) of not selecting your highest ranked goal as an overarching institutional goal?

7. Assuming your highest ranked item were adopted as an overarching institutional goal for the next five to ten years, what institutional objectives should we adopt for the next two to five years. Place them in rank order from most to least important.

   1.

   2.

   3.

8. What are the benefits (positive aspects) of selecting your highest ranked objective?

9. What are the costs (negative aspects) of selecting your highest ranked objective?

10. What are the costs (negative aspects) of not selecting your highest ranked objective?

ABSTRACTS

ABSTRACT 4.1
WHAT BUSINESS SCHOOLS AREN'T TEACHING

Bruzzese, Anita
Incentive (IMK), Vol. 165, Issue 3, March 1991, pp. 29–31

It was at the University of Chicago that Dr. Deming, as a graduate student in the late 1920s, first encountered the sweatshop working conditions at the famous Bell Labs which influenced forever the course of total quality. After sixty years, it is finally coming full circle, as outlined in this provocative article by Bruzzese. The author argues that as total quality and teamwork replace traditional management methods in the real world, educators and executives are stressing the urgency for curricula teaching total quality management (TQM). Companies such as Motorola and Xerox charge that the majority of business schools do not immerse students in the concept of TQM or provide them with the people skills needed to motivate a U.S. workforce reeling from recession, layoffs, and tough foreign competition. One reason business schools have neglected TQM is that many consider it only a buzzword for traditional subject matter.

Of particular interest are the findings of a panel of business leaders, who recommend ten action items/strategies for introducing total quality in university business schools. Finally, with the advent of the Malcolm Baldrige National Quality Award and the proliferation of total quality seminars, some campuses are beginning to incorporate TQM into their curricula. At the University of Chicago, the LEAD (leadership, education, and development) teamwork program has some 500 students who work in 10 groups called cohorts. These groups study and learn together, as well as function as a social network.

ABSTRACT 4.2
INDUSTRY TO B SCHOOLS: SMARTEN UP ON TQM OR ELSE

Jörgensen, Barbara
Electronics Business (FB), Oct. 1992, pp. 66-70

Several industry leaders have begun to talk about the importance of supplier quality in their businesses. While this may be nothing new, one must recognize that they are not talking about electronics components but about the flood of new MBAs that they must retrain because many American business schools include very little on total quality management (TQM) in their curricula or in their service areas. This results in multi-billion dollar retraining efforts for American industries each year, and in some cases, MBAs not trained in the principles of TQM are being overlooked by prospective employers.

Additionally, several barriers appear to be keeping TQM from gaining widespread acceptance in business schools. For example, many still view TQM as just another management fad, and perhaps more importantly, many universities are still promoting individual effort over team-oriented learning. Sadly, many schools, bombarded with an endless array of TQM theories, gurus, and industry models, cannot agree on which system to implement or what to teach.

However, there is light at the end of the tunnel! The TQM University Challenge, sponsored by Procter & Gamble, matches industry leaders with universities to integrate TQM principles into their courses and daily operations. First, the university would conduct an internal audit using a questionnaire similar to the Baldrige criteria. Next, a customer survey and vision were developed, and employees given a week of on-site training en route to forming internal steering committees. Several tangible gains resulted from the TQM University Challenge, and a number of subcommittees were formed, in part to help assess what employers want from graduates. In many cases they want TQM to be part of required, not elective, course work, and competition frequently forces universities to comply. No references are provided, but some excellent sidebar articles are included.

ABSTRACT 4.3
TOTAL QUALITY MANAGEMENT IN BUSINESS AND ACADEMIA

Stuelpnagel, Thomas R.
Business Forum (LAB), Vol. 14, Issue 1, Fall 1988/Winter 1989, pp. 4–9

This article by Stuelpnagel was an early wake-up call for colleges and universities to begin thinking about and developing total quality management (TQM) master plans and study guides. Written in 1989, the key points raised remain as relevant five years later. His major premise is that every graduating class without total quality in education is one more group that will have to be retrained at a later date. He views total quality as a management "unification" process which can be compared to organized common sense. He also points out that TQM is an improved management process that originated in the United States and was perfected in Japan. In large measure, industry and government are making the transition directly with the assistance of private and government training organizations, thus bypassing the business schools. Universities need to become aware of the revolution that is occurring in the TQM field, develop TQM master plans, and work toward developing studies and curricula in support of TQM

The author's list of major areas to be addressed includes reduction of waste in management and introduction of statistical thinking, as well as instillation of pride and accountability in all employees. His definition of quality is simple and direct: giving customers what they have a right to expect. This is achieved with a system designed to keep the customer continuously in the product cycle. A total of thirteen features of TQM are covered, including using statistical methods to control both management and product processes and making all processes in the management–product/service chain subject to continuous improvement. Finally, TQM provides the opportunity for all employees within the organization to participate as team members, to help and be heard, to be rewarded and excel. Although somewhat dated, there are enough salient points to make the reading worthwhile, such as "Deming suggests that the 'critical mass' of the leadership group might be the square root of the number of people involved." References are provided.

ABSTRACT 4.4
A MATTER OF METAPHORS: EDUCATION AS A
HANDMADE PROCESS

Sztajn, Paola
Educational Leadership (GEDL), Nov. 1992, pp. 35-37

Total quality management suggests that we stop viewing schools as factories and begin looking at them as enlightened corporations. Thus, the author develops the notion that total quality management for universities and schools cannot be mass produced. Each must be considered to be unique, for it is in uniqueness that the added value of the endless range of possibilities that Sztajn suggests is available, through the clustering use of metaphors. The concepts of metaphors as shapes of social reality and as self-fulfilling prophecies are addressed. Thought-provoking material is provided, independent of practical realities. Limited references are given.

ABSTRACT 4.5
TQM AT OREGON STATE UNIVERSITY

Coate, L. Edwin
Journal for Quality and Participation (JCQ), Dec. 1990, pp. 90-101

The top management of Oregon State University (OSU) began their quest for quality in 1988 with a question: How adaptable are the methods of the quality gurus to the education industry? Whereas the learning processes are far less predictable than the manufacturing processes, the service areas of a university (billing, registration, etc.) are far more controllable and provide a good beginning point for total quality management. (Educators will need time to be trained to gather and interpret data regarding pupil achievement, long-term effectiveness, and process variation.) Frustrated by apparent contradictions between the quality gurus, management at OSU developed a model closely related to the Hewlett-Packard and Florida Power & Light Japanese-based approach. They also incorporated the Baldrige Award criteria to help develop their five-year plans.

Therefore, a nine-point implementation approach was initiated by the top management of OSU, beginning with point one, exploring total quality management. The senior managers at OSU conducted several awareness-raising activities such as research, benchmarking, and even a visit and speech by W. Edwards Deming. These activities, however, did not include lower echelon employees, and suspicion of the new system grew, leading to the decision to begin pilot programs with the service areas of the university. During point two, a pilot team was commissioned to address a specific high-priority issue that had a high probability of success, was customer focused, and was selected by top management. The pilot team discovered many problems with the remodeling process and helped implement several changes which improved both customer relations and employee morale. Point three was designed to define customer needs through quality function deployment, an organized system to identify and prioritize customer needs and translate them onto a workable matrix pinpointing priorities. (The House of Quality matrix originally developed by the Japanese Union of Scientists and Engineers [JUSE] was modified for this purpose.) Also, three customer surveys were conducted in 1989; as a result, a marketing committee was created to begin to realign the classes that were offered with the classes that were needed.

CHAPTER 5

PROCESS MANAGEMENT

The second managerial level of total quality is the initiation of total quality improvement (TQI) through process management. It is at this level where the implementation plan of the TQI process is developed. *Webster's New World Dictionary* defines process as: "(1) a series of *changes* by which something develops; (2) a method of doing something with all the steps involved" (italics added).[1] Thus, for the purpose of this chapter, process is the way in which the work of the college or university is accomplished. All work involves process—changes or transformations by which something different develops.

This is also the second pillar and second foundation of the House of Quality, as highlighted in Figure 5.1. According to Voehl,[2] the purpose of process management is to ensure that all key processes work in harmony to maximize organizational effectiveness. The goal is to achieve a competitive advantage through superior customer satisfaction. A principal activity of this level is to develop overall continuous improvement and problem-solving processes. The principal tools and techniques of TQI used in this process are flowcharting, brainstorming, multi-voting, Pareto charts, graphs, and causal diagrams. If effectively implemented, three major outcomes result: (1) a common

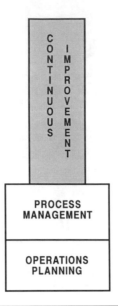

Figure 5.1 House of Total Quality.

language for documenting and communicating activities and decisions for key TQI processes, (2) a college- or university-wide system of linked TQI indicators, and (3) both initial and long-term gains due to the elimination of waste, rework, and bottlenecks.

Managing transforming processes is critical because the college or university has no products or services without them. In turn, without products and services, the visions of the institution cannot be achieved or its missions fulfilled. There is a lower risk of failure when introducing TQI at the process management level than at the strategy level because the entire organization may not be involved. However, implementation at this level still involves the territorial domain of division or subdivision of the college or university and may generate considerable concern, if not opposition, from those directly involved.

To begin this discussion of process management, a basic model of the transforming process is presented in Figure 5.2. As illustrated in this model, it is assumed that any work process, no matter how large or small, complicated or uncomplicated, involves three major components:

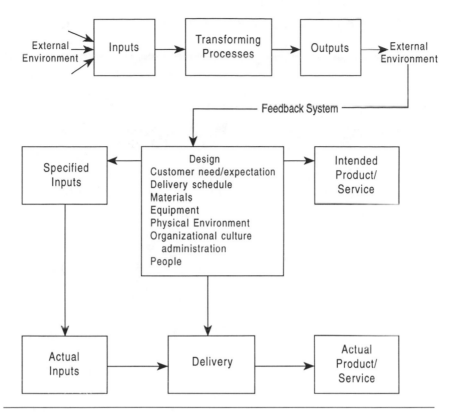

Figure 5.2 Basic Transforming Process Model.

- *Inputs:* Resources from the external environment, including the products or outputs from other subsystems of the college or university. Inputs may include raw materials, equipment, methods, etc. Also included are the physical environment, organizational culture, and people.
- *Transforming processes:* The work activities that transform the inputs, adding value to them and making them the outputs of the subsystem.
- *Outputs:* The products and/or services generated by the subsystem, intended for another subsystem in the college or university or a system in the external environment.

Using this model helps to identify three major targets for process improvement:

- *Design Stage:* Improving efforts that focus on (1) information about customer needs; (2) design steps in the transforming process; (3) specification of input requirements for materials, equipment, methods, physical environment, organizational culture/administration, and people; (4) delivery schedule; and (5) information about supplier capabilities.
- *Delivery Stage:* Improving efforts that focus on inputs to produce the desired product and/or service. These include issues related to (1) conformity to design specifications; (2) effectiveness and efficiency, i.e., mistakes, failures, and rework; (3) timeliness of delivery of the product and/or service; (4) costs; (5) meeting the resource needs of employees; and (6) complying with regulatory requirements, e.g., the work environment of employees.
- *Feedback System:* Improving efforts that focus on enhancing the information received from two feedback systems: (1) information from the internal environment on the effectiveness and efficiency of the delivery stage (i.e., design complexity, conformity of output to design expectations, and consistency of output, particularly negative variation) and (2) information from the external environment, or the customers, pertaining to the degree to which the product/service meets their needs and expectations (quality).

IMPLEMENTING PROCESS MANAGEMENT

Is there a need for colleges and universities to deal with the issues of process management? Such a need does exist, because process management focuses attention on the missing link in quality assurance efforts in higher education. As discussed in Chapter 1, the approaches to assure quality in higher education are accreditation and outcome assessment (see Figure 1.2 in Chapter 1). These two approaches address the two ends of the quality assurance process. Accreditation focuses attention on inputs such as faculty degrees, finances, and facilities, often without any significant understanding of the needs and expectations of the constituents or customers of the college or university. To the degree that this is true, then the input assessment approaches of accreditation are severely limiting, particularly if quality is

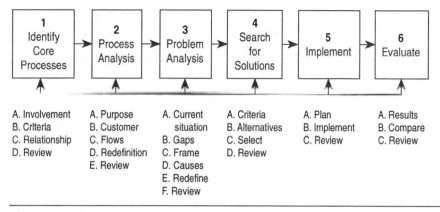

Figure 5.3   Process Management Steps.

to be defined in terms of the needs and expectations of the constituents. Chaffee and Sherr[3] argue that inputs should not be discussed in terms of producing quality.

> The inputs do not create quality design, processes, or outputs; rather they are derived from them. Design, processes and outputs, based on the needs of beneficiaries, define appropriate inputs. Proper inputs maximize the system, while improper inputs create limitations on the system. Therefore, it is more sensible to think of inputs as "proper" or "appropriate" rather than in terms of "quality."

Outcome assessments focus on the educational outputs or products. Unfortunately, knowledge of outputs does not provide a basis for identifying problems incurred during the process of providing the product. For example, knowledge of educational outputs does not provide insight into the teaching–learning process. If the teaching–learning process does furnish an educational output, then simple outcome assessments presents a major problem. How can educational outputs be improved if the teaching–learning process is not assessed? How can educational outputs be improved if the processes creating the outputs are not understood? Total quality management, with its emphasis on process management, provides the basis for obtaining the knowledge and understanding of the relationship between causes and effects. Total quality management provides the basis for applying the knowledge, understanding, and skill required to implement the entire input, transformation, and product process. (For additional information, see Abstract 5.1 at the end of this chapter.)

The six key steps in implementing process management (Figure 5.3) are (1) identification of the core processes, (2) process analysis, (3) problem analysis, (4) searching for solutions, (5) implementation, and (6) evaluation. The questions that must be asked and answered in order to fully carry out each step are listed in Exhibit 5.1.

Exhibit 5.1 Process Management Questionnaire

Questions to Be Asked and Answered for Each Process Management Step

1. **Identification of Core Processes**
   A. *Level of Involvement:* What level (division, subdivision, etc.) of the college or university is being studied?
   B. *Process Selection:* What criteria will be used to identify the core processes? What processes are critical to fulfilling the mission and achieving the vision of the college or university? Why?
   C. *Relationships between Core Processes:* What are the relationships between core processes?
   D. *Review:* Have we involved the right people in this step. Have we identified all the right core processes?

2. **Process Analysis**
   A. *Identification of Purpose(s):* What purpose is to be achieved by the targeted process?
   B. *Customer (Beneficiary) Identification:* Who are the customers (beneficiaries) of the process? Primary? Secondary? Internal? External? Who are the most important customers? Why? What needs and expectations do the customers have? How do others define the needs and expectations of the customers?
   C. *Analysis of the Flows in the Process:* Who are the major players in the process, including suppliers and customers? What are the detailed steps in the process? How are the steps related?
   D. *Redefinition of Purpose (if necessary):* Does the specified purpose meet the needs and expectations of the customers?
   E. *Review:* Have we involved the right people? Are all of the needed perspectives represented? Do we have adequate knowledge concerning the targeted process?

3. **Problem (Nonproblem) Analysis**
   A. *Assessment of the Current Situation:* Are customer needs and expectations being met? How effective and efficient is the process?
   B. *Identify Quality Gaps:* What are the gaps between desired and delivered quality of product/service resulting from the process?

C. *Frame (Define) the Problem:* What is the problem? What is the reason for seeking improvement?

D. *Determine Causes of the Problem:* What are the assumed causes of the problem? What are the major causes of the problem? What data are there to support the causal model?

E. *Redefine the Problem (if necessary):* Does the problem need to be redefined?

F. *Review:* Have we involved the right people? Is our description of desired quality appropriate? Is our description of the current situation sufficient? Are there different (better) ways of framing the problem? Did we have sufficient data? Is the problem worth solving? Why?

4. **Search for and Select Alternative Solutions**

A. *Specify Selection Criteria:* What criteria will be used to select solutions? Why? How will they be weighted? Why? What measures will be used to evaluate the success of new solutions?

B. *Identify Alternative Solutions:* What is the range of possible solutions to the problem? What problems will be created by alternative solutions?

C. *Select Preferred Solution:* Which solution best meets the selection criteria?

D. *Review:* Were the right people involved? Are all of the needed perspectives represented? Did we identify alternative solutions? Did we consider negative consequences? Were we objective? How well does the solution meet the selection criteria? Are there better solutions?

5. **Implementation**

A. *Plan for Implementation:* What individuals (groups) need to be involved in the planning and implementation process? What should the implementation plan include? What should the evaluation plan include?

B. *Implementation:* What actions are taken during implementation? How did they conform to the implementation plan? What were the reasons for deviations?

C. *Review:* Have we involved the right people? Have we developed a plan to gain commitment to implementation efforts? Does our implementation plan identify people, dates, and resources? Do we have a contingency plan if difficulties arise? Do we have a plan for evaluating the effort?

6. **Evaluate**

A. *Results:* What results were achieved? Why?

B. *Comparison:* How do the achieved results compare with the original conditions? How do the achieved results compare to the expected (desired, promised) results?

C. *Review:* How well did we follow our implementation plan? What changes were made during actual implementation? Did we implement our evaluation plan? Did we achieve our goals/objectives? What were there unintended consequences of our efforts? Were they positive or negative?

The guiding principle in developing these steps is the belief that there are definite advantages to be gained in maintaining clear distinctions between a number of activities. For example, process analysis should be distinct from problem identification, and problem identification should be separate from efforts to identify solutions. If these distinctions are not maintained, there is a tendency to invoke preconceived solutions prior to defining the problem, i.e., to the person who has a hammer, every problem is a nail. Each of the six steps is distinct and each must be carried out in sequence.

An action plan for initiating process management efforts is provided in Exercise 5.1 (all exercises appear at the end of the chapter). Use of this plan keeps the focus on the activities to be performed and the individuals who need to be involved.

Step 1: Identification of core processes. Step 1 appears to be simple for colleges and universities, at least at the institutional level. This is not always the case, however. Most college and university mission statements identify education or teaching, research, and community service as their fundamental purposes. Some even go so far as to identify education as the primary mission. However, far less than unanimity occurs when operationalizing the stated mission and establishing priorities concerning core processes. For example, while teaching, research, and service are expounded, some faculty members believe that the institution exists so that they may do research, and institutional reward systems often support this notion. Nor is there agreement on the degree to which colleges and universities are responsible for the affective as well as cognitive development of students. As one moves farther away from the overall institutional mission and core processes, this disparity increases. However, the issues involved in identifying core processes remain the same whether the total institution or subdivisions are involved.

Operationally, the activities included in Step 1 must involve a cross-functional team effort among key members of the organization. Cross-functional teams are important because most core processes span organizational boundaries. For example, faculty are the recipients of student recruitment efforts. Thus, they have a vested interest in the success of the recruitment program. Conversely, students have a vested interest in the nature and success of faculty recruitment efforts. Cross-functional teams are important because they help to ensure that different perspectives are represented; they also help to break down barriers, enhance communication, create a synergistic effect, and develop commitment.

An example of the core processes of a university is provided by Oregon State University (see Figure 5.7). These are discussed in the final section of this chapter.

Step 2: Process analysis.   This step starts with an effort to specify the purpose of the core process under study. Again, cross-functional teams provide the best approach to operationalize this step. Appropriate questions at this time include what is the purpose, why do we do it, and what does it accomplish.

Identification of customer needs and expectations must directly involve the customers as the primary source of information. These efforts may involve surveys, focus groups, or other activities designed to obtain direct data on their needs and expectations. In many cases it may be appropriate to combine data collection of customer needs and expectations with analysis of how well these needs and expectations are being met (see Step 3).

It is usually helpful to develop a flow diagram of the process being studied. A pictorial representation of a process can be a powerful tool because it provides a detailed, integrated view of the process. Examination of a flow diagram can provide considerable insight into sources of trouble, such as unnecessary steps and points of delay. An example of a basic flow diagram for selecting faculty members is given in Figure 5.4. A framework for the step-by-step collection and analysis of process data is provided in Exercise 5.2. This type of record keeping may be developed by the individuals directly involved in the target process, by direct observation, or both.

The procedures for developing a process flow diagram include:

1. *Boundary definition:*   The boundaries (beginning and ending) of the process being studied need to be specified.
2. *Data collection:*   Data on the process and all related activities need to be collected. The data collection efforts may involve direct participation in the activities, direct observation of the process, and asking others to describe how the work gets done.
3. *Sequential listing of activities (activity steps):*   The steps involved in the process should be identified in the order in which they occur, e.g., input, supplier, first actions, output of activity, who receives the output, etc.
4. *Drawing the flow diagram:*   Process flow diagrams are usually constructed using three standard symbols (see Figure 5.4).
5. *Study the flow diagram:*   Studying the flow diagram will provide insights as to missing data, redundant steps, potential delays, etc.

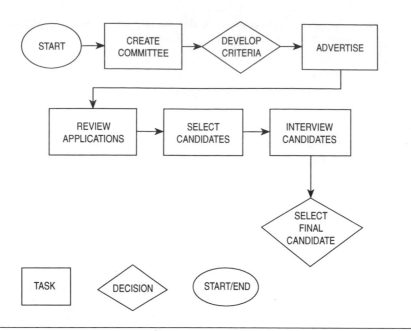

Figure 5.4   Process Flow Diagram: Selecting Faculty.

Step 3: Problem identification.   Step 3 involves the identification of performance measures and the collection of data on the process being studied. For example, data on student admissions may be used to study the admissions process, or student evaluations of faculty teaching may be used to study the teaching–learning process. These data are used to identify gaps in effectiveness, efficiency, or meeting the needs and expectations of customers. Where a gap is identified, it is stated as a problem. A framework of the problem is developed. Framing the problem is an important activity, because how a problem is framed sets perceptual and conceptual boundaries around the problem and ultimately determines the range of solutions to be considered. Criteria for framing the problem should include specificity, objectivity, and avoidance of assumed causes and potential solutions.

A framework for identifying gaps between the desired and actual quality of the product or service resulting from the target process is provided in Exercise 5.3. Data collection for this activity may require interviews with individuals responsible for the targeted process and/ or direct observation of the process.

Once the problem is framed, its causes need to be determined. Brainstorming is an effective tool to identify the range of possible causes. Usually, it is helpful to organize the ideas generated into a causal, or fishbone, diagram. Such a diagram is presented in Figure 5.5, which indicates barriers to the teaching–learning process. This diagram shows a number of causes of poor academic performance. A detailed analysis would involve identification of the "causes of the causes" presented in Figure 5.5. For example, the causes of poor study skills/habits would need to be identified. Additional efforts are required to produce data to verify the assumed causes. For example, a Pareto diagram of the reasons students give for leaving school is presented in Figure 5.6. These data may be used to verify a causal model for dropouts and to identify the major causes of the dropout problem.

Step 4: Search for solutions. This step involves the search for and the selection of solutions to the problem. In many cases it is useful to identify the criteria by which solutions will be evaluated before potential solutions are identified. This approach helps to avoid becoming fixated on a specific solution (e.g., only using a hammer). The criteria may include such factors as feasibility, costs, effectiveness, efficiency, time needed to implement, and even political acceptability. Each factor should be weighed in terms of its perceived importance. At this point, attention should also be devoted to identifying the measures to be used to evaluate the success or failure of the implemented solutions.

It may not be easy to find and agree upon solutions. In some cases, generating ideas for solutions is problematic. In other cases, agreement is difficult to achieve because individuals are committed to specific solutions. Brainstorming and other similar techniques are usually helpful in generating ideas for solutions. This is also the point at which benchmarking (i.e., seeking information on the best practices for the same or similar processes) may be valuable.

Coming to agreement on the best solution is facilitated if (1) consensus is reached on criteria for evaluating alternative solutions and (2) the causal logic of proposed solutions is made explicit. How will the solution change the identified causes of the problem? A framework to more explicitly examine the causal impacts of proposed solutions is provided in Exercise 5.4.

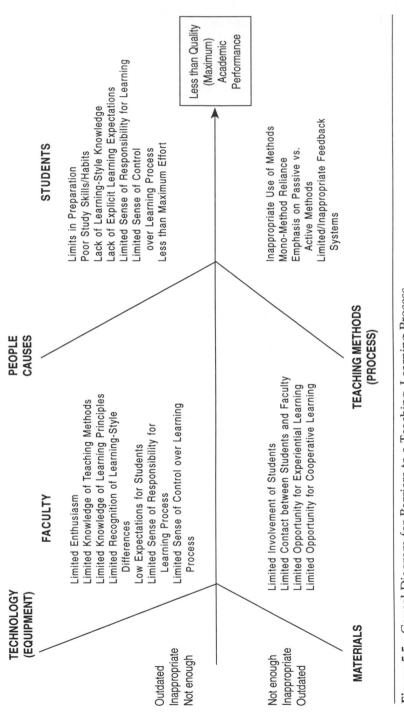

TECHNOLOGY (EQUIPMENT)

Outdated
Inappropriate
Not enough

FACULTY

Limited Enthusiasm
Limited Knowledge of Teaching Methods
Limited Knowledge of Learning Principles
Limited Recognition of Learning-Style
   Differences
Low Expectations for Students
Limited Sense of Responsibility for
   Learning Process
Limited Sense of Control over Learning
   Process

PEOPLE CAUSES

STUDENTS

Limits in Preparation
Poor Study Skills/Habits
Lack of Learning-Style Knowledge
Lack of Explicit Learning Expectations
Limited Sense of Responsibility for Learning
Limited Sense of Control
   over Learning Process
Less than Maximum Effort

Less than Quality
(Maximum)
Academic
Performance

MATERIALS

Not enough
Inappropriate
Outdated

Limited Involvement of Students
Limited Contact between Students and Faculty
Limited Opportunity for Experiential Learning
Limited Opportunity for Cooperative Learning

TEACHING METHODS (PROCESS)

Inappropriate Use of Methods
Mono-Method Reliance
Emphasis on Passive vs.
   Active Methods
Limited/Inappropriate Feedback
   Systems

Figure 5.5 Causal Diagram for Barriers to a Teaching–Learning Process.

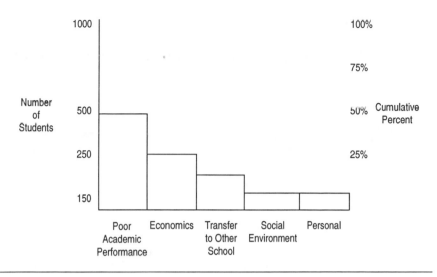

Figure 5.6 Pareto Diagram: Student Reasons for Leaving School (based on student exit interviews).

Step 5: Implementation. Issues related to implementation are often neglected, usually with unfortunate results. Planning for implementation should involve detailed efforts, including developing a contingency plan to deal with problems that may arise if something goes wrong. Tools that may be useful in these efforts include deployment flowcharts, Gantt charts, PERT charts, checklists, and force-field analysis. Attention must also be paid to the actual implementation of the solution. This may be identified as monitoring, or formative evaluation. Whatever it is called, it must be done. This is also the point at which a formal plan should be developed to evaluate the success or failure of the proposed solution.

Step 6: Evaluation. The sixth and final step is the natural extension of all the preceding steps. In most cases, evaluations do not have to be complicated. They do, however, have to address the issue of results, both intended and unintended. Evaluation efforts should involve all team members, although their particular functions may vary. After the results have been reviewed, it must be determined whether it is necessary to return to any previous steps.

THE CULTURE OF PROCESS MANAGEMENT

It must be stressed that there is a culture associated with the concept of process management. The essentials of this culture have been well articulated by Chaffee and Sherr[4] in a recent book on the transformation of postsecondary education, where they make the following points:

> You cannot inspect quality into a product or service at the end of the line. Quality requires not just the detection of defects, but also their prevention. It requires elimination of unnecessary steps and assurance of appropriate procedures.

> All work is process. The details of organizational processes are important because they are the substance of organizational work that ultimately produces the results.

> If the details are wrong, the process is wrong. If the process is wrong, the results are wrong. Quality requires attention to detail.

> You cannot improve a process without data. And often the data yields surprises.

> Common causes of problems are inherent in every process and are not attributable to the worker.

> Special causes of problems come from exceptions to the normal process. Eliminating them requires detecting them as quickly as possible.

> Adding steps to a process adds opportunities for new problems. Make each process as simple as possible to improve.

Individuals interested in initiating process management activities should carefully review these points to ensure that a supporting value system is brought to the effort. (For additional information, see Abstract 5.2 at the end of this chapter.)

APPLICATION OF PROCESS MANAGEMENT AT OREGON STATE UNIVERSITY

The implementation activities conducted by Oregon State University (OSU) integrally reflect the core functions of process management. In their first year (1990) they carried out their version of the process management implementation steps (Figure 5.3). The core processes of the president were identified. These processes were important, because while they were identified as the principal responsibilities of the president, they were the critical processes of the university. The twelve processes and their performance measures are presented in Figure 5.7.

Steps 2 (process analysis) and 3 (problem analysis) were applied in a focused identification of their internal and external customers. Four surveys conducted in 1989–90 provided data about their customers. The image survey evaluated the image of OSU perceived by six important customer groups: the general public, college-bound Oregon high school students, OSU alumni living in Oregon, OSU undergraduate students, classified staff, and faculty. The admitted students survey provided additional information about student customers, those who

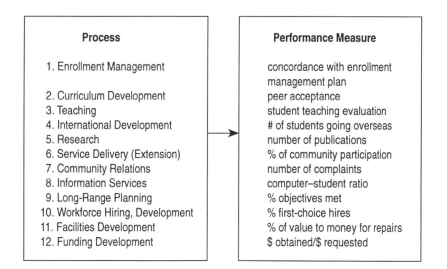

Process	Performance Measure
1. Enrollment Management	concordance with enrollment management plan
2. Curriculum Development	peer acceptance
3. Teaching	student teaching evaluation
4. International Development	# of students going overseas
5. Research	number of publications
6. Service Delivery (Extension)	% of community participation
7. Community Relations	number of complaints
8. Information Services	computer–student ratio
9. Long-Range Planning	% objectives met
10. Workforce Hiring, Development	% first-choice hires
11. Facilities Development	% of value to money for repairs
12. Funding Development	$ obtained/$ requested

Figure 5.7 Oregon State University's Twelve Critical Processes. (Source: Coate, L. Edwin (1992). *Implementing Total Quality Management at Oregon State University*. Corvallis: Oregon State University, p. 13.)

either did or did not enroll at OSU. Respondents compared OSU with other institutions they considered. A faculty survey and a staff survey provided information about the internal customers of the university.

Steps 2 and 3 were also applied in the establishment of a pilot "daily management" study or work team in the physical plant, to address the problem of time spent in the building remodeling process. The team included ten managers and frontline workers, a team leader, and a training facilitator. In the first six months the team worked through two phases of problem solving (discussed in Chapter 6). Their process flowchart uncovered 33 causes of overlaps, delays, and unnecessary paper flow which led to many immediate process improvements and five major changes in areas of customer service, communication, and procedures in the remodeling process. The team's solutions during these two phases resulted in a 23 percent reduction in the average duration of a remodeling job (see Figure 5.8). The success of this pilot work team project was as a beneficial learning experience and a model for future teams. "The process showed top managers internal problems they had not recognized before and exposed workers to problems managers face in day-to-day operations. The result is cooperation. Productivity has increased, and a survey of customers showed that they are more satisfied, knowing that they've been listened to."[5]

Step 4 (search for solutions) resulted in redefining an increasingly important concept—marketing:

> Universities have traditionally avoided marketing. The idea of designing courses to fit the market has been foreign to our university's way of thinking. Faculty know what students need, not the other way around. To begin to deal with this, we created a marketing committee to look at OSU's image and the products we deliver, a first step in beginning to realign classes offered with the classes customers say they need. Total commitment to developing "customer-driven" systems will not come easily. However, the curriculum committee, responding to industry comments about students not writing well, completely revised our curriculum to require writing courses during all four years of a student's academic career.[5]

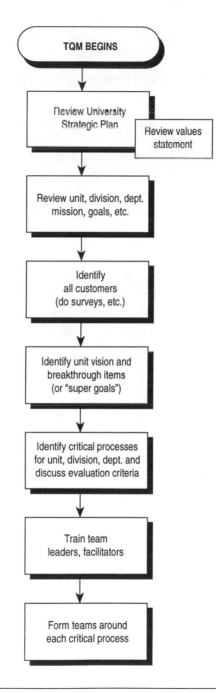

Figure 5.8 Total Quality Management at Oregon State University: Strategic Planning. (Source: Coate, L. Edwin (1992). *Total Quality Management at Oregon State University*. Corvallis: Oregon State University, p. 12.)

Step 5 (implementation of total quality management) began at OSU with top management of the university focusing on what was identified as "strategic breakthrough planning," which consisted of five activities: defining the mission (discussed in Chapter 4), developing the vision (also discussed in Chapter 4), understanding customers (discussed earlier), identifying the critical processes (also discussed earlier), and identifying breakthrough items. Three breakthrough items, or activities to generate quality improvements in basic systems, were identified: increased computing capability of the university, increased internationalization of the university, and increased administrative efficiency by implementing total quality management. A five-year plan based on these priority breakthrough items was then developed.

A second activity of the implementation step (Step 5) was the development and utilization of a planning process model, presented in Figure 5.8. Use of this model resulted in the identification of the critical processes for every unit of the university. This is presented in Figure 5.9. Although lengthy, review of these processes reveals the critical identification of each unit's areas of responsibility. This can then be used to assess the scope of products and services provided (or not provided), cross-functional relationships, and areas of collaboration for the development of total quality management and continuous improvement processes.

The final step in the implementation process was the development of daily management study or work teams. This was considered to be the most important step in OSU's implementation of total quality management and is discussed at length in Chapter 6 on project and team management.

President's Critical Processes

Admissions	Testing	Research	Community relations	Long-range planning
Curriculum development	International development	Service delivery (extension)	Information services	Workforce hiring and development
				Funding development

OSU Vice Presidents' Critical Processes

Provost and Vice President for Academic Affairs

Faculty recruitment, retention, development	Teaching and advising	College and departmental administration	Cultural diversification	Precollege programs	Planning	Research	Statewide services
Promotion and tenure		Curriculum development		Registration, articulation, admission		Faculty governance

Associate V.P.
- Faculty development
- Academic recruitment and hiring
- Promotion and tenure
- Faculty retirement and benefits
- Continuing higher education
- Faculty recognition and awards
- Family employment program
- Faculty appeals
- Academic budgeting

Assistant V.P., Special Programs
- Precollege programs
- Educational opportunities program (EOP)
- Student appeals
- Holocaust observance
- Minority initiatives
- University seminars

Assistant V.P., Undergraduate Studies
- Curriculum
- Community college articulation
- Accreditation and assessment
- Instructional computing
- Registration/student information system
- Communication media center (CMC)
- Horner Museum
- ROTC

CMC
- Equipment distribution
- Nonprint materials collection
- Graphic arts services
- Photographic services
- Electronic distance education
- Electronic equipment design and maintenance
- Television production
- TV distribution, engineering
- Training and consultation

Continuing Higher Education
- Credit programs
- Noncredit, special projects
- Summer session

Horner Museum
- Collection and curation
- Public education
- Museum studies
- Collection access
- Museum practices
- Extension

EOP
- Student recruitment
- Academic advising
- Academic development
- Academic support

Library
- ARL status
- Technical development
- Staff training
- Continuing reorganization
- User orientation
- Access to information

Faculty Senate
- Leadership
- Representation
- Communication

Academic Units
Agriculture, business, education, engineering, forestry, health and human performance, home economics, liberal arts, oceanography, pharmacy, science, veterinary medicine, ROTC

Shared critical processes*
Teaching and advising
Research
Service

*Additional critical processes are specific to particular units.

Figure 5.9 Oregon State University Critical Processes. (Source: Coate, L. Edwin (1992). *Total Quality Management at Oregon State University*. Corvallis: Oregon State University, pp. 45–47.)

Vice President for Finance and Administration

Process headers: Fiscal services · Workforce hiring development · Information services · Long-range planning · Budgeting · Community relations · Facilities management · Law enforcement · Safety

Budget Services
Archives/records management
Budget administration
Management communication
Management information
Planning and analytical studies

Personnel Services
Benefits
Classification
Employment
Employee relations
Quality
Staff development

Business Services
Accounting services
Other fiscal support
Research fiscal support
Student loans

Printing Services
Mailing service
Printing service
Quick copy service

Computing Services
Academic computing
Administrative computing
Computer support
Computer training
Networking

Support Services
Contracting support
Motor pool service
Purchasing support
Surplus property service
Telecommunications service

Facilities Services
Building operations
Campus planning
Construction
Custodial
Delivery
Engineering
Parking
Police
Safety
Utilities

Radiation Services
Research
Service
Teaching

Vice President for Research, Graduate Studies, and International Programs

Process headers: Program development · Program promotion · Program facilitation · Program integrity · Program assessment · Facilities improvement · Long-range planning

Research Office
Research promotion
Research proposal review
Data collection, reporting
Program integrity
Interdisciplinary research development

Hatfield Marine Science Center
Facilities management
Public education
Community relations
Information dissemination
Program facilitation

Graduate School
Program development
Program assessment
Program standards
Procedure/policy monitoring
Minority recruiting
Interdisciplinary program development

Sea Grant Program
Program development
Program management
Project monitoring
Information dissemination
Industry/government liaison

International Research and Development
Program development
Project design
Project management
Internatl. research coordination
Fund raising

International Education
Program development
Program promotion
International networking/coordination
Counseling and advising
Information dissemination
Study abroad program management
Student orientation
International faculty/student exchange liaison
Scholarship management
Testing and evaluation

Vice President for Student Affairs

Planning | Student development | Enrollment management | Service delivery | Workforce development | Constituency development | Facilities maintenance | Financial management | Advocacy

Recruitment and Admissions
Enrollment management
Recruitment
Information dissemination
Admissions
Reporting
Scholarship management
Residency determination

New Student Programs
New student orientation
Retention
Scholarship management
On-campus visitations
Mom's/dad's clubs
Advising and referral
Information delivery

Student Housing Services
Facilities management
Residence life management
Fiscal management

Student Aid Delivery
Student aid delivery
Data collection and reporting
Scholarship management
Student aid coordination

Counseling and Testing
Counseling and advising
Teaching
Testing

Student Support Services
Student academic support
Student life support
University support services
Instruction and advising

U. Community Food Service Delivery
Purchasing Inventory management
Production
Education
Program support

Career Planning and Placement Processes
Job placement
Employer recruitment
Work experience
Information delivery and marketing
Training and education
Legal rights monitoring
Information systems management
Donations and solicitations

U. Community Program Services, Facilities
Retail goods and service monitoring
Events management
Student involvement
Information gathering and dissemination
Recreational sports administration
Marketing and research
Facilities management

Health Services
Diagnosis
Treatment
Patient education
Health promotion
Disease prevention
Administrative services

Figure 5.9 (continued)

Vice President for University Relations

Resource development   Timely response   Voluntary participation and involvement   Building pride and ownership   Providing useful information

Alumni Relations
Marketing OSU
Colleges/units alumni management
Establishing alumni clubs
Assisting with student recruiting
Producing *Oregon Stater*
Maintaining alumni database
Legislative liaison support

Development
Raising private funds for university use
Cooperating with OSU Foundation in matters involving gift receipting, acknowledgment, management as needed
Responding to donor interests
Focusing on major gifts fund raising to meet university and unit priority needs
Building staff, systems, and volunteer structure for campus-wide capital campaign

University Marketing, Conferences, and Special Events
OSU Portland Center
Marketing OSU statewide, nationally, internationally
Facilities, coordination, and organizational services for meetings, conferences, events
Maintaining campus activity calendar
Providing venue for cultural activities, i.e., Giustina Gallery, Austin Auditorium

News and Communication Services
Providing comprehensive public information services
Providing publicity program that articulates OSU's strengths
Promoting internal relations and understanding within OSU
Servicing relationships with all media
Providing public relations training for OSU departments
Assisting with needs for professional public relations support service

Community and Government Relations
Local and state government relationships
Legislative information and service to university units
Providing direction to OSU alumni advocates program
Informational programs on governmental and legislative issues
High school relations
Representing OSU at governmental hearings and meetings
Local business relationships

Publications
Producing OSU's publications
Providing professional support and consultation in concept development, editing, design, production, control, distribution
Reviewing production of publications for compliance with laws, rules, policies
Developing policies and encouraging cooperation among all publication production units
Managing OSU Press

Figure 5.9 (continued)

ENDNOTES

1. *Webster's New World Dictionary* (1982). Compact School and Office Edition, New York: Simon and Schuster.
2. Voehl, Frank W. (1992). *Total Quality: Principles and Processes within Organizations.* Coral Springs, Fla.: Strategy Associates, pp. 1–2.
3. Chaffee, Ellen and Sherr, Lawrence (1992). *Quality: Transforming Postsecondary Education.* ASHE-ERIC Higher Education Report #3, p. 24.
4. Chaffee, Ellen and Sherr, Lawrence (1992). *Quality: Transforming Postsecondary Education.* ASHE-ERIC Higher Education Report #3, p. vi.
5. Coate, L. Edwin (1992). *Total Quality Management at Oregon State University.* Corvallis: Oregon State University, p. 9.
6. Figure 5.1, Exhibit 5.1, and Exercises 5.1 to 5.4 ©1992 Strategy Associates, Inc.

EXERCISES

EXERCISE 5.1 ACTION PLAN FRAMEWORK FOR PROCESS MANAGEMENT

Operational Steps	Planned Actions	Persons	Target Dates

1. Identify core processes

2. Process analysis
   Specify purpose
   Identify customers
   Identify needs
   Analyze flows

3. Identify problem
   Assess current situation
   Identify gaps
   Frame problem
   Determine causes

4. Search for solutions
   Criteria
   Alternatives
   Select

5. Implement plan
   Implement

6. Evaluate
   Evaluate

EXERCISE 5.2   PROCESS FLOW IDENTIFICATION FORM

	Input Step	Who Receives	Action	Output	Disposition
1.					
2.					
3.					
4.					
5.					
6.					
7.					
8.					
9.					
10.					
11.					
12.					
13.					
14.					
15.					

EXERCISE 5.3 TRANSFORMING PROCESS ASSESSMENT FORM

Inputs	Process	Outputs

Step 1
Expected
Actual
Gap

Step 2
Expected
Actual
Gap

Step 3
Expected
Actual
Gap

Step 4
Expected
Actual
Gap

Step 5
Expected
Actual
Gap

EXERCISE 5.4 INTERVENTION MODEL: CAUSAL FLOWS OF CHANGE EFFORTS

An intervention model is used to identify: (1) the goal (desired result) of change efforts, (2) the objectives that will lead to goal achievement, (3) the activities that are the means to achieving the objectives, and (4) the inputs needed to perform the activities. In developing an intervention model, the best approach is start with the goal and work backward. This is known as reasoning from Z to A. The actual interventions may be substantially more complicated than the one shown below, but complexity can be addressed by breaking the model down into smaller units.

Input	$\rightarrow$	Activity	$\rightarrow$	Objective	$\rightarrow$	Goal
Input 1						
		Activity 1				
Input 2						
				Objective 1		
Input 3						
		Activity 2				
Input 4						
						GOAL 1
Input 5						
		Activity 3				
Input 6						
				Objective 2		
Input 7						
		Activity 4				
Input 8						

ABSTRACTS

ABSTRACT 5.1
MAKING TOTAL QUALITY WORK:
ALIGNING ORGANIZATIONAL PROCESSES,
PERFORMANCE MEASURES, AND STAKEHOLDERS

Olian, Judy D.; Rynes, Sara L.
Human Resources Management (HRM), Vol. 30, Issue 3, Fall 1991, pp. 303–333

Throughout this article, four 1991 survey sources are used: the KPMG survey of 62 companies, 2 Conference Board surveys of 149 firms and 158 Fortune 1000 companies, and the AQF/Ernst & Young study of 500 international organizations. The cornerstone of this 30-page article revolves around the authors' statement: "The goals of total quality can be achieved only if organizations entirely reform their cultures. Total quality (TQ) is increasingly used by companies as an organization-wide system to achieve fully satisfied customers through the delivery of the highest quality in products and services. In fact, TQ is the most important single strategic tool available to leaders to effect the transformation of their organizations. Traditional management, operations, finance and accounting systems are reviewed against changes that are needed in organizational processes, measurement systems, and the values and behaviors of key stakeholders to transform the status quo and shift to a total quality culture that permeates every facet of the organization."

Total quality must reflect a system-wide commitment to the goal of serving the strategic needs of the organization's customer bases, through internal and external measurement systems, information and authority sharing, and committed leadership. The article contains the following pertinent data: (1) organizational synergies critical to achieving a pervasive culture; (2) the essentials of TQ; (3) organizational processes that support TQ; (4) establishing quality goals, including a look at "Six Sigma" and "Benchmarking;" (5) training for TQ; (6) recognition and rewards; (7) measuring customer reactions and satisfaction; (8) developing four areas of measurement: operation, financial, breakthrough, and employee contributions; and (9) stakeholder support. Of significant added value are over 60 references on the subjects discussed, which is reason enough to obtain a copy of this extremely worthwhile article, in spite of its formidable length.

ABSTRACT 5.2
HOW SYSTEMS THINKING APPLIES TO EDUCATION

Detto, Frank
Educational Leadership (GEDL), Nov. 1992, pp. 38–41

As the call for systemic change in education becomes increasingly vocal, many educators claim to be using a systems approach, but almost no one really is. School boards and senior management need to comprehend why current approaches are not working and understand the advantages of the systems approach to education.

Whereas the main function of higher education is to prepare students for life after school, the most important aspect being "critical and creative thinking for problem solving and decision making," increasingly, education has run into paradigm paralysis. *Webster's* defines paradigm paralysis as "persistence in a mistaken belief" using old models that are no longer useful. The new paradigm must be an approach to systems thinking, and the conclusion drawn from this thinking is that the old system is no longer up to the task. Betts states that this new participative organizational style is a shift from the "system in which one teacher provides information to many students toward a system in which there are many information resources accessible by one student." By adopting a systems approach to education, the United States can move from an emphasis on instruction to an emphasis on learning. Selected references are provided.

ARTICLES

THE QUALITY MOVEMENT'S CHALLENGE TO EDUCATION*

Ron Brandt

When I first heard about Total Quality Management I thought, "Oh no, another gimmick from the management training people." It is indeed the latest hot topic in management training, but now that I have read more about it, I think the idea is crucial to the future of the United States—and every other country that expects to compete in today's global economy.

The quality movement is deceptive because most parts of it are familiar. Sadly, they are familiar only in the abstract, because most organizations, including schools, apply them erratically and inconsistently. For example, the model is based on the assumption that people want to do good work and it is management's job to make that possible. "Well, sure," we say, "that's McGregor's Theory Y. So what's new?" What is new is that large corporations are taking Theory Y seriously, assigning authority and responsibility to frontline workers. Of course TQM is much more than delegation; it also requires teamwork, focused training, and extensive use of data.

In schools, practices in harmony with the quality movement include site-based decision making, quality circles, outcome-based education, team teaching, action research by teachers, cooperative learning, and teaching thinking. All these things are advocated in the literature, and all exist here and there, but few schools have been able to implement them throughout the system.

Practices that many experts say violate quality principles include issuance of detailed directives at state and district levels, setting quantitative goals and quotas, teaching obsolete curriculum, using norm-referenced testing, and grading students competitively. Again, these practices have long been criticized by some educators, but they continue anyway, partly because policymakers, many of whom are not educators, insist on them.

* Reprinted from *Leadership (Journal of the Association for Supervision and Curriculum Development)*, Vol. 49, No. 6, March 1992.

The quality movement is too complex to explain in a few sentences. For those who want to know more, several articles in this issue provide an introduction. And we will be hearing more—much more— in the years ahead. Numerous books, such as *Quality or Else* (Dobyns and Crawford-Mason 1991) show than Japan's phenomenal success and America's economic decline over the last two decades resulted from Japanese devotion to quality and long-term thinking while most U.S. corporations emphasized quantity and short-term profits.

Education's role in this situation has been not cause but collusion. It was not education but poor management that lost whole industries, such as consumer electronics, to other countries in less than two decades. It was political irresponsibility, not education, that transformed the United States from the world's largest creditor nation to the largest debtor nation.

But schools reflect the society they serve. American schools have the same problems, and face the same challenges, as American corporations. Like corporate CEOs, school executives have emphasized quantity over quality. Like top-down industrialists, state and large-district officials have sought to prescribe how schools should function. Like alienated factory workers, some teachers and principals have resisted efforts to make schools more productive.

If the U.S. is to remain a world leader, that cannot continue. The challenge to education is well defined by Ira Magaziner and Hillary Clinton (p. 10), chairs of the commission that produced America's Choice, and Marc Tucker (p. 19), head of the National Center on Education and the Economy (1990), which sponsored it. Unless businesses opt for quality, it will make little difference whether schools do or not. But if business leaders get the message, they will need a better-qualified work force. In that case, to attain significantly higher standards of student performance, educators too must make the commitment to quality.

REFERENCES

Commission on the Skills of the American Workforce. (1990). *America's Choice: High Skills or Low Wages!* Rochester, N.Y.: National Center on Education and the Economy.

Dobyns, L. and C. Crawford-Mason. (1991). *Quality or Else: The Revolution in World Business.* Boston: Houghton Mifflin.

CHAPTER 6

PROJECT MANAGEMENT/ TEAM MANAGEMENT

The third managerial level for the initiation of total quality is project management. The central role of project management in the quality process, and the related role of teams empowered to carry out the projects, are examined in this chapter. *Webster's New World Dictionary*[1] defines project as: "That which is projected or designed; something intended or devised; a scheme; design; plan."

This managerial level is represented by the third pillar and the third foundation of the House of Quality, as highlighted in Figure 6.1. The purpose of this level, as described by Voehl,[2] is to establish a practical system to effectively plan, organize, implement, and control all resources and activities needed for the successful completion of the primary projects for total quality and continuous improvement. The major tasks include developing the project-centered vision; identifying critical success factors (CSFs); developing control systems and estimat-

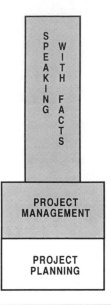

Figure 6.1 The House of Quality.

ing, scheduling, and tracking mechanisms; and identifying the skills required and performance indicators. It is at this level that the total quality tools (described in Chapter 3) are extensively used for effective data collection and analysis. This enables the organization to "speak with facts."

The people involved in and responsible for project management are the managers, supervisors, and workers at the operational level of the organization. This is where, for the first time in the total quality process, the plans become operational. It is at this level that "the talk is walked," or as one engineering faculty member stated, "where the rubber meets the runway, and the craft is tested to see if it will move, let alone fly."[3]

Projects are assigned or delegated to groups of managers, supervisors, and workers. A growing trend is to identify these groups as *teams*. A closer look at the importance of teams is necessary.

THE CENTRAL ROLE OF TEAMS IN QUALITY IMPROVEMENT

While organizations have traditionally been formed around task or work groups, the concept of teams and *teamwork* has become important in the last two decades. The focus of human resource management has historically been on the recruitment, placement, compensation, development, and evaluation of individuals rather than groups. It has recently become apparent that this contributes to rivalries, competition, favoritism, and self-centeredness, which collectively counter the focus on the two most important functions of any organization: accomplishing the mission and service to customers.

The central role of the team, and the need for such team skills as cooperation, interpersonal communication, cross-training, and group decision making, is a fundamental shift in how work within colleges and universities is viewed. Presently, cooperation among administrative divisions and academic departments is not encouraged. The predominant practice is individual advancement. This is encouraged by administration with such practices as management by objectives and individual performance evaluation and promotion. On the academic side, faculty members are expected to work alone and even compete for limited resources, such as grant money.

A major theme emphasized throughout this book is that the success of every organization fully rests on the effectiveness of each work group—each team. The key differences between groups and teams are presented in Table 6.1. Groups can be productive, but it is becoming increasingly evident that just bringing a group of individuals together to complete specific tasks is ineffective and unproductive. The term *team* has come to be accepted to describe a group of people who are goal centered, interdependent, honest, open, supportive, and empowered. Members of a team develop strong feelings of allegiance that go beyond the mere grouping of individuals. The productive outcome is synergistic, and the accomplishments often even exceed even the original goals of the task.

Consider the rewarding experience of working on a team where a great sense of unity and commitment toward accomplishing a highly motivating project prevails. The achievement of putting a man on the moon and the defeat of the Russians by the U.S. Olympic hockey team are often cited as readily recognized examples of highly focused team efforts. Most people have at some time had the opportunity to enjoy

Table 6.1 Groups Versus Teams

Groups	Teams
• Members think they are grouped together for administrative purposes only. Individuals work independently; sometimes at cross purposes with others.	• Members recognize their interdependence and understand that both personal and team goals are best accomplished with mutual support. Time is not wasted struggling over "turf" or attempting personal gain at the expense of others.
• People tend to focus on themselves because they are not sufficiently involved in planning the unit's objectives. They approach their jobs simply as hired hands.	• Members feel a sense of ownership toward their jobs and units because they are committed to goals they helped establish.
• Members are told what to do rather than being asked what the best approach would be. Suggestions are not encouraged.	• Members contribute to the success of the organization by applying their unique talents and knowledge to team objectives.
• Members distrust the motives of colleagues because they do not understand the roles of other members. Expressions of opinion or disagreement are considered divisive or nonsupportive.	• Members work in a climate of trust and are encouraged to openly express ideas, opinions, disagreements, and feelings. Questions are welcomed.
• Members are so cautious about what they say that real understanding is not possible. Game playing may occur, and communication traps may be set to catch the unwary.	• Members practice open and honest communication. They make an effort to understand each other's point of view.
• Members may receive good training but are limited in applying it to the job by the supervisor or other group members.	• Members are encouraged to develop skills and apply what they learn on the job. They receive the support of the team.
• Members find themselves in conflict situations which they do not know how to resolve. Their supervisor may put off intervention until serious damage is done.	• Members recognize conflict as a normal aspect of human interaction, but they view such situations as an opportunity for new ideas and creativity. They work to resolve conflict quickly and constructively.
• Members may or may not participate in decisions affecting the team. Conformity often appears more important than positive results.	• Members participate in decisions that affect the team, but understand that their leader must make a final ruling whenever the team cannot decide or an emergency exists. Positive results, not conformity, are the goal.

Source: Adapted from Maddux, R. B. (1988). *Team Building: An Exercise in Leadership.* Oakville, Ontario: Crisp Publications.

the experience of participating in a team that was highly focused and driven, developing a shared vision, spending whatever hours were needed to complete the task, and possibly surpassing the original goal. Such examples in higher education include fund raising drives, student recruitment, building programs, service projects for special students, highly focused research experiments, and the great catalytic experience of a winning football, basketball (or any sport) season. These experiences are greatly fulfilling, but often short-lived. It is the goal of quality-centered project management to create these or similar experiences within an organization that empowers each person through the creation and continuous development of effective teams.

FOUR TYPE OF TEAMS

To effectively implement total quality improvement, four types of teams are necessary. The first is the *lead team*, also identified as the *Quality Council*. This team is responsible for the strategic management of the quality process (refer to Chapter 4). It functions as the steering committee in that it sets policy, establishes guidelines, and handles overall logistics and communication for the teams operating under it.

Membership of the lead team differs, depending on its position in the organization. The *executive level*, system-wide lead team is composed of the president and vice presidents. The *activity-centered level* is led by a vice president, director, or manager, who provides the leadership for a specific activity, e.g., academic affairs, admissions, registration, student affairs, etc. The *location-centered level* is led by the chief officer and staff of a campus or center. It provides the same kind of leadership at the local level that the executive level lead team provides overall.

The other three teams operate under the lead team and are located throughout the college or university. The *functional team* is the work group from a single work or functional area. Membership is voluntary and the team is continuous. The ideal size of a functional team is six to eight persons. The *cross-functional team* includes people from more than one work area. This team is responsible for projects that cut across functional lines. Like the functional team, membership is voluntary and the team is ongoing. The *task team* includes people from one or more functional areas. It is formed to solve a specific problem or group of problems and is then disbanded. Members of this team are selected on the basis of background and experience. Membership and tasks are typically assigned by management (the lead team). Examples of a cross-functional team and a wide variety of functional work teams at Oregon State University are described later in this chapter. (For additional information, see Abstract 6.1 at the end of this chapter.)

TEAM DEVELOPMENT

Creating empowered, effective teams requires a process of four facilitative steps, as described by Schultz.[4] While this process is beneficial for all four types of teams previously described, it is most effective for the three ongoing teams (lead, functional, and cross-functional teams), because this four-step process assumes a long-term commitment. The initial step is to *create a vision statement* of the ideal team five to ten years into the future, answering the question, "What can we be?" The statement should be clear, inspiring, and "owned" by everyone on the team. It should also be consistent with the vision and mission of the organization.

The second step is to briefly *define the purpose,* or the need for this team in the college or university, answering the question, "Why does this unit exist?" The third step is to *define the principles and values* that will guide the actions of the team members, checking that they relate to the principles and values of the college or university. This step answers the question, "What are the principles and values we consider most important in working toward our vision?"

From this, the fourth step, *develop a unit mission,* serves as a guideline for decision making by everyone on the team. It answers the question, "How will we move toward our vision?" The mission should (1) be consistent with the mission of the college or university and (2) identify the areas for which the team has responsibility. (For additional information, see Abstract 6.2 at the end of this chapter.)

A framework for team responses to these four questions is provided in Exercise 6.1 (all exercises appear at the end of the chapter). Examples of statements for teams in the area of registration as well as an academic program are also given.

PROJECT MANAGEMENT

Numerous texts and manuals have been published to describe the management of projects. Two project management processes are provided in this chapter. The first process is known as the quality improvement story. It is, by design, a process that can be summarized using a few key steps and presented in summary form (Figure 6.2). It is also based on a framework of total quality/continuous improvement, using appropriate measurement tools (e.g., flowchart, Pareto, fishbone, etc.).

As shown in Figure 6.2, all seven steps are presented on one page. The task or problem is stated at the top. The first step, *define the problem*, asks for a factual statement of the problem and provides space for a flowchart of the problem and other data display (e.g., control chart). The second step, *observe the problem*, examines the problem from various viewpoints, relying less on narrative and more on such tools such as bar graphs and control and/or Pareto charts. Step three, *determine the causes of the problem*, consists of first identifying possible reasons for the problem and then analyzing these reasons. A cause-and-effect, or fishbone, diagram is an effective tool for identifying reasons, and a Pareto chart is useful in the analysis.

Based on these three analytical steps, appropriate *action to eliminate the main causes* (step 4) can be taken. Data sources should be listed in order to evaluate root causes and proposed solutions. The focus is on action (i.e., Plan, Do, Check, Act). Try a solution and carry it out. Then, step 5, *study the results*, can be initiated. Data must be evaluated, and the situation before and after the action was implemented should be compared. If the result is not what was desired, another solution should be considered. Study each result (step 5) and be prepared to try another.

Standardize the changes (step 6) after the desired results are achieved. Communicate the changes to everyone. Appropriate training must be provided and a feedback system developed to determine compliance with the new standard. In step 7 (the last step), *state the final conclusions* for future reference. Describe what was learned, both the benefits and the mistakes.

Exercise 6.2 is a blank copy of a quality journal. A completed chart was provided in Figure 6.2. Creating a quality journal is a standard quality improvement process used widely in industry. Its applications in higher education are numerous. Few good examples are available at

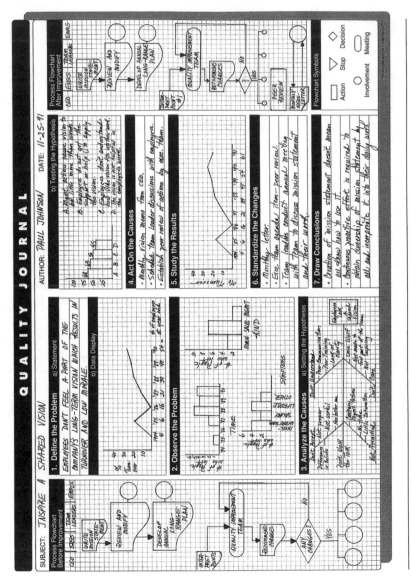

Figure 6.2 Example of a Quality Journal. (Source: Schultz, Louis E. (1989). *Personal Management.* Minneapolis: Process Management International, p. 28.)

the present, and the reader is encouraged to prepare such a journal detailing his or her experience with the quality improvement process (for possible use in future publications).

The second example of a project management process comes from Oregon State University, where a ten-step problem-solving process was developed (Figure 6.3). The process begins with the customer and focuses on root causes/barriers to improvement to ensure that decisions and actions are based on real data. The process is initiated by identifying a critical process for study and improvement. The process may be identified by using surveys and/or by the team sponsor (usually the immediate supervisor of the team). The ten steps developed by Oregon State University are

1. The team identifies and interviews key customers of the process to determine which services do not meet their expectations.
2. The team charts customer problems and reviews the most important ones, including their potential for "cost of quality" savings. The team selects a problem to study, prepares an issue statement to direct the study, and uses customer data to set a measure of improved performance.
3. The team constructs a flow diagram that shows the process that is being studied as it is currently configured.
4. The team brainstorms to identify possible causes of the process problem and then uses total quality management tools to select critical causes for further study.
5. The team collects data, graphs them concisely, and uses them to determine root causes of the customer problem. These data become a benchmark for measuring future progress.
6. The team develops possible solutions to the root causes that have been verified by data and then measures these solutions against criteria that reflect customer needs.
7. The team identifies benchmarks for the process being studied, i.e., processes used by other organizations or work areas that produce a high-quality product or service. Possible solutions are measured against the benchmarks.
8. The best solutions are implemented, and their performance is monitored. If they work, they are adopted.
9. The team measures the results of the improvements, including the "cost of quality," and continues to refine performance.
10. The team selects the next problem to be studied.

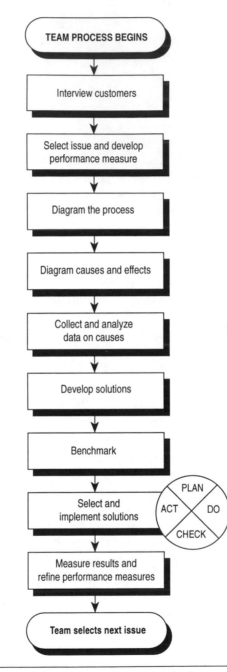

Figure 6.3   Total Quality Management Team Process. (Source: Coate, L. Edwin (1992). *Total Quality Management at Oregon State University*. Corvallis: Oregon State University, p. 12.)

The ten-step problem-solving process is summarized in Exercise 6.3, which provides a checklist to be used and expanded upon, i.e., include appropriate tools as needed.

IN CLOSING: EFFECTIVE PROJECTS = EFFECTIVE TEAMS

Teams are everything! Project management can only be as successful as the team managing the project. As stated in the Oregon State report, "Focusing teams on process improvement is what it is all about. Make sure they have adequate training before they begin. Then stick to the process. The Hawthorn effect is prevalent at first, but the TQM process will see that solutions get implemented. Team building is almost as important as process improvement."[5]

The synergy developed within effective teams can be substantial. The relationship, trust, and support will exceed the original expecta-

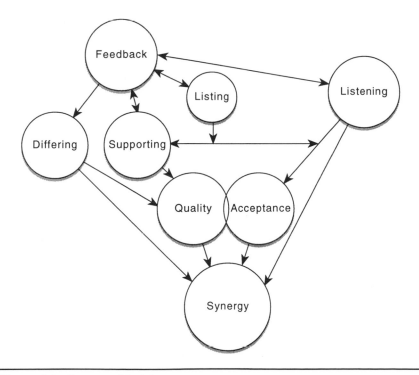

Figure 6.4 Synergy Model.

tions of the team (Figure 6.4). This is poignantly noted by Seymour,[6] who cites the comment of a faculty member at St. Francis College in Pennsylvania about the group (team) to which he belongs:

> We work as a group. We do all kinds of things as a group. Because we have outside accreditation agencies to answer to, we have to do self-studies and all kinds of other things that other departments in the school have never even thought of doing much less being required to do. But even with other programs that do go through accreditation procedures, the program director sits down and he writes the self-study or he writes a grant. We do all of it in groups. We have brainstorming sessions, we all write different sections, we all review those sections as a group, and make it work as one document—as one thought. It takes a lot of time but I really believe that it makes the individuals feel as though they have responsibility for the "whole" program, not just the course that he or she teaches.

APPLICATION OF PROJECT MANAGEMENT AND TEAM MANAGEMENT AT OREGON STATE UNIVERSITY

As previously stated, the teams at Oregon State University (OSU) were considered to be the core of the total quality program at that institution. In the beginning, it was apparent that the teams had to be effective, but awareness of the central importance of the teams grew over time. In the initial implementation, a pilot study team was conducted in the physical plant.

Based on the success of this pilot team, ten additional teams, called Daily Management Teams or Study Teams, were created in Finance and Administration. The study teams and team roles were described as follows:

> Study teams are composed of people who normally work together on the process being reviewed. The team studies a process that can be improved by using resources they control. Each team includes a team leader, most often the super-

visor of the process being studied, a facilitator/trainer, and no more than 10 team members. The division director usually serves as the team sponsor, ensuring that the team's work is linked to the university's critical processes and moves the university toward its vision.[8]

As of March 1992, 72 study teams had been created in 5 administrative areas. Each team had responsibility for a critical process (i.e., operational unit) and focused on a single issue or problem. The issues included:

Office of the President	Administrative processes
V.P. for Student Affairs	Undergraduate evaluation
V.P. for University Relations	Alumni relations, record keeping
V.P. for Academic Affairs	Course approval process in continuing education
V.P. for Graduate Studies, Research, and Intl. Programs	Service delivery in reception area
V.P. for Finance and Administration	Energy management system Personnel reclassification system

A second key element in the total quality management process was the creation of cross-functional management teams. As stated in the March 1992 report, "we realized that cross-functional management is where the biggest process improvement action will be. Universities already operate with committees that cross administrative and academic lines. Many organizational problems are cross-functional. Teams that cross departmental lines are best able to initiate cost-saving efficiencies for the university."[9]

Participation in a cross-functional team was preceded by involvement in a study team in order to learn the tools of the total quality management process. "We learned that cross-functional management, especially, requires well-developed team skills. Individuals from different units must be able to move beyond 'turf protection' to cooperation for the good of the institution."[9] As of March 1992 ten cross-functional teams were established, as shown in Table 6.2.

How effective were the teams at Oregon State? Two views illustrate the collective benefit of team management and problem solving. The first perspective is derived from summaries of two of the ten pilot teams initiated in 1990.

Table 6.2 Cross-Functional Teams at Oregon State University

Units involved	Team issue
Budgets & Planning, Physical Plant	OSU space inventory process
Business Affairs, OSU Foundation	Receipting of donations
Environmental Health & Safety, Human Resources	Workers' compensation
Environmental Health & Safety, Radiation Safety	Radiation Safety inspection of university labs
Human Resources, Business Affairs, Budgets & Planning	Processing of INS I-9 forms
Public Safety, Oregon State Police	Bicycle theft problems
University Computing Services, Printing, Physical Plant, Telecommunications	Billing/accounting processes
Admissions, University Relations	Recruiting/marketing
Admissions, Academic Affairs	Undergraduate evaluation process
Admissions, Graduate School	Graduate admissions process

Source: Coate, L. Edwin (1992). *Total Quality Management at Oregon State University.*
Corvallis: Oregon State University, p. 18.

Staff Benefits Team. Study issue: Increase speed of initial response in the information dissemination process. A survey and a two-week collection of phone data told the team that their OSU customers needed quick, human responses to phoned-in questions, and they were getting them only 58 percent of the time.

Solutions included: Adding phone lines and another phone; extending the number of rings before a caller received a message, giving employees longer to catch a call; and a busy signal rather than a message on the manager's phone to let callers know she is in; changing phone messages each day or when employees are away for four hours or more; and returning all calls within four hours.

Another solution cut the number of calls by providing more printed information to customers and encouraging use of E-Mail.

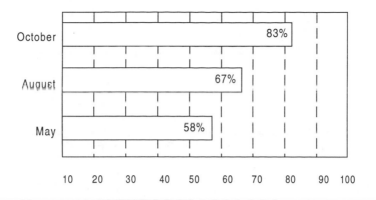

Figure 6.5 Percentage of Calls Receiving Initial Human Response. (Source: Coate, L. Edwin (1992). *Total Quality Management at Oregon State University.* Corvallis: Oregon State University, p. 13.)

Results: One year after the data were first collected, calls answered by a person on first try had increased from 58 to 83 percent (see Figure 6.5). A team member said, "We thought we knew what our problems were. TQM helped us find out what they really were. TQM has given us a process to use in the future."

Research Accounting Team. Study issue: Reduce the time expended in processing grant and contract documents. A flow chart of the team's process showed several time-wasting loops: waits for signatures of authorities outside OSU, return of contracts to researchers for amendment of incorrect award language, routing of awards for review within OSU, and time spent hunting for account files in use by another person.

Solutions included: communicating correct contract award language to researchers, developing a locator system for account files, and give other time-saving changes in office procedures. The team's efforts improved procedures in the state system of higher education. Their data documenting delays caused by signature loops resulted in the Chancellor's agreement to eliminate one of them.

Number of Days

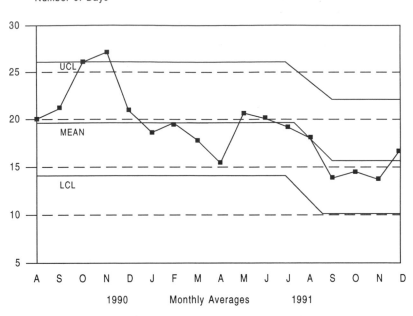

Figure 6.6 Number of Days to Set Up Grant/Contract. (Source: Coate, L. Edwin (1992). *Total Quality Management at Oregon State University*. Corvallis: Oregon State University, p. 15.)

Results: Eliminating one state system signature loop reduced average processing days for some contracts from 12.7 days to 0.3 days. By September 1991, average processing days for all contracts had moved down by 34 percent (Figure 6.6).[10]

The second view of the effectiveness of the teams is presented as a summary of the ten pilot teams and what each achieved in terms of improved procedures and savings (Table 6.3). (For additional information, see Abstract 6.3 at the end of this chapter.)

ENDNOTES

1. *Webster's New World Dictionary* (1982). Compact School and Office Edition, New York: Simon and Schuster.

Table 6.3   Total Quality Management Pilot Team Results

Physical Plant Team: Remodeling
Reduced average duration of remodeling jobs by 23%. Estimated cost savings: $219,539.

Physical Plant Team: Fixed Equipment
Developed plan to decrease department responsibility for costs of maintenance, service, repair, and replacement of fixed equipment by 31%. Estimated cost savings to departments: $249,510.

Printing/Mailing Team
Implemented six solutions to reduce lost time in the pre-press process by 50%. Estimated cost savings: $16,224.

Budgets and Planning Team
Improved Budget-Status-at-a-Glance report to meet customer needs and cut preparation time by 50%. Estimated cost savings: $3,600.

University Computing Services Team
Implemented 10 solutions to improve delivery of network information by 6%. Estimated cost savings: $937.

Business Affairs Team: Journal Voucher Process
Decreased number of journal vouchers returned to departments for error correction by 94%.

Business Affairs Team: Research Accounting
Decreased number of days to process grant/contract documents by 15%. Estimated cost savings: $73,128.

Public Safety Team
Increased number of daily building security checks by 17%.

Radiation Center Team
Implemented 6 new services and process improvements in response to customer surveys. Estimated cost savings: $8,000.

Human Resources Staff Benefits Team
Increased number of phone calls getting an initial human response by 83%. Estimated cost savings: $6,667.

Source: Coate, L. Edwin (1992). *Total Quality Management at Oregon State University.* Corvallis: Oregon State University, p. 14.

2. Voehl, Frank W. (1992). *Total Quality: Principles and Processes within Organizations.* Coral Springs, Fla.: Strategy Associates, p. 35.
3. Comment made during a seminar conducted by the authors in February 1993 in Miami.
4. Schultz, Louis E. (1989). *Personal Management.* Minneapolis: Process Management International.
5. Coate, L. Edwin (July 1990). *Implementing Total Quality Management in a University Setting.* Corvallis: Oregon State University, p. 22.
6. Seymour, Daniel (1992). *On Q: Causing Quality in Higher Education.* New York: Macmillan, p. 46.
7. Coate, L. Edwin (1992). *Total Quality Management at Oregon State University.* Corvallis: Oregon State University, p. 12.
8. Coate, L. Edwin (1992). *Total Quality Management at Oregon State University.* Corvallis: Oregon State University, p. 11.
9. Coate, L. Edwin (1992). *Total Quality Management at Oregon State University.* Corvallis: Oregon State University, p. 18.
10. Coate, L. Edwin (1992). *Total Quality Management at Oregon State University.* Corvallis: Oregon State University, pp. 13, 15.
11. Figures 6.1 and 6.4 ©1992 Strategy Associates, Inc.

EXERCISES

EXERCISE 6.1
FOUR STEPS FOR DEVELOPING EFFECTIVE TEAMS

1. **Vision Statement.** Create a vision statement of the ideal team five to ten years into the future. Answer the question, "What can we be?"

   Examples: To provide quality registration service to the students, such that the level of complaints is one per thousand students (1:1000) To be recognized as one of the top five departments in the field, as indicated in the semi-annual survey conducted by the professional association.

2. **Purpose.** Define the need for this team in the college or university. Answer the question, "Why does this unit exist?"

   Examples: Provide registration, records management, and information service to present and former students. Provide effective instruction and applied research, and service that is complementary to the instruction and research.

3. **Principles and Values.** Define the principles and values that will guide the actions of the team members. Be sure they relate to the principles and values of the college or university. Answer the question, "What are the principles and values we consider most important in working toward our vision?"

   Examples: (1) Continuously seek ways to improve the department processes. (2) Develop and practice listening skills. (3) Encourage everyone's opinion. (4) Encourage initiative. (5) Work as a team, supporting each other. (6) Continue to learn. (7) Maintain a positive attitude. (8) Serve our students' needs. (9) Assist other departments with improving their processes. (10) Feel pride in and derive satisfaction from our work.

   (1) Serve our students' needs. (2) Continuously seek ways to improve our instructional program in both content and delivery. (3) Provide support in seeking and conducting research projects. (4) Work as a team, supporting each other. (5) Encourage collaborative activities with other programs throughout the campus. (6) Actively engage in professional activities nationally and internationally. (7) Contribute to related local and regional services. (8) Maintain a positive attitude. (9) Feel pride in and derive satisfaction from our program.

4. **Mission Statement.** Develop a unit mission, which will serve as a guideline for decision making by everyone on the team. Be consistent with the mission of the college or university, and identify the areas for which the team is responsible Answer the question, "How will we move toward our vision?"

Examples: Our mission is to plan for and execute the development and delivery of the finest registration services possible, continually striving to improve upon what is presently being provided. The services will enable students, present and past, to be fully served within the minimum possible time. We will cooperatively pursue this mission and will provide the tools needed to successfully meet work challenges and achieve pride of accomplishment.

Our mission is to plan for and execute the development and delivery of the finest possible student-centered instructional program. Our research will complement our teaching and contribute to our field. We will cooperatively pursue this mission and will provide the resources needed to successfully meet the needs and challenges of the program.

EXERCISE 6.2
COMPLETING YOUR QUALITY IMPROVEMENT STORY

Refer to Figure 6.2 and the instructions in the text for completing this form.

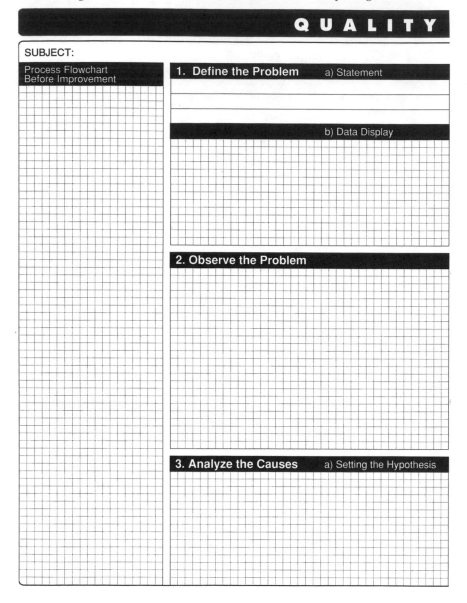

JOURNAL

AUTHOR: DATE:

| b) Testing the Hypothesis | Process Flowchart After Improvement |

4. Act On the Causes

5. Study the Results

6. Standardize the Changes

7. Draw Conclusions

Flowchart Symbols

| Action | Stop | Decision |
| Involvement | Meeting |

Source: Schultz, Louis E. (1989). *Personal Management*. Minneapolis: Process Management International, p. 27.

EXERCISE 6.3
THE TEN-STEP PROBLEM-SOLVING PROCESS

Step 1	Identify and interview key customers to determine which services do meet their expectations.
Step 2	Chart customer problems. Review the most important problems, including their potential for "cost of quality" savings. Select a problem, prepare an issue statement to direct the study, and use customer data to set a measure of improved performance.
Step 3	Construct a flow diagram to show the process that is being studied as it is currently configured.
Step 4	Brainstorm to identify possible causes of the problem. Then use total quality management tools to select critical causes for further study.
Step 5	Collect data, graph concisely, and use to determine root causes of the customer problem. Use the data as a benchmark for measuring future progress.
Step 6	Develop possible solutions for the root causes verified by data. Measure them against criteria that reflect customer needs.
Step 7	Identify benchmarks for the process being studied, i.e., processes used by other organizations or work areas. Measure possible solutions against the benchmarks.
Step 8	Implement the best solutions and monitor their performance. Adopted a solution if it works.
Step 9	Measure the results of improvements, including the "cost of quality." Continue to refine the performance of the process.
Step 10	Select the next problem for study.

ABSTRACTS

ABSTRACT 6.1 PRACTICAL MATTERS

Stuller, Jay
Across the Board (CBR), Vol. 30, Issue 1, Jan./Feb. 1993, pp. 36–40

The author is a San Francisco-based journalist and author of several corporate histories. His major theme is that executive training needs to be customized in order to provide a working as well as a theoretical education. He states that in recent years, the nature of business management has changed from an emphasis on U.S. and European markets, discreet operating units, and top-down administration to a transition toward globalization; at the same time, a movement has begun toward total quality management programs, customer focus, flattened hierarchies, and employee empowerment. "Business schools have long offered open-enrollment advanced management programs…but practical application of classroom insights was secondary." By contrast, Stuller argues, customized courses are as much a working education as a theoretical one, designed to immerse large groups of managers from a single company in a new business focus or practice.

Teamwork and the development of personal leadership skills are common themes among customized executive education programs. In addition to classroom learning, customized education programs often send executives away from the classroom with on-the-job applications projects. Overall, the article shows the value of immersing teams of executives from one organization in practical on-the-job projects in conjunction with theoretical learning. The author's half-page comparison insert of the major executive education programs is one of the major highlights of the article. No references are provided.

ABSTRACT 6.2   GET QUALITY PERFORMANCE FROM PROFESSIONAL STAFF

Fitz-enz, Jac; Rodgers, James
Personnel Journal (PEJ), Vol. 70, Issue 5, May 1991, pp. 22, 24

"Quality has jumped the fence," the article begins—and so do the authors' viewpoints, with a leap and a bound. The principles and process of total quality can be applied to managerial and professional performance, in that the total quality approach strips away ambiguity, improves communication, fosters better performance, and improves customer relations. This approach is effective for professionals involved in any staff function— from human resources and accounting to management information systems and marketing, regardless of the industry.

The central argument is all-encompassing: everyone—including professionals—must turn out quality in an efficient manner. This is a reasonable demand in today's highly competitive (higher education) environment. The most effective approach is to start by clarifying the quality requirements of the end result or output. Focusing on the product allows the professional the latitude to exercise both personal judgment and the skills to accomplish that objective. An interesting procedure for creating a total quality work process is offered to test whether the specifications, measures, and perhaps the work process itself must be changed in order to adjust to changing requirements. Although the purely creative aspects of some professionals may not be subject to process management, the authors allow that the majority of professionals and their managers can be held accountable for quality standards and will find that the total quality process can be a help, rather than a hindrance, in this effort.

ABSTRACT 6.3   BENCHMARKING: TALES FROM THE FRONT

Flower, Joe
Healthcare Forum (HPF), Vol. 36, Issue 1, Jan./Feb. 1993, pp. 37–51

This article by Flower discusses the value of competitive benchmarking in a cooperative environment. The author uses the experiences of several nonhealthcare organizations as a resource to aid hospitals and other organizations interested in benchmarking. Oregon State University (OSU) at Corvallis identified a half dozen peer institutions and determined which one within that particular universe was best in its class by a host of measures. The section of the article that deals with OSU provides some interesting notes to the case study and details their focus on clearly measurable processes and benchmarking activities. When the worker compensation premium at OSU surpassed $2 million per year, they analyzed the problem and adopted a few measures that were standard elsewhere, providing a savings of up to $1 million. OSU then turned those processes over to total quality management teams to be implemented. They did what was necessary, including benchmarking (as previously mentioned), to resolve problems. This has saved the university a significant amount of money and time and has given OSU a competitive edge.

Cleveland Memorial Hospital has cut 200 overtime hours annually from its admissions operation through benchmarking with fellow members of the SunHealth Alliance. When a coalition of over 30 employers in Kalamazoo, Michigan began demanding less expensive, high-quality healthcare, Borgess Medical Center took action. Borgess decided to target its more than 650 open-heart cases per year, using MediQual Systems Inc.'s MedisGroups database. After the first stage, benefits were already apparent. For example, fine-tuned pharmacy procedures saved about $525 per patient. Although most of the article is geared toward total quality management in healthcare, the section on OSU provides a good description of their benchmarking activities and is worth reading. Useful documentation and contacts for best practice situations are provided.

CHAPTER 7

INDIVIDUAL MANAGEMENT and TASK MANAGEMENT

The responsibility for quality in higher education is not something that resides in special offices or with selected persons. Causing quality requires the energy, commitment, and knowledge of everyone within the organization.[1]

Organizations intent on building shared visions continually encourage members to develop their personal visions. If people don't have their own vision, all they can do is "sign up" for someone else's.[2]

The fourth managerial level for the initiation of total quality is individual/task management. The focus at this level is on the development of each person, within the framework of his or her work or tasks. The definition of *work* from *Webster's New World Dictionary* is "effort in doing a particular task, job, or undertaking."[3] *Task*, in turn, is defined as "work to be done, assigned, or found necessary."[3] A plan for individual management is described in this chapter, with emphasis on the potential for personal growth through involvement in quality-centered tasks within a work team.

As emphasized in Chapter 6, it has been repeatedly validated that organizations committed to quality through continuous improvement succeed when a work team functions effectively. While the focus is appropriately placed on the *team* to ensure organizational success, the team is comprised of *people*. The success of the team is dependent on *every person* on the team. A college or university is only as good as its people, and total quality is ultimately dependent on people—the faculty, the administration, and the professional, technical, and clerical staff.

While an individual may be part of a team, his or her primary thoughts are, first, about himself or herself. Individual perceptions of self-esteem are very important. Self-esteem is addressed primarily through interactions with the world, including work and co-workers. Thus, the greater the success of the team, the greater the potential for increased individual self-esteem. Positive relationships with people and activities considered to be important foster feelings of empowerment and commitment toward continued self-growth. This is the focus of this chapter.

RESPECT FOR PEOPLE

The fourth pillar and fourth foundation of the House of Quality are highlighted in Figure 7.1. This is the most important of the four pillars, because it is based on an absolute for all organizations implementing total quality: commitment to and continuous demonstration of a total *respect for people*. Deming considered it so important that eight of his Fourteen Principles are directed to personal respect. If there is a perceived genuine respect for everyone, from the newest employee in housekeeping to the most senior faculty member, the commitment to initiating the necessary steps toward quality and continuous improvement will be achieved. If, however, respect for people is perceived to be a facade, with criticism prevailing rather than encouragement and support, the weakness of this fourth pillar will eventually become evident, and the total structure will be weakened.

Figure 7.1 Respect for People and Quality Planning within the House of Quality.

PERSONAL IMPROVEMENT

Personal respect is realized through the support of personal improvement. A guide for implementing personal quality planning and continuous improvement is provided in this chapter. This is achieved through a process consisting of five functions or steps: (1) the creative development of a personal *vision*, (2) upon which a meaningful *mission statement* can be written, based on the roles to be fulfilled. (3) Personal *objectives* can then be developed for implementing the mission, (4) which will require specific *projects* to accomplish the objectives and (5) the listing and completion of specific *tasks* to complete the projects. These steps are the action core for fulfilling an individual plan for continuous growth by establishing an effective relationship between personal vision and mission and profession or career requirements, within the vision, mission and operational objectives, projects, and tasks of the college or university. (For additional information, see Abstract 7.1 at the end of this chapter.)

The five steps will now be more fully described. The basic guideline, presented in Exhibit 7.1, facilitates the fulfillment of each function.

Exhibit 7.1 General Guidelines for Implementing the Five Steps: Vision, Mission, Objectives, Projects, Tasks

1	Purpose. What you will be doing:
2	You will know you are done when:
3	Techniques or instruments you can use for this activity (refer to Chapter 3):
4	Reality check. How will I know this plan "fits" me?:
5	Guidelines for implementation:

The initial activity is to define the purpose of the step, describing what will be done in each step, and prepare a statement describing what will have been accomplished when each step is completed. Next, techniques such as brainstorming, tools such as the fishbone diagram and flowchart, and instruments such as the histogram and Pareto chart (refer to Chapter 3) are used. This is followed by a reality check, which asks, "How will I know that this (vision, mission, objective, project, or task) fits me?" Finally, specific guidelines for implementing each step are given.

To further illustrate the use of this guideline, the personal plans of six people with various occupations at a university are presented to fully explore the positive potential of carrying out the five steps. The first two steps are personal vision and mission statements, while the three operational steps (objective, project, and task) are work team related to emphasize achieving personal growth and management through work.

Step 1. Create a Personal Vision

Developing a plan for personal growth is not new. Most self-help books, tapes, and videos provide guides for developing a personal plan. They usually begin, however, with identifying and developing personal objectives. A major difference in this plan is the first two steps: creating and developing a personal vision and writing an inclusive mission statement.

Creating a personal vision asks what someone wants to be doing five, seven, and even ten (or more) years from now. Through various activities (described later in this chapter), an individual is guided through the development of a picture (or, more accurately, a video) of his or her life as he or she would like to live it (to lead it) in the foreseeable future. This powerful tool has been a source of strength for many who have had an impact throughout history (e.g., Ghandi, who visualized an independent India; Martin Luther King, who clearly saw "from the mountain top" true equality for all people; and Sister Teresa, who lives her vision through true love for everyone, particularly the poor).

When personalized and truly owned, a vision provides the incentive—the drive toward fulfillment. It creates the commitment, the motivation, and the drive for initiating the mission, objectives, projects, and tasks necessary to realize the vision. The guidelines and steps for developing a personal vision are presented in Exhibit 7.2.

Developing a vision, as described in the guidelines in Exhibit 7.2, requires three or four weeks. This may seem like a long time, but consider that the vision is to be a portrayal of what life could be like five or ten (or more) years from now. Time is allowed for dreaming and brainstorming, along with categorizing random thoughts to ensure a comprehensive and realistic vision.

Step 2. Write a Mission Statement

If the vision is the *what* of life; the mission is the *why*. Covey[4] states that in the vision, the individual is the creator, creating what he or she wants to be. A mission statement is the first creation of the vision. It identifies the roles or activities to which an individual is committed and provides the overall direction for achieving the vision. As described by Covey,[4] "It focuses on what you want to be (character) and to do (contributions and achievements) and on the values and principles upon which being and doing are based."

Should the mission statement come before the vision? The implementation of the total quality program described in this book calls for developing the mission statement and then the vision of what the college or university should be in, say, ten years from now. While not critical, it is recommended that the personal vision be clearly developed, so that a personal mission statement can be based on it. The

Exhibit 7.2   General Guidelines for Implementing the Five Steps

---

Step: Vision, Mission, Objectives, Projects, Tasks

1   **Purpose. What you will be doing:**   Putting in writing a personal vision of your life seven to ten years from now.

2   **You will know your are done when:**   You have developed a long-range vision that you "own" and are excited about.

3   **Techniques or instruments you can use for this activity** (refer to Chapter 3):   The two techniques appropriate from the 21 listed in Chapter 3 are affinity diagram and brainstorming. In addition, techniques used in life planning exercises would include daydreaming, journaling, and scenarios.

4   **Reality check. How will I know this vision "fits" me?:**   I have a clear picture or "video" of what I will be doing in a typical week seven to ten years from now. This will include the "important others" in my life (as they will be seven to ten years from now), what and where I will be working as a part of my career plan, my role(s) in community and religious activities, and my recreation activities. This picture is also based on timeless, proven principles.

5   **Guidelines/instructions (KISS):**

    1   If you have not been doing keeping a journal, begin keeping a brief record of your daily life and activities. Assess your activities, identifying those things you like and don't like to do. If there are some things you don't like, but must do *for your growth and development,* are there some changes you can make in order to enjoy them more?

    2   Find about an hour of quiet time alone and brainstorm about all the possible images that come to mind of what you want to be doing seven to ten years from now. Put each one on a separate card. Daydream about this list, and then brainstorm again a week or so later. Then, put the cards aside for one or two weeks. Let the ideas percolate.

    3   Review the cards and combine similar activities. Then, edit and briefly rewrite any that need to be more personal for you.

    4   List at least the following five categories: Relationships, Career, Community, Religious, Recreation. You may have other names for these items and additional categories, but keep the number to a minimum. Then place each card (brainstorming statement) under the heading that it best fits. Put this aside for a week, if possible, to percolate some more.

    5   Again, find an hour alone and write a scenario of a typical week seven to ten years from now, using the lists you compiled. If you have time, you might want to write a *best-case* and a *worst-case* scenario (thesis and antithesis) and then a composite scenario (synthesis) that appears to be most realistic *at this time.*

    6   **Your vision statement.**   Your scenario may serve as a vision statement, but you may want to develop a succinct statement of your vision that you can use as the basis for your mission statement. A vision statement should be something you want to move toward, not move from.

---

important point is that both the vision and the mission statement must be completed before clear objectives, projects, and tasks can be developed and implemented.

Mission is shorter term (two or three years) than vision, because roles change. For example, the role and mission of a parent change as children grow older, or a job or position may change as experience is gained and new responsibility assumed.

The guidelines and steps for developing a personal mission statement are presented in Exhibit 7.3. It begins with a short, positive statement (twenty to thirty words) of the vision. It should then identify personal areas of activity (family, work, community, friends) and/or present and desired roles (worker, change agent, spouse, parent, child, brother/sister, friend, etc.). Then, specific statements can be written for each role and activity, based on present and desired functions and relationships. From this base of a personal vision and mission, practical objectives can be developed.

Step 3. Develop Operational Objectives

If the vision is the *what* of life and the mission is the *why*, objectives, projects, and tasks are the *hows*. They are the operational functions of the personal action plan. An effective vision is long term (five, ten, or more years) and provides the drive and emotion. The mission statement identifies the activities and roles to be fulfilled over the next two to three years. Objectives are the action statements of the personal plan, identifying specific functions to be accomplished in order to fulfill the mission. They are measurable and designed to be achieved within a maximum of twelve months. The basic question to be answered is whether a specific, observable change or transformation will have occurred when this objective has been completed.

The guidelines and steps for developing operational objectives are presented in Exhibit 7.4. Objectives reflect the mission statement, using the activities and roles for identifying the objectives to be initiated first. The objectives are action oriented, with a specific time frame, and written in the past tense in order to create a mental image of the goals being accomplished. They should also provide the framework upon which the projects and tasks can be developed and implemented. Examples of two objectives are given, one administrative and the other academic.

Exhibit 7.3 General Guidelines for Implementing the Five Steps

Step: Vision, **Mission,**ª Objectives, Projects, Tasks

1 **Purpose. What you will be doing:** Develop a personal mission statement that focuses on what you want to be and what you want to do. Like the U.S. (or any other country) Constitution, it is a personal constitution. It is personal and positive, written in the present tense, and provides a direction for achieving your vision. Finally, it defines the roles you consider important in your life, e.g., worker, spouse, parent, citizen.

2 **You will know your are done when:** You have a fairly brief, but succinct, statement that clearly states who you are, the roles important to you, and how you are fulfilled through these roles.

3 **Techniques or instruments you can use for this activity** (refer to Chapter 3): The techniques appropriate from the 21 listed in Chapter 3 are affinity diagram, brainstorming, fishbone diagram, flowcharting, surveys. In addition, techniques used in life planning exercises would include journaling and mindmapping.

4 **Reality check. How will I know this plan "fits" me?:** I have a written statement that represents the best that is within me. It provides direction and purpose upon which I can develop functional objectives. In sum, this statement inspires me.

5 **Guidelines for implementation:**

   1 First, review your vision. This is what your mission will be based on—your mission or goal is to actualize your vision. Conduct a mindmap, putting your vision in the center and identifying the strategies you will use to realize the vision.

   2 Continue the journaling started while developing your vision. Record the activities you do over, say, a two- or three-week period. Another way is to identify all the activities you do, with the help of the brainstorming technique.

   3 From this activity list you will begin to identify the roles that are important to you. Through the use of an affinity diagram and/or fishbone diagram, group the activities under major roles, such as worker, spouse, parent, citizen. By identifying your life roles, you will gain perspective and balance.

   4 After identifying the roles, project yourself into the near future and write a brief statement of how you would most like to be described in each role. In writing these descriptive statements, you begin to visualize your highest self—what you want to be through these roles.

   5 In step 1 you identified your vision—what you want to be and do in the future. Now you have listed your life roles and defined what you want to be and do in the immediate future. Drawing heavily from this, create a rough draft of your mission statement.

   6 Evaluate this draft, asking the following questions (they should also be asked periodically in order to keep your statement in harmony with yourself):

1 Is my mission based on my personal vision and upon proven principles?

2 Does this mission statement represent the best that is within me?

3 Do I feel direction, purpose, and challenge when I review this statement?

4 Am I able to develop operational objectives from this mission statement?

7 Revise your rough draft based on these questions. Then, keep it for a while to further revise and evaluate. Write a permanent draft, and try to commit it to memory so that you keep your vision and your mission clearly in mind. A second alternative is to keep it on your calendar or a place where you will frequently look at it.

---

[a] Portions of the material for this step are taken from Covey, Stephen (1989). *Seven Habits of Highly Effective People*. New York: Simon and Schuster.

Steps 4 and 5. Implement Projects and Tasks

Projects are very specific activities that are necessary in order to move toward accomplishing an objective. Tasks are the specific steps to be completed in order to accomplish a project. Each objective usually requires multiples projects, and each project of course requires many tasks.

The guidelines and steps for implementing projects and tasks are presented in Exhibit 7.5. A disclaimer is given regarding the guidelines (i.e., project and task development, implementation, and management require more description and guidelines than is the intent of this book). Specific techniques and a personal project list are presented. Examples of projects and tasks based on the two objectives in Exhibit 7.4 are also presented. (For additional information, see Abstract 7.2 at the end of this chapter.)

Implementing a Personal Plan: Six Examples

To further illustrate the potential impact of developing a personal plan, six selected visions reflecting a cross section of university employees are presented in Exhibit 7.6. They are presented to emphasize the applicability of this activity to all individuals. While the process requires time and energy, the benefit of having a personal vision upon which a mission statement (and related objectives, projects, and tasks)

Exhibit 7.4 General Guidelines for Implementing the Five Steps

---

Activity: Vision, Mission, **Objectives**, Projects, Tasks

1   **Purpose. What you will be doing:** Develop performance-based, operational objectives that are based on specific mission statement(s). The objectives are written in the past tense to establish a mindset of their being accomplished. Two examples would be (1) *I developed and pilot tested a survey questionnaire for assessing the students' perception of our registration process. This was completed in the fall semester.* (2) *I coordinated the revision of our baccalaureate program, including the development and approval of any new courses and deletion of the old. This took four terms (fall, spring, summer, fall) to complete.*

2   **You will know your are done when:** You have an action-oriented, time-focused statement upon which projects can be developed.

3   **Techniques or instruments you can use for this activity** (refer to Chapter 3): Affinity diagram, brainstorming, competitive benchmarking, flowcharting, nominal group technique, surveys, trend chart.

4   **Reality check. How will I know this plan "fits" me?:** The objective is clear in what will be accomplished, challenging, and achievable within the designated time frame. It enables me to identify specific projects and tasks which I am able to complete.

5   **Guidelines for implementation:**

    1   Your mission statement, if done as described in step 2, lists the roles you wish to fulfill, as well as a statement of how you would most like to be described in each role. You also listed the activities and developed an affinity diagram, or fishbone diagram, to group the activities within each role. This is the basis for your objectives.

    2   From the above, identify (with the help of brainstorming) the activities that focus on your role statements. With the help of the fishbone diagram, expand on the activities, coding each one if space does not allow an adequate description or statement.

    3   Establish a time frame (e.g., twelve months) and identify those activities you wish to focus on first. If this is the first time you have done this type of activity, select those that have the greatest chance of succeeding.

    4   Develop a draft of specific objectives, using the examples above as guidelines. The objective should be action oriented, with a specific time frame, and written in the past tense, i.e., you have already completed the objective.

    6   Evaluate this draft, asking the following questions:

        1   As stated, does the objective establish a mindset of being accomplished?

        2   Can the objective be realistically completed within the stated time?

        3   Is there clear direction and challenge in this objective?

        4   Am I able to develop specific projects and tasks from this objective as stated?

    7   Revise your draft based on these questions. Then, quickly move on to the development of the required projects and tasks.

Exhibit 7.5 General Guidelines for Implementing the Five Steps

Activity: Vision, Mission, Objectives, **Projects, Tasks**

1 **Purpose. What you will be doing:** Develop and implement specific projects and related tasks that are based on a single objective. An objective usually requires numerous projects, and a project requires numerous tasks. Two examples, based on the objective stated in step 3, are[a]

    3 *Start-up project* (student survey of registration process—the third of eleven projects for this objective)
        3.1 Develop project schedule (control chart, PERT chart)
        3.2 Develop initial list of project tasks (flowchart, checksheet)
        3.3 Organize meeting of project team
    4 *Gather information* (the fourth of eleven projects)
        4.1 Develop questions for information gathering (brainstorm)
        4.2 Interview selected students (small survey)
        4.3 Contact other universities (benchmarking)
        4.4 Summarize data obtained (histogram, Pareto diagram, trend chart)
    2 *Gather information* (revision of the baccalaureate program—the second of nine projects)
        2.1 Conduct student focus group (brainstorm, survey)
        2.2 Conduct alumni focus group (cause-and-effect diagram, checksheet, survey)
        2.3 Interview other universities (benchmarking)
        2.4 Prepare summary report (histogram, Pareto diagram, trend chart)
    3 *Design the new program* (the second of nine projects)
        3.1 Review summary data with faculty (affinity diagram, cause-and-effect diagram)
        3.2 Brainstorm revised program with faculty (brainstorm)
        3.3 Chart proposed revisions (control chart, flowchart)
        3.4 Design the new program
        3.5 Review program with faculty, students, and alumni
        3.6 Accept design

2 **You will know your are done when:** You have developed all the projects and related tasks and are able to design a flowchart that is logical and understandable to others.

3 **Techniques or instruments you can use for this activity** (refer to Chapter 3): Affinity diagram, block diagram, brainstorming, cause-and-effect diagram, checksheet, competitive benchmarking, control chart, histogram, interview, Pareto diagram, run chart, scatter diagram, survey, tree diagram, trend chart

4 **Reality check. How will I know this plan "fits" me?** I am able to "walk" through the project without missing a step (task) and complete the journey within the designated time.

Exhibit 7.5 (continued)   General Guidelines for Implementing
the Five Steps

---

5   **Guidelines for implementation:**   As noted in the footnote to step 1, it is not
the intent here to describe in detail the development and implementation of
projects. It is strongly recommended that you at least read a text or manual
on project development and management or, preferably, attend a seminar
for your own benefit and your team's benefit. What can be provided is a
personal project checklist as a start in the development of productive projects.

1	Define the project	7	Monitor progress
2	Select a strategy	8	Take corrective action
3	Develop tasks	9	Provide feedback
4	Develop measures	10	Test final outcome
5	Develop a schedule	11	Evaluate project
6	Develop a budget	12	Initiate the next project

---

[a] It is not possible in this book, nor is it the intent, to describe in detail the development
and implementation of projects. Illustrative examples are given here to emphasize
the benefit of this process, from the vision to the specific projects and tasks that are
governed by commitment to the vision.

is focused can have the same impact for each individual that this
process can have for the college and university. The plans present the
vision statements only, as illustrations of their personal diversity. A
complete list of the related personal mission statements, objectives,
projects, and tasks would include all the roles that these individuals
identify and is beyond the scope of this book. As mentioned earlier,
Exhibit 7.4 presents two objectives, and Exhibit 7.5 presents four projects
and the related tasks for two personal visions and mission statements.

APPLICATION OF PERSONAL MANAGEMENT AND TASK MANAGEMENT AT OREGON STATE UNIVERSITY

While the documented activities of the implementation of total
quality management at Oregon State University (OSU) fully describe
the application of strategy, process, and project management, little was
recorded about personal and task management. Extensive discussion
was directed toward the central role of training all team members,
particularly facilitators, and recognition of the need to provide increased applicable training.

Exhibit 7.6 Vision and Mission Statement of Six University Employees
(Two Faculty, Two Administrative, Two Hourly)

FACULTY

Associate Professor: Tenured and in his present position for 11 years, this is his second position since receiving his doctorate. He is proceeding well in his career, averaging about one article published every two years, at least one presentation a year at a national conference, and a record of service to his profession, although he is not on any national committee at this time. He is married (his wife is a teacher in the local school system) and has three children (the older two not at home and the youngest graduating from high school). He and his wife are active in their community and parish and are just starting to think about retirement, which is at least fifteen years away.

Ten-year vision: I am in my mid 50s. I am a full professor. My wife will also be in her 50s, fulfilling her vision. Our children will either be in college or just graduated. Our home will hopefully (!) be empty, enabling us to travel more. We are providing at least partial care for our parents.

Assistant Professor: Tenure earning and in her present faculty position for three years, this is her first position after receiving her doctorate. She is proceeding well in her career, having published one article from her dissertation and presented at two national conferences. She is active in her profession and has just been elected to a national committee on professional development. She is single, with no present commitments. Because of her work, she is moderately active in a community rights group and at a singles group in a local church.

Seven-year vision: I am tenured. While I like where I was (seven years ago), there is 50/50 chance that I will be at another university. I just completed a year as president-elect of the national association of my profession. While I would enjoy being married, I am equally satisfied if I am not. Part of my consideration in relocating is based on being closer to my aging parents.

ADMINISTRATIVE/PROFESSIONAL

Associate Vice President, Institutional Planning: She has been in this position for four years, having been selected in a national search and coming from a similar position at a smaller college, where she worked for seven years. She has a doctorate in higher education administration and is fairly active in her profession, having published one article, presented at national conferences occasionally, and served on two committees previously. She is liked by her president and the V.P. for administration (her boss), but because of various tough positions on resource allocations, she is tolerated by the other V.P.s and the academic deans. She is married, and her husband is a human resources manager at an area hospital. They have two children, one just starting college and the other just starting high school. They have been active in the schools their children have attended and in community and church youth programs.

Exhibit 7.6 (continued)   Vision and Mission Statement of Six University Employees (Two Faculty, Two Administrative, Two Hourly)

Ten-year vision: I am V.P. for Administration, hopefully at this university. The current V.P. will have retired four years ago. While the odds of the president remaining here for ten years are slim, I was viewed by my colleagues as the strongest candidate. My husband is at the hospital in some expanded human resources role. We spend many weekends at the vacation house we bought three years ago. Our children, having completed school, are establishing themselves in their respective careers. I am active in the yearly Youth Fair and continue serving on the board of Boys Club.

Director of Academic Computer Systems: He has been with the university for twelve years and in this position for five years. His responsibilities have grown with the increased use of academic computer applications, the installation of more computer labs, and greater access by students. He has been too busy to consider any professional involvement other than occasionally attending a conference or seminar to stay current with the field. He is divorced and has no children, with little thought of remarriage at this time. He has been active in a computer users group, but his new "love" is to escape to hiking trails throughout the state and nation.

Five-year vision: I can only create a vision five years from now. I am either still Director of Academic Computing or, preferably, Associate V.P. for Computer Services, with university-wide responsibilities. Computer technology has continued to rapidly expand, with the university constantly struggling to keep current. The focus will be on networked PCs. Turning to my personal life, I have hiked most of the major trails in the U.S. and am now traveling to other countries at least every other year. I am active in the local hiking club and am trying to get some youth involved.

HOURLY (CLERICAL/MAINTENANCE)

Departmental Secretary: She has been with the college for eight years, having previously worked for two local businesses and a government agency. She is one of two secretaries to a department of twelve faculty. She received an associate degree in office practices and pursues what training is provided by the college. Married, her husband is a manager at a local department store. They have two boys; the oldest is in the military and the youngest in high school. She is very active in her parish, where she assists in personal growth seminars.

Seven-year vision: I am in my early 50s; my husband is in his mid-50s. Both boys are on their own; hopefully we will have grandchildren. I am now in an Administrative Assistant position, specializing in computer technology. I am active at St. Mary's, assisting in mass and small group programs.

Maintenance Electrician: He has been with the university three years, having been in a similar position for ten years at a local plant that shut down. One of four electricians, he is the oldest in years and experience, but the youngest in length of employment. Divorced, his teenage son lives with him. He is moderately active in Big Brothers, but quite active in an investment club.

Six-year vision: This is as far as I can see, right now. I am 44 years old and have been an electrician at the university for nine years. I have been the supervisor for three years, with a crew of five. I just received my bachelor's degree in business administration. My son is in college and I pay most of his expenses. It's a 50/50 chance whether I am married.

A poignant quotation reflects the personal impact of total quality management. It is also an appropriate conclusion to this discussion of personal growth and development through personal quality improvement. In one team member's words, as written in an evaluation survey:

> I have been at OSU for nearly 10 years, and I've experienced a lot of stumbling blocks to getting things done. I had pretty much decided that I was just going to come to work, do my job, and not make waves. I got into a rut, and didn't see much hope. Now TQM has opened another door, and I see a chance to make some changes that just make common sense. Total Quality Management seems to be OSU's answer.[5]

For additional information, see Abstract 7.3 at the end of this chapter.

ENDNOTES

1. Seymour, Daniel T. (1992). *On Q: Causing Quality in Higher Education.* New York: Macmillan, p. 96.
2. Senge, Peter (1990). *The Fifth Discipline.* New York: Doubleday, p. 210.
3. *Webster's New World Dictionary* (1982). Compact School and Office Edition, New York: Simon and Schuster.
4. Covey, Stephen (1989). *Seven Habits of Highly Effective People.* New York: Simon and Schuster, p. 106.
5. Coate, L. Edwin (1992). *Total Quality Management at Oregon State University.* Corvallis: Oregon State University, p. 43.
6. Figure 7.1 and Exhibits 7.1 to 7.5 ©1992 Strategy Associates, Inc.

ABSTRACTS

ABSTRACT 7.1 IMPROVING PRODUCTIVITY IN SPONSORED RESEARCH ADMINISTRATION

Kirby, Bill
SRA Journal, Fall 1992, pp. 41–54

This article by Bill Kirby, who is a senior executive at the Federal Quality Institute (FQI), examines the role of research administration in the context of a major issue facing the economy and the research system—productivity. The author challenges the research enterprise to improve competitiveness and quality and maximize the cost effectiveness of research. Research administrators need to examine how their profession contributes to the research process and what needs to be done to improve its quality and productivity. Various themes and strategies for addressing the issue of productivity are discussed, including the importance of leadership and management, new approaches for designing work processes, the need for purposeful cooperation among all sectors of research administration, and new structures for developing federal policies in sponsored research. The crisis in the economy and pressure from the government sector further intensify the need to explore the issues of productivity and quality. What is needed is a transformation into an organization in which management empowers research administrators to explore the existing links between different factions of the research administration community.

Ideally, the focus should rest on the areas that are the foundation of the federal project grant system: the system that controls the creation of federal policies for research administration and the system of accountability that assures federal university financial integrity, quality, and productivity. Overall, the following issues are dealt with: (1) productivity and research administration, (2) roles of research administration, (3) managing for quality and productivity, (4) a quality management model, (5) examples of total quality in action, (6) importance of integration, (7) process management and timeliness, (8) new structures for the administration and stewardship of federally funded academic research, and (9) conceptual basis of a model policy. The argument Kirby raises for simplifying the information-usage process, rather than trying to simplify the requirements, is a central issue around which this work revolves. Substantial references are provided, as well as an interesting exhibit for stewardship models.

ABSTRACT 7.2   TOTAL QUALITY MANAGEMENT: AN AMERICAN ODYSSEY

Krone, Bob
The Bureaucrat, Fall 1990, pp. 35–37

The author is Chair of the Systems Management Department at USC and a specialist in total quality in academia. Along with Curt Tompkins, a dean at West Virginia and also a total quality in academia specialist, a cast of four other total quality "experts" have come together to explore the premise that "The paths to TQM and total national security have many crossings. Achievement of both will benefit us all." The views of the six panelists of the 51st national conference of the American Society of Public Administration are categorized into the following areas: (1) What is TQM? (2) Why does America need TQM? (3) How is it going? (4) What are the implementation barriers? (5) The future is America's challenge. The article is enhanced with notes and remarks from the six panelists. "Those of us in the academic world have a long way to go to contribute to total quality management in the U.S. We're really at a primitive stage." (Tompkins, West Virginia University). The article is worth reading for the panelists' insights alone. Limited references are provided.

ABSTRACT 7.3   APPLYING DEMING'S PRINCIPLES TO OUR SCHOOLS

Leonard, James F.
South Carolina Business Journal, Vol. 11, 1991

The gauntlet is laid down in the opening paragraph: "The overwhelming challenge facing America today is the need to regain competitive position in the world...a challenge for all of our major institutions: business, government and education." The article focuses on how Deming's principles can help educators improve the quality of teaching and learning (and living) in our schools by (1) understanding the school as a system, (2) focusing on process, (3) recognizing changing roles in the school system, and (4) redefining obligations of the chancellors, school boards, and administration. Although the article was written for schools in general, the "systems perspective" advocated can readily be applied to higher education. This is a basic introductory article with limited references.

CHAPTER 8

IMPLEMENTATION: theTRANSFORMING PROCESS

There is nothing more difficult to carry out, nor more doubtful of success, nor more dangerous to handle, than to initiate a new order of things. For the reformer has enemies in all those who profit from the old order, and lukewarm defenders in all those who would profit by the new order.[1]

Almost twenty years ago, Hargrove[2] identified implementation as the installation of new policies and/or programs in organizations. He also stated that it is the "missing link" in organizational planning and design. What he meant is that when compared to planning or even evaluation of policies and programs, issues and actions related to their actual implementation received little attention. Unfortunately, this is still the case, despite the fact that implementation failure has long been identified as a source of policy or program failure. For example, Lewis and Green[3] identified it as one of three reasons why policy and program innovations appear to languish:

- *Programmatic overexpectation:* Unrealistic expectations for success.
- *Conceptual failure:* The theories about causation and the relationships underlying the policies and programs are inaccurate or incomplete.
- *Implementation failure:* The failure to carry out the policy or program as designed.

There is very little one can do to avoid failures due to programmatic expectations except to (1) warn potential customers to be careful (if it sounds too good to believe, it probably is) or (2) warn advocates to avoid excess (do not promise what you can't deliver).

Regarding the second and third causes of failure, stories abound of how quality improvement efforts have been tried and have failed. A review of these stories seems to indicate that many (perhaps most) of the presumed failures are do to programmatic overexpectations and/or implementation failure. They are replete with similar phrases (e.g., "we thought the situation would be turned around in six months," or "the President told us we were now 'empowered' to make decisions," or, "the President didn't even attend the training sessions for the quality improvement program").

The focus of this chapter is the implementation of quality improvement efforts. The implementation of any policy or program is complicated and is compounded by the unique combination of the history, the personalities, and the social, technical, and management systems of every college and university. Because of these complexities, specific implementation plans must be developed. A standard operational "blueprint" for implementation cannot be provided. (For additional information, see Abstract 8.1 at the end of this chapter.)

GUIDELINES FOR IMPLEMENTATION

Guidelines for implementation can be provided, but even this may prove perplexing. The growing literature in total quality is inundated with techniques, prescriptions, and procedures. Little attention is devoted, however, to how total quality has been implemented, the hurdles encountered by organizations, and how they adapted the principles of total quality to existing cultures. Even the leaders in the field cannot agree, as noted by Coate:[4]

Furthermore, the lack of agreement among the TQM gurus produces contradictions and inconsistent prescriptions that are puzzling to would-be users. Deming says "eliminate slogans," while Crosby uses the slogan of "zero defects." Deming says "drive out fear," while Juran says "fear can bring out the best in people." Deming's process starts at the top and works down, while Juran starts with middle management and works both ways.

From this rich and diverse milieu, six models for implementing total quality can be identified:[5]

1. *Total Quality Element Approach:* Uses elements of quality improvement programs rather than full implementation of total quality, such as quality circles, statistical process control, and quality functional deployment.
2. *Guru Approach:* Uses the writings of Deming, Juran, and Crosby for analysis and implementation. Deming's fourteen-point model is an example.
3. *Japanese Model Approach:* Uses the writings of such Japanese writers as Kaoru Ishikawa and the educational guidelines of the Union of Japanese Scientists and Engineers (JUSE).
4. *Industrial Company Model Approach:* Leaders from one organization visit an organization using total quality, identify its system, and integrate this information with their own ideas to create a customized approach. Visiting winners of the Baldrige Award is an example.
5. *Hoshin Planning Approach:* Focuses on successful planning, deployment, and execution and monthly diagnosis. Developed by the Japanese firm Bridgestone and used successfully by Hewlett-Packard.
6. *Baldrige Award Criteria Approach:* Uses the criteria for the Malcolm Baldrige National Quality Award to identify areas for improvement.

All of these approaches work and have been applied in hundreds of organizations. Which approach, or approaches, is most applicable to higher education? In this book the use of a variety of total quality techniques and tools was described in Chapter 3. The fourteen points of Deming and the seven Baldrige criteria were also described in Chapter 3, modified for educational application. The four managerial levels for implementing total quality were described in Chapters 4 to 7, maintaining that total quality can begin at any of these levels. Exercises to encourage a methodical process of analysis and implementation have been provided throughout. The experience at Oregon State University in implementing total quality has been discussed at length. In sum, the strategy advocated in this book is an eclectic hybrid of all of these approaches: taking the best and configuring it into a framework is most applicable to the higher educational environment. (For additional information, see Abstract 8.2 at the end of this chapter.)

DEVELOPING AN IMPLEMENTATION PLAN

The focus of this chapter is the development of a plan for implementing the total quality improvements advocated throughout this book. A model and supportive framework are provided to assist in the development of this plan. The model for the total quality transformation process is presented in Figure 8.1. Several points should be noted about this model:

- It identifies activities related to adopting quality improvement efforts as a distinct phase in the process.
- It recognizes the need for completing institutional assessment efforts (speaking with facts) as a critical phase in the developmental process.
- It identifies four levels at which quality improvement efforts may be initiated: *strategy management and concept development* (Chapter 4), *process management and development* (Chapter 5), *project management and development* (Chapter 6), and *task management and implementation* (Chapter 7).
- It recognizes the need for continual evaluation of the college or university and its quality improvement efforts, with the evaluation based on facts.

The material in Figure 8.1 presents a flow from *total quality goal setting*, to *assessment*, to the *four management levels* listed above, to *evaluation*. This holistic approach to implementation is necessary, if feasible. As indicated previously, beginning at the initial, organization-wide stages (goal setting, assessment, and strategy management) may not always be feasible. In such situations, intervention at other levels (e.g., process management, project management, or task management) may be the most appropriate approach for initiating quality improvement efforts at the college or university.

A descriptive summary of an implementation action plan based on the total quality transformation process model (Figure 8.1) is presented in Table 8.1. Each action is based on the coded statements in the model, with descriptors that provide guidelines for *what* should be done, *who* should be doing it, *why* this particular action is necessary, *how* the action should be carried out, *when* it should be done, and what *indicators* are required to ensure that it has been implemented. While still a framework upon which a specific plan applicable to the college or university must be designed and developed, this summary provides an extensive guide for initiating a thorough and, hopefully, more effective and productive total quality transformation plan.

APPLICATION OF THE TOTAL QUALITY MANAGEMENT IMPLEMENTATION PLAN AT OREGON STATE UNIVERSITY

The implementation of total quality management at Oregon State (OSU) was based on an extensive review of various approaches (refer to the preceding summary). Their model was most closely associated with the Hoshin Planning Model used by Hewlett-Packard. The Baldrige Award criteria were used to develop a five-year plan. The nine phases in the OSU model are similar to the seven actions steps presented in this chapter. The OSU model is presented very similar to the implementation model shown in Figure 8.1 and illustrates the commitment of both models to a sequential process of analysis, goal identification, mission and vision development with related objectives, projects (teams), and task initiation. The process may vary somewhat, but the intent and desired outcome are the same.

Phases of Implementation

The implementation of each phase was described in a July 1990 report.[6] The following are some notable highlights and insights derived from each step.

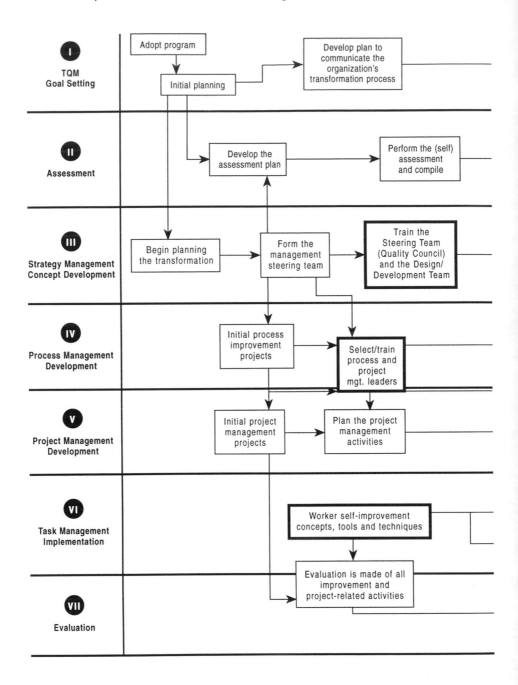

Figure 8.1 Total Quality Transformation Process.

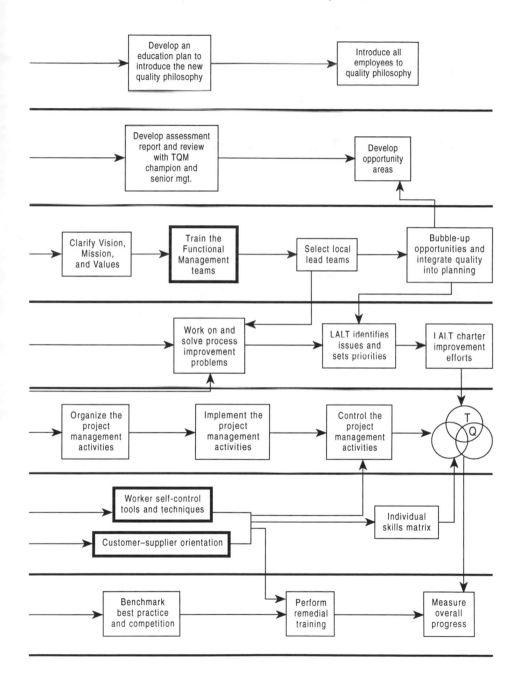

Table 8.1 Action Plan for Total Quality Transformation Process

No.	Action	What	Who
1 Total Quality (TQ) Goal Setting			
1.1	Adopt program	Explore quality issues and adopt total quality program	President (head of sponsoring unit), and Executive Committee
1.2	Initial planning	Develop mission, vision, guiding principles, and goals for Quality Council	President and the Quality Council
1.3	Communications plan	Plan to communicate the program and process	President and Quality Council, Design and Development Team
1.4	Education plan	Develop plan to introduce the quality program and quality principles	President and Quality Council, Design and Development Team
1.5	Introduce quality improvement	Introduce all members to quality improvement principles and techniques	President and Quality Council, Design and Development Team
2 Assessment			
2.1	Develop assessment plan	Develop a plan to assess the college/university and its leadership in terms of quality improvement principles and issues	President and Quality Council, Design and Development Team
2.2	Conduct assessment	Conduct the assessment with customers (internal and external) and suppliers (see Chapter 3); analyze the results	Design and Development Team
2.3	Prepare and circulate report	Prepare assessment report; circulate to the President, Quality Council, and key individuals	Design and Development Team
2.4	Identify opportunities	Identify opportunity areas for quality improvement	President and Quality Council, Design and Development Team
3 Strategy Management Concept Development			
3.1	Begin planning the transformation	Develop basic plans for the quality improvement effort at the strategic level	President and Executive Committee

Table 8.1 Action Plan for Total Quality Transformation Process

No.	Why	How	When	Indicators
Total Quality (TQ) Goal Setting				
1.1	To ensure top level commitment to the effort	Appoint Quality Council (Chapter 4)	Month 1	Executive Committee minutes
1.2	To develop the framework for the quality improvement effort	Consultations with Quality Council	Months 1 and 2	Quality Council minutes, written documents
1.3	To ensure systematic and consistent communication about the quality effort	Appoint a Design and Development Team to report to the Quality Council	Month 1 and continuously throughout the program	Written materials, Quality Council minutes, Design and Development Team minutes
1.4	To initiate the transformation process with all members of the college/university	Publication of the plan, newsletters, meetings, seminars, workshops	Month 2	Quality Council minutes, Design and Development Team minutes, written documents
1.5	To initiate the transformation process with all members of the college/university	Official documents, newsletters, meetings, workshops	Month 2	Quality Council and Design and Development Team minutes
2 Assessment				
2.1	To obtain data to assess the current state of "quality" in the college/university	Review existing literature for assessment, gather benchmarking data and internal data, seek consultants (see Chapter 4)	Month 2	Assessment instrument
2.2	To collect data on quality in the college/university	Surveys, preview of documents, existing databases	Month 2	Completed data files
2.3	To share data, obtain feedback, and involve members	Formal meetings, written reports, newsletters	Month 3	Assessment report, other related documents, record of the meetings
2.4	To select target areas for quality improvement efforts	Analysis of report(s), discussions with key members	Month 3	List of target opportunities
3 Strategy Management Concept Development				
3.1	To ensure top level commitment to the effort	Appoint Quality Council	Month 1	Minutes of the Executive Committee

Table 8.1 (continued)   Action Plan for Total Quality Transformation Process

No.	Action	What	Who
3.2.1	Form the Quality Council	Appoint Quality Council from key positions in the organization (Executive Committee, administrative groups, unions, faculty, other employee groups	President
3.2.2	Form the Design & Development Team	Create the Design and Development Team	Quality Council
3.3	Training	Train the Quality Council and the Design and Development Team	Qualified individuals, which may include outside consultants initially
3.4	Clarify mission, vision, guiding principles, and goals	Conduct meetings (workshops) focused on the college/university vision, mission, guiding principles, and overarching goals	Quality Council, Design and Development Team
3.5	Train functional management teams	Select and train teams from the major functional areas of the college/university, e.g., Academic Affairs, Business, Finance, Student Affairs, Athletics, etc.	Coordinated by Design and Development Team in consultation with the Quality Council; training done by appropriate persons (may be outside consultants)
3.6	Work on improving own process	Functional management teams focus on internal process improvement efforts	Functional management teams, Design and Development Team

Table 8.1 (continued) Action Plan for Total Quality Transformation Process

No.	Why	How	When	Indicators
3.2.1	To provide ongoing leadership in establishing and maintaining total quality effort	Appoint Quality Council; identify Quality Council mission, vision, guiding principles, goals (Chapter 4)	Month 1	Minutes of the Executive Committee, minutes of the Quality Council
3.2.2	To have the college or university team responsible for developing and monitoring the TQ plan; to encourage everyone to contribute to the quality improvement effort	Select people from critical divisions and departments (Chapter 6); identify the mission, vision, and guiding principles for the team (Chapter 4)	Month 2	Minutes of the Quality Council, minutes of the Design and Development Team
3.3	To increase the understanding of quality improvement principles and improvement to the process	Intensive workshops (a location away from work would be very beneficial); combine initial training with follow-through sessions	Months 1 & 2, with follow-through session continuous during the project	Training designed and delivered; written initial vision, mission, guiding principles, and goals
3.4	To ensure a collective on and commitment to the mission, vision, guiding principles, and overarching goals	Discussion of assessment report and sessions focused on the review and development of material related to the mission, vision, principles, and goals (Chapter 4)	Months 1 and 2	Quality Council, and Design and Development Team minutes; revised statement of vision, mission, guiding principles, and goals
3.5	To increase understanding of and commitment to quality improvement efforts among key persons in the major functional areas	Select and appoint functional management teams (Chapter 6); train functional management teams	Months 3 and 4	Design and Development Team minutes; training designed and delivered to functional management teams
3.6	To provide team members with the opportunity to analyze and improve internal processes	Process and problem analysis (Chapter 5)	Months 5 and 6	Design and Development Team minutes, functional management team minutes

Table 8.1 (continued)   Action Plan for Total Quality Transformation Process

No.	Action	What	Who
3.7	Local Area Lead Teams (LALTs)	Select and train LALTs	Coordinated by the Design and Development Team, in cooperation with the functional management teams; training done by appropriate persons
3.8	Identify opportunity areas, "bubble-up"	Identify opportunities for quality improvement efforts based on process and problem analysis	LALTs, functional management teams, Design and Development Team
3.9	Integrate quality into planning	Integrate quality improvement principles and techniques into college/university planning	Led by the Quality Council, in cooperation with the other teams that have been formed
4 Process Management Development			
4.1	Initial process improvement projects	Identification of the core processes	Quality Council and Design and Development Team
4.2	Select and train teams	Select and train the functional management teams and LALTs	Quality Council and Design and Development Team
4.3	Process improvement problems	Identify and solve process improvement problems; select and train-cross-functional improvement teams	Cross-functional process improvement teams, in cooperation with the Quality Council and Design and Development Team
4.4	LALTs	Select and train LALTs	
4.5	College/ university issues and priorities	Identify issues and priorities of the college/university	LALTs

Table 8.1 (continued) Action Plan for Total Quality Transformation Process

No.	Why	How	When	Indicators
3.7	To have local area teams address issues related to major core processes	Select persons directly involved in the processes to be addressed, and appoint LALTs (Chapter 6); train LALTs	Months 6 and 7	Minutes of functional management teams; training designed and delivered to LALTs
3.8	To assist the Quality Council in identifying opportunities for quality improvement efforts	Analysis of all materials produced by the assessment and process management activities	Months 6 and 7	Reports to functional management teams and to the Design and Development Team and Quality Council
3.9	To institutionalize quality improvement principles and techniques into ongoing planning of activities of the college/university	Train all team members in quality improvement principles and techniques, development of policies and procedures	Month 6 and continuously throughout the program	Training designed and delivered to all team members; written policies and procedures
4 Process Management Development				
4.1	To assure that all key processes are working in harmony to maximize organizational effectiveness	Systematic effort by the Quality Council and Design and Development Team to identify core processes of the college/university (Chapter 5, step 1)	Months 3 and 4	List of core processes of the college/university
4.2	To enhance the understanding of and commitment to quality improvement principles and techniques	Selected reading materials on quality improvement principles and techniques, workshops on improvement principles and techniques	Months 4 and 5	Training designed and delivered to the functional management teams and LALTs
4.3	To ensure that the major processes of the college/university are effective, efficient, and meet customer needs and expectations	Systematic efforts using cross-functional teams (Chapter 5, steps 2 and 3, and Chapter 6)	Months 5 and 6	Process improvement problems identified and addressed by cross-functional process improvement teams
4.4				
4.5	To have an accepted set of issues that need to be addressed by the college/university	Cross-functional teams, following a systematic process (Chapter 5, steps 2, 3, and 4)	Months 6 and 7	Reports on activities and results of crossfunctional teams

Table 8.1 (continued)   Action Plan for Total Quality Transformation Process

No.	Action	What	Who
4.6	Charter improvement efforts	Process management improvement efforts recommended and approved	LALTs, Design and Development Team, Quality Council

5 Project Management Development

No.	Action	What	Who
5.1	Initial project management projects	Identify the initial projects based on the list of core processes of the college/university (step 4.1)	Functional management teams and LALTs in cooperation with the Design and Development Team and Quality Council
5.2	Plan the project management activities	Initiate the overall plan for each of the selected projects	Functional management teams and LALTs
5.3	Organize the project management activities	Coordinate the organizational framework of each project; conduct training on shared responsibilities (cross-training)	Functional management teams and LALTs
5.4	Implement the project management activities	Begin each project based on the developed plan and organizational framework	Functional management teams and LALTs
5.5	Control the project management activities	Utilize the control strategies developed in the overall plan of each project	Functional management teams and LALTs
5.6	Complete the projects	Complete each project within the designated objective, specified time, and budget	Functional management teams and LALTs

Table 8.1 (continued)   Action Plan for Total Quality Transformation Process

No.	Why	How	When	Indicators
4.6	To ensure selection of appropriate processes, authorization, commitment, and support	LALTs recommend priorities and target processes; they are reviewed and approved by Design and Development Team and Quality Council	Months 7 and 8	Approved reports on process improvement priorities and target processes
5 Project Management Development				
5.1	To ensure that projects are based on the core college/university processes and to select problems with a high chance of success as the initial projects	Each functional management team and LALT identifies the problem processes they would like to initially address	Months 8 and 9	Approved list of initial projects
5.2	To identify all the necessary steps, required resources, and areas of collaboration with other teams for each project	Each functional management team and LALT develops the overall plan and strategy for the selected projects	Months 8 and 9	Fully developed plan for each selected project
5.3	To organize all the necessary steps, required resources, and areas of shared responsibilities for each project	Each team collaboratively organizes its project, with the help of a lead person as the facilitator; conduct workshops on cross-training	Months 8 and 9	Fully developed and understood organizational framework for each project
5.4	To initiate the selected team-centered quality improvement projects	"Just do it;" get started with the projects, applying PDCA and the appropriate quality tools and techniques (Chapters 3 and 6)	Months 9 and 10	Visible indication of projects beginning, initial progress reports
5.5	To assure the progress of each project, based on planned control systems	Utilize the appropriate quality evaluation and feedback tools and techniques (Chapters 3 and 6)	Months 9 and 10	Scheduled progress reports
5.6	To demonstrate the success of team-centered project management	Successful implementation of steps 4.6, 5.1–5.5, and 6.4	Months 10 and 11	Scheduled progress and end-of-project reports

Table 8.1 (continued)   Action Plan for Total Quality Transformation Process

No.	Action	What	Who
6 Task (Personal) Management Development			
6.1	Personal self-improve-ment	Provide education and develop-ment for self-improvement of everyone	Each person in the college/university on a voluntary basis, and preferably in teams to facilitate co-development
6.2	Personal self-control	Provide education in developing personal vision, mission, and objectives plans (Chapter 7)	Each person in the college/university on a voluntary basis, and preferably in teams to facilitate co-development
6.3	Customer–supplier orientation	Sensitivity to meeting, even anticipating, needs of customers/constituents; establish long-term relations with suppliers	Each person in the college/university within the frame-work of the teams, and in coop-eration with the Design and Development Team and Quality Council
6.4	Personal skills matrix	Development of personal skills matrix and database	Each person in the college/university within the frame-work of the functional manage-ment teams and LALTs
7 Evaluation			
7.1	Process and project evaluation	Evaluation criteria and procedures built into *all* quality improvement efforts; quality improvement efforts reviewed and evaluated	Functional management teams and LALTs responsible for improvement effort, with reports reviewed by the Design and Development Team and Quality Council
7.2	Benchmark best practices	Identification of best practices and performances on target processes and projects	Functional management teams and LALTs responsible for improvement effort, with reports reviewed by the Design and Development Team and Quality Council

Table 8.1 (continued) Action Plan for Total Quality Transformation Process

No.	Why	How	When	Indicators
6 Task (Personal) Management Development				
6.1	To develop the institution's most important resource, its people, for the benefit of the people and the college/university	Provide courses and seminars on personal and team-related education and development	Begin in month 4 (see step 4.2) and continue throughout the project	Positive evalua tion of the courses/seminars, measurable impact on team effectiveness
6.2	To demonstrate the college/university's commitment to personal/self-growth and control; to enforce team development with personal development	Provide courses and seminars in developing personal vision, mission, and objectives plans	Begin in month 4 (see step 4.2) and continue throughout the project	Positive evalua- tion of the courses/seminars; measurable impact on personal effective- ness
6.3	To actualize the two basic purposes of the project: implement the basic mission of the college/university and totally serve the customers/constituents	Provide courses and seminars on customer service; team-based projects addressing customer service process (steps 4.1–4.6 and 5.1–5.6)	Begin in month 6 (see step 4.5) and continue throughout the project	Successful completion of and measurable impacts on customer service and supplier orientation projects
6.4	To provide a personal skills matrix for each person, identifying present and future skills; facilitate the cross-training of each team and its members	Establish a personal skills matrix database for each person; coordinate with a team-centered database	Begin in month 6 (see step 3.7) and continue throughout the project	Personal skills matrix database of each person established, coordinated with a team-centered database
7 Evaluation				
7.1	To learn whether the improvements occurred in terms of effective- ness, efficiency, and meeting the needs of the customers; to maintain orientation to continuous improvement	Application of total quality tools such as control charts and other more formal evaluation techniques (Chapters 3 and 5)	Begin with initiation of the project (steps 4.1–4.6 and 5.1–5.6) and continue throughout the project	Evaluation criteria and procedures identified for each project; periodic project reports
7.2	To maintain continuous improvement orienta- tion; to obtain data on best practices	Review of data concerning the performance of out- side quality leaders in each process area (field, related fields, similar functions)	Begin with initiation of the project and continue throughout the project	Benchmarking data, internal reviews compar- ing process/ project perform- ance with outside quality leaders

Table 8.1 (continued) Action Plan for Total Quality Transformation Process

No.	Action	What	Who
7.3	Training, remediation, and enhancement	Develop and deliver additional training for persons identified in steps 4.1 and 4.2 or on topics identified through the benchmarking process (step 7.2)	Design and Development Team, in cooperation with the functional management teams and LALTs
7.4	Measure overall programs	Develop and conduct efforts to monitor and evaluate the overall impact of the quality improvement efforts	Quality Council and Design and Development Team, in cooperation with the functional management teams and LALTs

Phase 1. Exploring Total Quality Management

Companies with total quality management programs were visited. Dr. Deming also met with them. A number of books and articles on total quality were read. The president and two top managers attended a class on the seven total quality tools, taught by Hewlett-Packard. Excitement about total quality was generated; potential resistance, particularly from the academic side, was recognized.

Phase 2. Initial Pilot Study Team

A total quality study team was formed in the physical plant to apply total quality processes on a small scale. The issue of turnaround time in remodeling projects (a major problem) was addressed. The pilot was very successful, and results included shortening the remodeling process by ten percent, improved customer relations, and improved attitudes and behaviors of workers and managers.

Phase 3. Defining Customer Needs through Quality Function Deployment

Customers were identified (discussed in Chapter 3), and three customer surveys were conducted: an image survey, an admitted stu-

Table 8.1 (continued) Action Plan for Total Quality Transformation Process

No.	Why	How	When	Indicators
7.3	To maintain the relevance of the established education and training program; to enhance the knowledge, skills, and attitudes of everyone	Formal training programs, newsletters with an educational focus, written material (job aides, manuals, performance guide-lines)	Begin with initiation of the project and continue throughout the project	Additional train-ing completed and evaluated; written materials published
7.4	To obtain data on the impact of the quality improvement efforts; to ensure a fact-driven organizational environ-ment	Development of overall evaluation design that builds on and synthesizes the team project reports	Begin with initiation of the project and continue throughout the project	Team project evaluation reports, synthesized evaluation reports

dents survey, and a faculty survey. Based on the results, a cross-functional marketing committee was created to examine OSU's image and the products it delivers. Potential problems were acknowledged: "Total commitment to developing 'customer-driven' systems will not come easily."[7]

Phase 4. Top Management Breakthrough Planning (Hoshin Planning)

Five major steps were identified for this phase: (1) clarification of the mission, (2) clarification of the customer, (3) identification of the critical processes of the university, (4) development of the university's vision, and (5) identification of priority breakthrough items (e.g., en-suring that all employees understand the vision and providing more detailed plans and operational detail). From this, it was recognized that this must be an iterative process, with continual modification as the process cascades down. It was also recognized that it would take at least five years for implementation to reach all facets of university life.

Phase 5. Divisions Do Breakthrough Planning

Finance and Administration initiated its five steps, resulting in the implementation of total quality management throughout this division.

Phase 6. Form Daily Management Teams

"Teams are at the very heart of TQM."[8] Work teams (identified as "study teams") were formed, typically led by the supervisor. The teams addressed processes that could be improved by resources controlled by the team. Roles were identified, and a ten-step problem-solving process was used (discussed in Chapter 6 on project management). Ten teams were initially created, all of which were in Finance and Administration. It was estimated that 400 teams would be required for full implementation of total quality management at OSU. The teams found surveys and a flowchart to be very helpful and were able to identify and refine the issue addressed, recognizing that some teams would move more rapidly than others. Time (release from regular tasks) and additional training were acknowledged to be needed.

Phase 7. Cross-Functional Pilot Projects

Processes and problems usually cross work unit (team) boundaries, and cross-functional coordination is needed. The pilot cross-functional team was composed of the division directors in Finance and Administration, who selected improvement of the total quality implementation process as their issue. They flowcharted the total quality process, using survey data to identify implementation problems. Using brainstorming, they identified a list of twenty possible solutions and then narrowed the list to four criteria: measurably reduce implementation time, improve the issue process, address an identified customer need, and be practical when initiating the solution.[9]

Phase 8. Cross-Functional Management

Cross-functional management was recognized as the area in which the greatest process improvement would occur. Because the university operated with committees that crossed departmental lines, existing committees were provided with training in total quality processes;

daily management and the tools and techniques of total quality were key items. From the pilot (phase 7), they learned that well-developed team skills are very important. "Individuals from different units must be able to move beyond 'turf protection' to cooperation for the good of the institution."[10]

Phase 9. Reporting, Recognition, and Awards

Feedback through regular reports is important in the total quality implementation process. Monthly reports were sent to the Vice President for Finance and Administration, focusing on the performance measures. The improvements were reviewed annually with each division director, and goals for the coming year were established. Salary increases were based on measurable improvements.

In terms of recognition and awards, three categories of awards were developed: (1) quality award, to recognize persons who make a significant measurable impact on the university; (2) beaver award (named for OSU's mascot), to recognize employees or teams who sustain continuous, high-quality work performance; and (3) great performance award, to spontaneously recognize and show appreciation to persons exceeding the "expectations in a specific activity or action, either unique or routine, showing at least one of the following: initiative, competence, customer service, flexibility, communication, cooperation, or tenacity."[11] OSU also participated in a regional "Teamwork Day," sponsored by Xerox Corporation, where quality teams exhibited their projects. From this experience, they sponsored a simpler version, a "Quality Fair," in April 1991. Teams displayed their projects, recognition was awarded, Xerox provided monetary awards, the president spoke, and "live music, balloons, streamers, and refreshments helped to keep the fair upbeat and celebrative."[12] (For additional information, see Abstract 8.3 at the end of this chapter.)

Beginning Total Quality on the Academic Side

Improving administrative and teaching processes on the academic side remains a major challenge in higher education. OSU addressed the academic side late in the second year of their total quality process, beginning with "a series of one and one-half day TQM strategic planning workshops for leadership teams from academic units, usually deans and department heads."[13] Numerous projects were launched from these workshops, and the following projects illustrate activities in four areas.

Improvement of Teaching

A professor of forest engineering had students form a total quality management team to help him improve his teaching. The teacher's performance was measurably increased from this process. An instructor in speech communication used a customer survey to ask students how they wanted to learn. Through a "nominal group" technique, the instructor helped the class identify the instructional techniques they most want (speakers, videos, lectures, etc.).

Teaching Total Quality

Graduate and undergraduate courses and internships are being offered in the Colleges of Business and Engineering. Student government leaders have participated in total quality classes and have used the total quality management manual to write a sample case study on the work of the student program council.

Total Quality Research

Research projects in total quality management applications are being conducted in the College of Business and OSU's Extension Service.

Academic Administration

The university's Extension Service is using total quality management to examine its functions. The College of Business conducted a comprehensive study to evaluate its mission and develop a "vision to guide critical decisions and processes through 2005. Central to the new strategy is the fundamental TQM philosophy that the output of the college (graduates and research) must be responsible to the needs of its customers."[14] The OSU library has three total quality management teams working to improve government document services, binding services, and stack maintenance.

Barriers to Total Quality

Oregon State University is committed to total quality management, but its deployment "was more challenging than many of us realized at first."[15] A deployment planning matrix (developed by Randy Schenkat) which can be used as a framework for getting started is provided in Table 8.2. In the March 1992 report,[16] seven barriers to total quality were described.

Skepticism

Total quality is being viewed as a fad—the latest in many management philosophies—and it too will pass. Based on the success that OSU has enjoyed, they maintain that "TQM is much more than a fad. It is the evolution of many systems built on behavioral science, and it is right for today's workplace. TQM goes beyond the classic management concept that 'there is one best way to do anything,'...TQM says that there are always better ways to do things and provides a process that can help all employees to discover them."[15]

Time

This remains a persistent problem, with total quality management viewed as another assignment rather than a way to achieve improvements. More time is being allowed for training and planning, but this will remain an issue to be addressed continuously.

Language

Total quality management originated in industrial settings, where such phrases as "quality control," "process performance measures," and "the customer is always right" are readily understood. In academia, suspicion is always aroused when jargon-laden language is used. Coate[17] recognized this issue, but tried to put it into perspective: "Experience today shows these arguments about language to be time-consuming and non-productive. We often substitute the word 'clients' for 'customers.' However, I believe that there are real advantages to the use of 'customers,' especially on the academic side. Our institution cannot afford to tolerate our high failure and low retention rates (wastage).

Table 8.2 Deployment Planning Matrix for Transformed Schools

	Stage		
	Starting a quality program	Operating a beginning quality program	Sustaining a quality program
Leadership for quality	• Learn the quality values and their implications for education • Develop personal support mechanisms • Link to broad-based community movement focused on TQM done thoughtfully	• Lead consistently day to day; model learning with staff; see things getting better • Push for 14 points daily in obvious ways by top management • Apply TQM through a trained middle management group (principals) • Communicate quality values to the public	• See an integration of quality in all major decisions • Sense a personal transformation
Assurance of product and service quality	• Understand constructivism and learning for conceptual change • Synthesize ongoing district efforts	• Design quality into curriculum development process • Build in mechanism of continuous improvement (time issues, action research, quality tools)	• Change naturally to interdisciplinary curriculum • Shift the ways schools provide learning
Human resource development and management	• Guarantee that no jobs will be lost from TQM (drive out fear) • Orient all employees to quality values through introductory program (consider joint training with other local firms) • Invest heavily in leaders and in envisioning learning communities	• Attain intended implementation through staff development • Reconsider existing evaluation practices • Foster professionalism set forth in NBPTS	• Improve continually in allocation of human effort • Unleash optimal motivation • Convey symbolically that employees are the district's most competitive asset

Table 8.2 (continued)   Deployment Planning Matrix for Transformed Schools

	Stage		
	Starting a quality program	Operating a beginning quality program	Sustaining a quality program
Strategic quality plan	• Keep communication focused on long-term support and constancy of purpose • Develop support for long-range budget to support quality initiative	• Secure funding for next 5–10 years related to employee learning needs • Link all facets of quality cohesively	• Carry out long-term design projects for 5–8 years with solid staff commitment • Scan futures for needed paradigm shifts
Information and analysis	• Benchmark on some quality practices in community • Develop measures to sense community support	• Benchmark to set high standards academically • Base decisions on data • Cease dependence on mass inspection	• Determine if data drive decisions and if schools are getting better in a variety of areas
Quality and operational results	• Begin discussion on needs for *all* to learn in new paradigm (moving away from normal curve of learning)	• Begin tracking costs that relate to the cost of inspection	• Show consistent trends in data collection • Spend fewer dollars in rework (compensatory education programs, costs of failure, etc.)
Customer focus and satisfaction	• Conduct community dialogue regarding new demands for work, civic, and personal life • Discuss distinction between information accumulation and understanding	• Work with community to accommodate new learning schedules • Look deeply at student growth, not just their opinions • Be responsive in solving problems (phones, voice mail)	• Establish an ongoing process to determine future needs • See that community is delighted

Note: TQM = total quality management; NBPTS = National Board of Professional Teaching Standards.

Souce: Randy Schenkat.

Faculty recognition of students as customers might reduce the attrition of our customer base."

Middle Management

"The teamwork approach to problem solving was unfamiliar to most of OSU's mid-level managers....Empowering employees to change processes is incompatible with a primarily top-down, authoritarian, command-and-control management style."[18] It is now recognized that managers at OSU were not provided with adequate education early in the process. The result was that some projects failed because traditional management practices were maintained.

University Governance

The focus on committee and task force decision making and faculty empowerment, while basic principles of total quality, can also be major detriments. The transition from task force or committee to total quality team is not entirely smooth, and "many subunits are accustomed to 'doing their own thing' without reference to the overall institutional mission and vision."[19]

Dysfunctional Units

All units, or work groups, fall somewhere along a continuum between functional and dysfunctional. The experience at OSU demonstrated that the total quality process will not heal a dysfunctional unit. It will bring hidden problems to the surface, perhaps intensifying them. Such a unit must be helped toward healing before initiating any total quality activities. Organizational development interventions were found to be beneficial at OSU.

Attitude

Such attitudes as "looking for the big and/or quick fix," "we don't need this, we have our act together," "it's new so we don't trust it," and "just try to change us" represent constraints to implementing any change in an individual and are exponentially more difficult in an organization.

For additional information, see Abstract 8.4 at the end of this chapter.

WILL TOTAL QUALITY WORK IN HIGHER EDUCATION?

Barriers are part of any change, but some are compounded in college and universities because of the nature, purpose, and culture of higher education. Therefore, can total quality ultimately be successful in the academy? The answer at OSU is an absolute *yes.*[20]

> OSU has seen results. Processes have been improved, saving time, material, and money. Employees have learned and used team-building and problem-solving skills. Job satisfaction and morale have increased as managers implemented TQM team recommendations.

> Most importantly, customers have been satisfied—often delighted—by the improvements TQM produced. In many areas of the university, numbers begin to tell the story. For example: turnaround time for students' financial aid documents decreased by more than 40 days; average duration of building remodeling jobs was cut by 45 days; the staff benefits office increased by 30 percent the number of immediate "human" responses to employee phone calls.

To accomplish these and other beneficial results, Coate[21] suggests six key recommendations for the successful implementation of total quality in a college or university:

- *Support from the top.* A firm commitment from the president or CEO is essential. Deming believes this to be the single most important factor.
- *Just do it!* "Don't study it to death. Learn about the steps the teams go through and get one started. Only then will you understand what TQM is all about and whether it will fit into your culture."
- *Teams are everything!* "Focusing teams on process improvement is what it is all about." Teams must have adequate training, but should be empowered to make process decisions and should be

responsible for what is decided. "The Hawthorne effect is prevalent at first, but the TQM process will see that solutions get implemented. Team building is almost as important as process improvement."

- *You need a champion.* "Implementation of TQM takes a long commitment (five years), a lot of time (up to 20 percent), and costs money (at least 60K/year)." Someone has to be the champion to get it going, keep it going, and make sure solutions are implemented.
- *Breakthrough (Hoshin) planning helps.* Identifying and clarifying the mission and vision, the customers, and the critical processes and priority breakthrough items helps to establish vertical alignment, integrate strategic planning processes already underway, and focus efforts on processes that can really make a difference.
- *Try the service or administrative side first.* It is easier to start here than on the academic side. "Start with a unit that is having trouble; they know they need help and will appreciate being helped. You need early success to get the momentum going."

ENDNOTES

1. An admonition from Machiavelli's *The Prince,* given by Donald Langenberg in his inaugural address as the Chancellor of the University of Maryland System in Baltimore on June 26, 1991.
2. Hargrove, Erwin (1975). *The Missing Link: The Study of Implementation of Social Policy.* Washington, D.C.: Urban Institute, p. 23.
3. Lewis, Ralph G. and Greene, Jack R. (1978). "Implementation Evaluation: A Future Direction in Project Evaluation." *Journal of Criminal Justice,* Vol. 6, No. 2, Summer 1978.
4. Coate, L. Edwin (1992). *Total Quality Management at Oregon State University.* Corvallis: Oregon State University, p. 6.
5. Initially presented in *Competitive Times,* Vol. I, 1990 (Methuen, Mass.: Goals/QPC); cited in Coate, L. Edwin (1992). *Total Quality Management at Oregon State University.* Corvallis: Oregon State University, p. 7; modifications and additions were also made for this chapter.
6. Coate, L. Edwin (July 1990). *Implementing Total Quality Management in a University Setting.* Corvallis: Oregon State University, pp. 7–21.
7. Coate, L. Edwin (July 1990). *Implementing Total Quality Management in a University Setting.* Corvallis: Oregon State University, p. 12.
8. Coate, L. Edwin (July 1990). *Implementing Total Quality Management in a University Setting.* Corvallis: Oregon State University, p. 16.

9. Coate, L. Edwin (November 1990). *An Analysis of Oregon State University's Total Quality Management Pilot Program.* Corvallis: Oregon State University, p. 23.
10. Coate, L. Edwin (1992). *Total Quality Management at Oregon State University.* Corvallis: Oregon State University, p. 18.
11. Coate, L. Edwin (July 1990). *Implementing Total Quality Management in a University Setting.* Corvallis: Oregon State University, p. 21.
12. Coate, L. Edwin (1992). *Total Quality Management at Oregon State University.* Corvallis: Oregon State University, p. 20.
13. Coate, L. Edwin (1992). *Total Quality Management at Oregon State University.* Corvallis: Oregon State University, p. 20.
14. Coate, L. Edwin (1992). *Total Quality Management at Oregon State University.* Corvallis: Oregon State University, p. 24.
15. Coate, L. Edwin (1992). *Total Quality Management at Oregon State University.* Corvallis: Oregon State University, p. 37.
16. Coate, L. Edwin (1992). *Total Quality Management at Oregon State University.* Corvallis: Oregon State University, pp. 37–41.
17. Coate, L. Edwin (1992). *Total Quality Management at Oregon State University.* Corvallis: Oregon State University, p. 38.
18. Coate, L. Edwin (1992). *Total Quality Management at Oregon State University.* Corvallis: Oregon State University, p. 39.
19. Coate, L. Edwin (1992). *Total Quality Management at Oregon State University.* Corvallis: Oregon State University, p. 40.
20. Coate, L. Edwin (1992). *Total Quality Management at Oregon State University.* Corvallis: Oregon State University, p. 7.
21. Coate, L. Edwin (July 1990). *Implementing Total Quality Management in a University Setting.* Corvallis: Oregon State University, pp. 21–22.
22. Figure 8.1 ©1992 Strategy Associates, Inc.

ABSTRACTS

ABSTRACT 8.1   THE NEW SOCIETY OF ORGANIZATIONS

Drucker, Peter F.
Harvard Business Review (HBR), Vol. 70, Issue 5, Sep./Oct. 1992, pp. 95–104

The author begins this article with gusto in the opening sentences of the first five paragraphs: "Every few hundred years throughout Western history, a sharp transformation has occurred. In a matter of decades, society altogether rearranges itself—its world view, its basic values, its social and political structures, its arts, its key institutions." Recent American history is such a period of transformation, beginning with the (G.I.) Bill of Rights, which provided to each American soldier returning from World War II money to attend a university, something that Drucker feels would have made no sense at the end of World War I. This signaled the shift to a knowledge-based society, in which land, labor, and capital have become secondary and knowledge is the product. For Drucker's managers, the dynamics of knowledge imposes one clear imperative: each organization must build the management of change into its very structure. Each organization must learn to exploit its knowledge in order to develop the next generation of applications from its own successes. And it must learn to innovate.

If the organization is to perform, it must be organized as a team. For more than 600 years, no society has had as many competing centers of power as the one in which we now live. Change is the only constant in the life of an organization. Drucker, as always, is the master storyteller, with his tales of Japanese business development (the soccer team), the Prussian army vs. Henry Ford's assembly line (models of teams), PTAs at suburban schools (perfunctory management), university freedom (the autonomous centers of power), who will take care of the common good (unresolved problems of the pluralistic society), and the failure of socialism/communism (leading to cohesion of power in knowledge-based organizations). This is Drucker's thirtieth article for this journal and undoubtedly one of his best.

ABSTRACT 8.2   GETTING STARTED WITH TQM

Freeston, Kenneth R.
Educational Leadership (GEDL), Nov. 1992, pp. 10–13

The total quality improvement efforts of the Newtown, Connecticut public school system provide an excellent case study for those who are not satisfied with prepackaged total quality management. Intrigued by the works of Deming and Glasser, Newtown wanted a system that acknowledged the psychological aspects of change and emphasized the work process. Citing the importance of knowledge and the need for a set of core beliefs, the Newtown Quality Council began to collect information, develop alternative forms of student assessment, and form teams of teachers to establish performance standards.

A mission statement was then developed, acknowledging that every student has unlimited and multiple abilities. Five of their objectives are given: (1) become a self-directed learner, (2) achieve cognitively and master the curriculum, (3) acquire process skills, (4) show concern for others, and (5) know the importance of self-esteem. The thinking has changed in Newtown over the past two years, and that new way of thinking is guided by their quality model. New teachers spend a week in training during the summer, and quality core groups in each school address quality issues. Adhering to Deming's principle of continuous improvement, however, they now seek to apply quality management techniques to problem solving at all levels of the school system. Although not specifically developed for colleges and universities, this case study provides insight for educators who want to implement total quality management. Selected references, concise graphs, and an exhibit showing barriers to total quality are provided.

ABSTRACT 8.3   QUALITY MANAGEMENT: A TEN-POINT MODEL

Heymann, Kenneth
Cornell H.R.A. Quarterly, Oct. 1992, pp. 51–60

In reading through various recent articles on quality management (QM), it seems that most are driven by a focus on one of three components of the QM process: (1) the importance of establishing and using standards, (2) the need for quality teams or circles, and (3) the value of empowering employees. The author points out, however, that most approaches offer a singular method which, standing alone, does not provide an appropriate long-term solution for all organizations. What is lacking is a flexible model that allows each organization to tailor the process to its unique circumstance and can serve as a guideline for future action.

Creating and maintaining organization-wide effectiveness requires an integrated approach that involves ten key components. While improving any single component may lead to better performance, a comprehensive organizational transformation requires action on all ten: (1) establish a culture of quality, (2) develop a team orientation, (3) develop leadership skills, (4) develop customer-driven policies and procedures, (5) set standards, (6) develop human resources, (7) plan for quality, (8) build systems to measure achievement, (9) evaluate performance, and (10) build reward and recognition systems.

The first three elements make up the informal components of an organizational response to quality management. They address the basic aspects of how people work together to accomplish their goals and objectives. The remaining seven deal with the systems and procedures used in day-to-day operations of the organization.

Each of the points is discussed in detail, and any one can serve as an appropriate place to start. Although originally written for the hospitality industry (and published in the Cornell Business School's *H.R.A. Quarterly*), the framework is useful for universities to consider as well. No references are provided.

ABSTRACT 8.4   TEN STEPS TO TQM PLUS

Kaufman, Roger; Hirumi, Atsusi
Educational Leadership (GEDL), Nov. 1992, pp. 33–34

"History is filled with examples of products and services that have satisfied individuals but, in the long run, proved to be unhealthy for society." DDT and leaded gas are only two such examples. The same is true for education. A 100 percent rate of graduating students who cannot find jobs is also a social failure of the university or school. The authors point out that piecemeal interventions within the current educational system have done little to increase productivity or usefulness. They discuss a new world that needs to begin with the "ideal vision" and offer a ten-step process for integrating social and environmental concerns into total quality management for the university or school. References are provided.

ARTICLES

MEETING THE CHALLENGE TO EDUCATION: AN INSTITUTIONAL RESPONSE*

Randy Schenkat

Change is not made without inconvenience, even from worse to better.
Hooker, cited by Samuel Johnson in the Preface to *English Dictionary*.

In the preceding chapters we have tried to present a strong case for a development-based, liberal-arts-oriented, teacher-education program; it includes mutually agreed-upon outcomes that are built into the syllabi of courses, not only in the teacher-education programs but, also, in the whole liberal arts curriculum. There is strong documentation of the need for this type of program. We also offer rational arguments for adopting the programs on other campuses. Most of the material in the appendixes are actual instructional packages for use by both faculty and students.

In this chapter, we take a look at the prospects of introducing needed changes in teacher-education programs throughout the country. At the College of Saint Teresa, the innovative efforts were grant dependent essentially; three major funding sources supported the projects to the extent of approximately $10,000 per faculty member.

The changes occurred at CST, however, mainly because faculty members were willing to operate in roles that went beyond the typical job description. For instance, a job description may call for the teaching of, say, eight courses per year and require attendance at departmental meetings and participation in college committees, but it does not call for extensive collaboration with peers within and across departments. At CST, the grant money bought the time for faculty members to work together summers to plan workshops or to give up a day or a half-day per month to work on project-related material. This is akin to the practices in public schools to develop staff members in curriculum and instruction by paying them on an hourly rate over and above the contract provisions or to provide substitute teacher days to make time for innovations.

*Reproduced from *It Stands to Reason*, published by the author, pp. 41–45.

Undertakings such as those at CST serve as model sites for how an innovative program can be accomplished. Publications, such as this book, can document situational facilitators as well as barriers to the innovation and become part of the collective body of knowledge on organizational change. It is assumed that people at forward-looking institutions will explore the possibilities of replicating the CST experience. It is also assumed that at some point the magic of the free market will influence students' preferences for institutions that incorporate forward-looking programs. Unfortunately, however, things do not work out exactly that way. (a) Good programs—even programs that are very good—seldom have a direct influence on the criteria students use to select colleges, and (b) hardly any institutions of higher education are able to command enough resource and development funds to pay faculty members for the time they spend in helping to bring about significant new modes of operations.

RELATIONS TO CORPORATE EXCELLENCE

The changes that occurred in the teacher-education program at CST, especially during the first three years of the project funding, were made possible by factors that parallel those responsible for the success of many American corporations (see Peters & Waterman, *In Search of Excellence*). These factors are as follows:

1. A bias for action.
2. Close to the customer.
3. Autonomy and entrepreneurship.
4. Productivity through people.
5. Hands-on, value driven.
6. Stick to the knitting.
7. Simple form, lean staff.
8. Simultaneous loose-tight properties (p. 13–15).

Parallels can be drawn between these factors or characteristics and the operations of the Department of Education at CST under the Dean's Grant project. The characteristics also can be juxtaposed to current operating conditions in schools, colleges, and departments of education at other institutions of higher education. The juxtaposition reveals an almost antithetical state between organizational characteristics of successful corporations and the current structures of education units.

At CST, "a bias for action" was demonstrated in the conduct of the project. A great deal was accomplished in three years through many faculty workshops and meetings and the collaborative efforts of faculty members. Perhaps grant timelines, which are often bemoaned by faculty members and administrators ("Project Director! You're trying to push us too fast! Don't you know change evolves?"), could collapse further. Typical teacher-education units often move more slowly. For example, they relegate problems to committees that may study the theoretical nature of one problem for a year, just as a starter. Successful companies, however, if they take an analytical approach to decision making, are not made inactive by the process.

> A Digital Equipment corporation senior executive says, for example—when we've got a big problem here, we grab ten senior guys and stick them in a room for a week. They come up with an answer and implement it. (Peters & Waterman, 1982, p. 13)

Excellent companies have techniques to maintain this fleetness of operations. To what degree is quick action important in teacher-education units? What must change to create conditions in which unit managers will allow their staffs to work with fleetness? These questions are central to teacher-education improvement.

The operations of the Education Department at CST was "close to the consumer" in that much of the redesign of the program was directed to maximizing teacher-education candidates' performances (e.g., using course audits, focusing on student-learner outcomes, adhering to a mastery model, and carefully interrelating course units). The external advisory committee of teachers and administrators that focused attention on K-12 schooling needs was another line to stay close to the consumer.

Currently, teacher-education facilities often distance themselves from their customers. At a campus level, the distancing occurs because of large lecture-type classes. At the K-12 school level, often it is only the lowest ranking faculty members or graduate students who supervise clinical and student-teaching experiences. In contrast, many innovative companies admittedly get their best product ideas by regularly and intently listening to the concerns of customers.

Staying close to the customer reflects a practice that is "value driven." In education, this would mean that the entire department has a common vision of what a good teacher should be and everyone contributes to realizing this vision. Project PRISE "stuck close to the knitting" of the Education Department because the "knitting" was to provide sound, regular education teacher preparation. Few add-ons were brought into the program at the time that Dean's Grants nationally were adding large quantities of content; rather, the delivery of instruction to students was refined and improved.

Research rather than "sticking" to the collective "knitting" of the unit is what is valued in many education programs. Indeed, college faculty members are reinforced to pursue individual professional interests, which often means narrow areas of academic specialization. There seems to be no common value base for faculty members and no common vision of what an institution's teachers should represent. Education management seems to be in a condition of anarchy because so much autonomy is vested in each faculty position, as if academic freedom had no other meaning.

Perhaps teacher education should be staffed by more teaching generalists who understand and can demonstrate good teaching and stay in touch with current practice. Faculty members need to go beyond intellectualizing and inculcating knowledge; they must be able to demonstrate performance. The research on coaching (Showers & Joyce, 1983) document this compelling need.

Significant research ventures might well be left to centers of collaboration by IHEs, state departments of education, and local education agencies. A premium should be placed on the application of significant research practices in both teacher-education units and school buildings, and experiences should be traded back and forth. Unfortunately, in many institutions published research, no matter how minor or impractical, is the only key to administrative recognition for promotion of salary increases. How much more efficient and productive it would be if all research was considered to be departmental rather than individual undertakings, and local resources and expertise contributed to the work!

Project PRISE was strengthened by adhering to "productivity through people." In an era when Dean's Grant projects commonly patronized the mainstreaming speaker's bureau, PRISE helped to develop its own "experts." Workshops were conducted by faculty members who found the experiences job-enhancing. It is ironic that faculty members who often supplement their incomes by outside consulting are seldom asked to serve as consultants on their own campuses.

PRISE also reflected what in organizational parlance is called "simple form." That is, no hierarchy was established and individuals were not distanced from each other; instead, faculty members formed an integrated work team with a high degree of interdependence. The difficulty in achieving the latter has been referred to under the characteristic "stick to the knitting." It is elaborated here in relation to the "course oriented" approach to teacher education.

Over time, courses take on an independent life; their relations to all other courses become obscured and regarded as administrative rather than programmatic. Each instructor tends to envision the course he/she teaches as an end in itself. In addition, each instructor tries to cover material which he/she considers essential for understanding key concepts that are interesting in themselves, indicative of the research and/or development in the area, and, perhaps useful for the student to know. Because course time is limited, more and more materials tend to be mentioned in passing or left for outside readings. Some instructors worry about whether it is more productive to expose students to a great deal of information which is not presented in depth or to the intensive study of central areas and key ideas.

Each instructor tends to hold students responsible only for the content covered in her/his course(s), which also simplifies the construction of tests. At the same time, the stress on courses rather than on a curricular body of knowledge seems to encourage students to regard each course as a discrete offering. For example, some proportion of students inevitably do not relate the theories of learning studied in educational psychology to the content of methods courses because they have no incentive to do so. However, if first-year students are aware that the content covered in, for example, the introductory psychology course will be directly drawn from in later courses, the relevance of the earlier material is thoroughly established. So, too, if instructors of first-year courses know that subsequent instructors will hold students accountable for previously learned material, the course content may be presented as part of the comprehensive curriculum and not as a separate area of knowledge. The focus of instruction must become how much students are able to master successfully rather than how much content can be crammed into allotted time periods.

Finally, Project PRISE supported "risk-taking." The impetus for the project, and the feature emphasized to the CST administration, was that the separate courses in learning disabilities could be eliminated and their content infused in the regular teacher-preparation sequences. This idea was palatable to the administration because it reduced the need for half of one faculty position. Although the infusion measure was acknowledged to be best for students it was also the most potentially problematic in dealing with state certification sections on the documentation of mainstreaming requirements. Another risk taken by PRISE was to focus on reasoning. As a rule, there is little in an institution's environment to support or encourage risk taking.

In organizational theory, the qualities found in excellent corporations reflect an open systems model in which a unit interacts with its environment's "input and output" ends to optimize the unit's function. Perhaps the environments surrounding teacher education are not in a sufficient state of flux to encourage this kind of interaction. Nevertheless, it is possible that many of the issues in teacher-education quality today can be related to the inability of the training organization to respond to the external environment.

The qualities of excellent corporations are in vogue today. However, the underlying wisdom that went into the generation of National Council on Accreditation of Teacher Education (NCATE) standards reflects a sense of the importance of corporate qualities. Standards call for a common vision in the design of curriculums. Faculty members are urged to stay close to the customer, and so on. Perhaps the frustration with standards that are meant to improve organization practices arises from the organizational constraints on working to achieve the standards. The costly time-consuming NCATE process basically reflects this process when it functions at a superficial yet voluminous and masking level.

In the current movement for excellence in American education, schools, colleges and departments of education are realizing that organizational considerations may be shutting them out of the local school inservice market. Teacher-education units in the past have offered campus-based courses or MA-degree programs for individuals who sought to advance on school districts' salary schedules. Today, however, schools are seen as the focal point of change. Needs for improvement are seen as specific to the building with a high degree of collegiality necessary to bring about the changes. Knowledge inculcation, the traditional university role, has some part in improvement but coaching to permit the application of that knowledge, and modification of building conditions to allow the use of the knowledge, and so on, are also needed. The university expertise, consequently, is only a small part of the improvement equation. Furthermore, in the institutions of higher education's reward systems, a low value generally has been placed on inservice. Faculty members obviously need incentives to get them into the field and to provide the depth of clinical training that will be useful to a school. So forward-looking institutions are seeking this change; without it, districts will turn more and more to developing their own training capabilities or hiring consultants that are not associated with IHEs.

If the characteristics of excellence in successful corporations bear replication in education, then teacher-education units should be moving to acquire the organizational conditions that permit their adoption. B. O. Smith (1980) suggested that current funding dictates an academic rather than a clinical form of pedagogy, that is, the use of lectures rather than clinical instruction, student evaluations on normative rather than absolute standards, emphasis on faculty research rather than teaching and supervision, and eclectic curriculums based on faculty specializations rather than professional training emphases. If members of schools, colleges, and departments of education pursue modifications of funding conditions in today's higher education climate, strong allies will be needed to support the adoption of changes. Externally, many organizations and lobbying groups have important stakes in teacher-education improvement. Rallying the support of professional associations and parent and citizen organizations is paramount.

Internally, in institutions of higher education, teacher-education units seeking and receiving a higher level of resources would make their gains at the expense of other academic units. In situations of limited governance or shared governance in teacher-education units, it is unlikely that no matter how compelling the argument, low-status teacher education would not be funded. If one accepts the fundamental similarities of the characteristics of success, in any profession—cognitive, interpersonal, and motivational skills (see Klemp, 1977)—then the problems of quality preparation in teacher education are very similar to those in any other profession. Rather than pitting disciplines against each other in win-loss situations, perhaps it is time for broad reform efforts to benefit all contributors to undergraduate education. The following two suggestions may be useful:

1. Institutions of higher education need to shift focus from "course orientation" to student outcomes to prepare graduates to join the fellowship of educated citizens. CST's Desirable Characteristics list suggests some potential outcomes. Then it becomes the responsibility of faculty members to be cognizant of these outcomes and to develop courses around their attainment rather than to the attainment of narrowly defined knowledge accumulation.

Furthermore, educational institutions should be obligated to measure their success by their graduates' ability to perform in the workplace, which would reflect the attainment of the institution's desired outcomes. This goal places a significant demand on the total institution and on individual faculty skills to evaluate students in terms of the outcomes desired. The CST model of evaluation suggests that perhaps only 50% of a student's learning would be reflected in traditional paper-pencil measures.

2. Extensive faculty development programs should be conducted in all institutions of higher education to develop proficiencies in teaching to a student development orientation and to evaluating students for outcomes. At CST, the understanding of college student cognitive development (e.g., the Perry and other models) has been an enlightening and rewarding experience for many faculty members. It is not an overgeneralization to suggest that most college faculty members are frustrated in teaching undergraduates precisely because they have never thought in terms of students' levels of cognitive development or of the instructional implications. The research reports gathered by the Perry network is beginning to offer very concrete suggestions to college instructors to make their experiences with undergraduates richer and more rewarding.

The notions of coaching and collegiality—central to public school improvement—have great relevance in higher education. Although at CST faculty members attended large group presentations on the Perry model of student development and considered the presentations highly interesting and rewarding, it was the chance to work in small groups that supported and sustained growth in instructional processes.

In an organizational sense, conditions must be created to allow faculty members to work within and across disciplines to learn to use new skills. Some universities have instructional improvement programs. Where such programs do not exist, Hufker (1980) has found that teacher-education units can serve productively as leaders in faculty development efforts.

It is unlikely that the directions of future changes, given the increasing complexity of society, will allow higher education to stay only at the knowledge-dispensing level. At CST, the synthesizing of three disparate grants melded the college's instruction into a developmental program for preparing teachers to be both professionals and citizens in the 21st century. The need for other preparation programs to move in this direction is pressing. It stands to reason.

CHAPTER 9

ISO 9000 in TRAINING and EDUCATION:
A VIEW to the FUTURE

Richard Freeman

Frank Voehl

PROLOGUE: THE COMING OF THE GLOBAL UNIVERSITY MARKETPLACE

Throughout history, most training and educational institutions have served only their local geographic regions, and their financial support has usually come from local or national public funds. All that is changing, as evidenced by two signs. The first is the development of global training and education markets. A student routinely travels thousands of miles for an MBA course. Also, satellite links are commonly used to join student and tutor across half the world. The second sign is the decreasing role of public funds, as governments push once public organizations to seek other sources of funding.[1] Training and education are becoming market oriented and are on the way to becoming market driven. Companies such as Motorola, Xerox, IBM, Procter & Gamble, G.E., and others are educating their executives and workers informally.[2]

Once competition enters the higher education market, each provider must find ways to distinguish the service it offers from that of its competitors. A competitive advantage must be identified. Some will seek that edge through providing special courses or facilities, others by providing flexible programs, and yet others by reducing price while adding value. Most, however, will have no option but to compete on the basis of quality.

While all providers undoubtedly like to think of themselves as supplying a quality service, any provider who complacently assumes that quality will somehow materialize will rapidly be overtaken by those who listen to the market. Only those providers who consciously strive to meet the demands of their markets will survive. What does strive mean? What it does not mean is expecting to be rewarded for hard work. The market rewards results, not effort. Clearly, striving for quality means working in some way which more effectively delivers results. Tom Peters would call this customer delight.

OVERVIEW

ISO 9000 Defined

What is ISO 9000? Let us start by first defining ISO as a term. According to Sprow,[3] it is short for *isos*, the Greek term for equal, homogeneous, or uniform—a deliberate transformation of the acronym for the International Organization for Standardization (IOS). This was done deliberately because IOS sounds too much like chaos, and the word order may be changed in different languages. One observer has quipped that ISO 9000 stands for International Strategic Opportunity for the '90s, which it certainly might be. (It sounds a bit like the transliteration of the Union of Japanese Scientists and Engineers into the acronym known as JUSE.)

Quality by Consensus

ISO 9000 began with the launch of Technical Committee 176 in 1979 to deal with generic quality principles—the need for an international minimum standard for how manufacturing companies establish quality control methods, not only to control product quality, but to maintain its uniformity and predictability. Customers wanted assurance that in the new world market—whether buying telephones, bread, wheat, or widgets—they would receive reliable quality for their money, today, tomorrow, or next year.

Twenty actively participating countries and half again as many additional observer countries met and created (by consensus) a series of quality system management standards called ISO 9000, which were finally issued in 1987. They were based in large part on the 1979 British quality standard BS 5750 as well as the Canadian standard CSA Z299, the American ASQC Z1.15 standard MIL Q 9858A, and to a limited degree on the JUSE-based Deming Prize guidelines.[3]

ISO 9000 was a huge success from day one. It was the first ISO standard to go beyond nuts and bolts and attempt to address management practices. It quickly became the most widely known, widely adopted ISO standard and sold more copies than any standard ISO has ever published. Although voluntary so far, over fifty countries have adopted it as a national standard. According to a recent survey, 82 percent of blue-chip European companies are familiar with its content and 64 percent have initiated action to become registered. Although the numbers on the other side of the Atlantic may not be as high, it is of interest in the United States.[3]

The Interrelationships between Quality Assurance and ISO 9000

To understand the potential impact of ISO 9000 on higher education, it is first necessary to focus on the interrelationship that exists between quality assurance (QA) and ISO 9000. The approach that manufacturing organizations have taken to achieve the quality edge has traditionally been QA. Over the past ten years, QA in the United States has evolved into total quality. Increasingly, training and education organizations are looking to use the same route to capture markets. Total quality involves a systematic approach to identifying market needs and honing working methods to meet those needs. Organizations can develop and implement their own QA and total quality management (TQM) programs, but many prefer to adopt a recognized standard and to seek external approval for their system. In the U.K., BS 5750 is the standard for QA and total quality systems. Internationally, BS 5750 is known as ISO 9000. The two standards are identical, except in name.

Many training and education organizations in Europe have begun to explore how they can adopt this standard; a few have attained the coveted British Standards Institute (BSI) "kite-mark" (certification symbol).[4] The main reason why so few organizations have achieved certification is the fact that BS 5750/ISO 9000 was initially designed for manufacturing industries. Its language and approach are alien to training and education. However, its underlying principles, which concentrate on meeting customer needs, are fully applicable in the new training and education marketplace of the global village. Somehow, then, ISO 9000 must be made applicable to training and education.

The ISO 9000 standards can be adapted for the benefit of teachers and students, without compromising the professional standards which teachers have developed over many years. Many of the consultants on ISO 9000 and TQM, whose backgrounds are in industry, are inadvertently persuading trainers and educators to apply the standard in a manner which is detrimental to good teaching and, hence, to students.[4] A different approach is clearly needed. (Richard Freeman[5] has written a book which provides some detailed guidelines on how BS 5750 can be applied to training and education.)

The ISO 9000 standards are a single system originally designed to cover all manufacturing, later extended to the service industries, and now being used experimentally in training and education. ISO 9000 certification could become a requirement for any university wanting to do business in the international marketplace, even though at this time that notion seems to be a bit of a stretch. While the strains of this stretching of BS 5750/ISO 9000 show all too clearly, it remains a very general set of principles for good management. As such, applying the principles to the teaching/learning process is often difficult. For example, the product of teaching is both the quality of what the student experiences (the teaching) and the outcome (what has been learned). It is easy to monitor the outcome, but very difficult for a quality measurement system to monitor the process. Of the twenty standards (modules) contained in ISO 9000, twelve have direct application, as shown in Figure 9.1.[6]

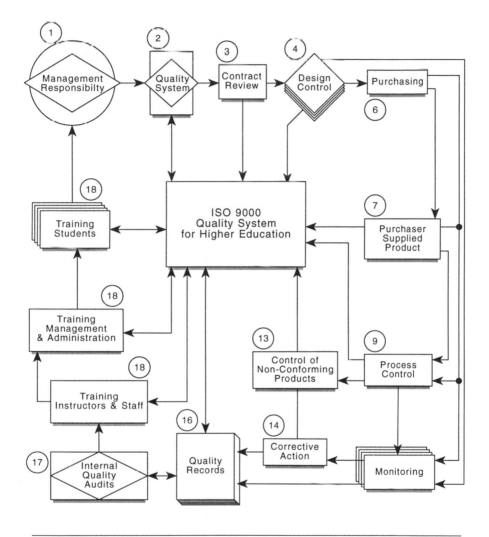

Figure 9.1 Flowchart of ISO 9000 Standards for Higher Education.

Getting a Feel for ISO 9000 Integration

The twenty separate standards (or modules) in the ISO 9000 series are not easy to relate to training and education. Indeed, some have almost no application in teaching and learning. In Figure 9.2, the twelve standards that seem to be highly relevant to the teaching process are related to a simple model for presenting a course.

The following are the ISO 9000 modules that are of particular importance to training and education:[7]

1. Management responsibility
2. Quality system
3. Contract review
4. Design control
6. Purchasing
7. Purchaser-supplied product
9. Process control
13. Control of nonconforming product

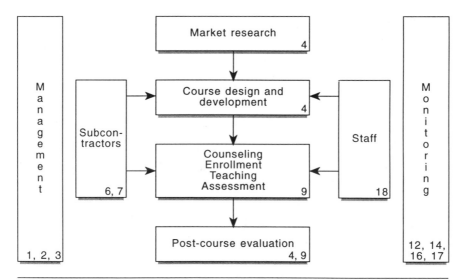

Figure 9.2 Relationship of ISO Standards to the Teaching Process. (Source: Freeman, Richard (1992). *Quality Assurance in Training and Education.* London: Kogan Page Limited.)

14. Corrective action
16. Quality records
17. Internal quality audits
18. Training

Fundamentals of the QA Management System

The words *quality assurance* in the context of total quality have a certain mystique, giving the impression of a complex set of skills which few will ever acquire. The early developers of QA no doubt kept themselves in the consulting business by continuing to foster that image. However, the reality is that QA is a fancy term for any well-run management system. This means that QA is not esoteric, or complex, or beyond the reach of nonspecialists. If it were, what would be the point? Any QA system which is going to work must be simple, fitting comfortably alongside—or even inside—everyday working practice.[8] It must be economical, in that it saves more than it costs, and it must be long lasting.

In essence, total quality involves an approach to organizing work to ensure that:

- The mission and objectives of the organization are clear and communicated to all.
- The systems through which work will be done are well thought out, foolproof as well as possible, and communicated to everyone.
- It is always clear who is responsible for what.
- What the organization regards as quality is well defined and thoroughly documented.
- Measurement systems are in place to verify that everything is working according to plan.
- When things go wrong—and they will—there are proven ways of correcting them.

These management systems can be divided into undocumented, documented and ISO 9000 (QA) type systems.

Undocumented System

In the undocumented system approach, the only way to find out how something is done is to ask someone. "Ask Harry, he always knows." "Try Mary, I think she's done that before." In very small organizations, this can often (although not always) work well, but as organizations grow, this system falls apart. Different people do things differently. Two different admissions officers apply differing admissions criteria. Two trainers find that they have both booked the same room through two conflicting systems. Essentially, the undocumented system is not a system at all. It is a *laissez-faire* approach in which the organization never decides how anything is to be done in a formal way. For many universities, this type of approach has traditionally been a way of life.

Documented System

Most undocumented systems are intensely frustrating and unproductive. Soon, task by task, methods are developed for how things should be done. An enrollment system here, a marking plan there…but do people adhere to these methods? Perhaps—and perhaps not. How would anyone ever know? That is one of the problems with the evolution of documented systems. It is one thing to set down on paper how tasks should be carried out, but quite another to ensure that those intentions become practice.

Additionally, even if a documented system is fairly well observed in practice, it still lacks any means of review and improvement. ISO 9000 overcomes that problem.

ISO 9000 QA Approach

The ISO 9000 QA approach to management is very similar to the documented method, but three essential extras are added:[9]

- A method to monitor how adherence to the system
- A method for correcting mistakes
- A method for changing the system if it has become obsolete

This error-correcting aspect of ISO 9000 is very important. Mistakes and failures will occur, and the ISO 9000 based quality system recognizes that possibility and prepares for it.

Three causes of failure are recognized:

- Human error
- Failure of nput materials
- Obsolescence of the existing method

The quality system carefully distinguishes among these causes. In the first case, the error or omission is corrected; in the second, the material method is amended. ISO 9000 is, therefore, both a self-correcting and a learning system. It changes to reflect changing needs. It is known as a QA rather than a traditional quality control type system.[10] (For additional information, see the Technical Supplements at the end of this chapter).

GETTING STARTED WITH ISO 9000

The Documentation Process

This section provides an overview of the heart of the documentation process for establishing a QA-based ISO 9000 system in the university. Four basic building blocks must be created: (Figure 9.3):

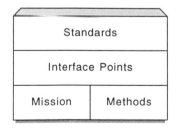

Figure 9.3 Documentation Building Blocks.

- Mission
- Methods
- Interface points
- Standards

Mission

ISO 9000 starts with a clear sense of what the university is to achieve: its mission. Deming calls this Constancy of Purpose. It is a timeless, qualitative statement, such as:

- To be the best provider of qualification courses in our area
- To maintain the highest possible level of repeat business in our area
- To have a reputation for excellence among parents in our area

In a well-established college or training center, it may seem unnecessary to document the mission. "We all know what we do here." "It's obvious what this place is for." Often, however, different individuals have different ideas of the purpose of the organization and where it is heading. It is pointless to install a QA-type ISO 9000 system in an organization which has no shared view of what constitutes success.

In summary, a mission statement is

- A statement of what the university is to achieve—its core purpose
- The vision of where the university will be in ten to twenty years
- The guiding principles and shared values that need to be internalized by all employees
- *Not* a set of objectives or targets

Methods

Once the mission has been agreed upon, QA systems compel the organization to document the methods by which tasks are to be accomplished. It is usually fairly clear what needs to be accomplished in an organization—enroll students, order books, train, clean classrooms—although in new organizations even the list of tasks may be unclear. In more mature organizations, despite superficial order, there may be strongly conflicting views about how each task should be done and, in particular, about who should do it. "No one told me I had to use a marking system. I've always done it my own way."

Essentially, the problems come down to a lack of agreement on:

- What needs to be done—*what*
- The method of doing it—*how*
- Who should do it—*who*

Interface Points

An additional concept in total quality is the interface point. According to quality theory, the critical point at which quality can effectively be assured is the interface between two functions: when person A gives a job to person B. For example:

- An editor gives a prospectus to a printer
- An administrator gives a trainer a list of students for a course
- A student turns in an assignment for assessment

An interface involves a preparer, a receiver, and a task, as illustrated in Figure 9.4. The receiver expects to carry out a particular stage of a process, e.g., teach a group of students. He or she can only do this if someone else first enrolls the students. One of the fundamentals of total quality is that clean handoffs at the interface points between departments or functions are necessary to ensure maximum quality and productivity.

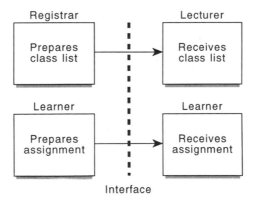

Figure 9.4 Interface Points. (Source: Freeman, Richard (1992). *Quality Assurance in Training and Education.* London: Kogan Page Limited.)

Some examples for education and training are shown in Figure 9.4 and illustrate how routine activities, such as preparing to teach a group or preparing to mark an assignment, depend on some prior work done by someone else. The lecturer cannot teach the group without a list of who is to be in the group. Nor can a lecturer mark an assignment which has not been completed.

This looks a bit abstract before considering what is expected to happen at an interface. The receiver expects that the preparer has done his or her job completely and in the agreed upon manner, because the receiver cannot do his or her job unless the preparer has done the same. Given that this handoff of work from preparer to receiver is so critical to doing a good job, the interface is often called a *critical interface*. By finding all the critical interfaces in an organization, fixing them, monitoring them, and continually improving them, a virtual total quality system is created. (In modern TQM jargon, the receiver is often called an *internal customer* and the preparer an *internal supplier*. However, these terms will not be used here because they are widely disliked by trainers and educators.)

In practice, everyone is both a preparer and a receiver. Few tasks are initiated in isolation by a tutor or trainer. Most involve carrying out the next stage in a sequence of processes.

Standards

As previously stated, the receiver expects that the task will be handed over in a completed state and in the agreed upon form. No instructor will mark half an assignment scribbled illegibly on a dozen old envelopes. Total quality systems assume that there are agreed upon standards and/or formats that define how tasks are handed over. For a class list, the instructor and administrator might agree that:

- The list is complete
- Names, ages, and sexes are accurate
- The list is documented

Meshing these standards is a critical part of setting up a total quality system. The process can often prove controversial, because opinions differ on how well tasks need to be done. One person might insist that all handouts be typeset, while another might think that typewritten (or even handwritten) will suffice. These problems are easily resolved if general agreement exists to use the most common definition of quality: fitness for purpose. This means ensuring that all debates on quality are tested against customer expectations. For example, the professional view of the trainer or lecturer bows to the reality of what purchasing is willing to pay.

The Building Blocks of an ISO 9000 System for Higher Education

As shown in Figure 9.1, twelve of the twenty ISO 9000 modules are considered to be directly applicable to the field of higher education. The following is a brief synopsis of these items.

Module #1: Management Responsibility for Setting Quality Policy

Management responsibility is central to ISO 9000. If there is any suspicion that management—at all levels, including the highest—is not taking the total quality system seriously, then the ISO 9000 assessors will conclude that the system is not effective. This is summarized forcefully in the introduction to ISO 9000:

> The management of a company should develop and state its corporate quality policy. This policy should be consistent with other company policies. Management should take all necessary measures to ensure that its corporate quality policy is understood, implemented and maintained. (BS 5750: Part 0: Section 0.2: 1987)

There is a very practical reason for this insistence on management involvement. Because total quality is itself a management system, and because an organization cannot run with two management systems, an ISO 9000 system can only work with total commitment from senior management.

A key management responsibility of setting up a quality system is defining a quality policy in a form which all employees, students, and stakeholders can use and understand. The policy documentation can be organized into four levels: the basic policy statements, the governing procedures, the work instructions to be followed, and the quality review. To be effective, they must be clear and specific.

Policy Statement

A quality policy statement might cover:

* Who is responsible for setting up and running the system
* How the system is to be monitored and reviewed by management
* For which functions/tasks defined procedures will be written
* How the implementation of those procedures will be monitored
* How failures to adhere to the procedures will be corrected

Procedures

Not everything that a university does can be subject to the full rigor of a quality system. To attempt to do so would be overwhelmingly time consuming. More practically, an organization identifies the functions or tasks where performance *critically affects* the service *as perceived by the users.* (In practice, ISO 9000 compels certain tasks to be covered, as will be explained later.) Meanwhile, an organization might decide that its critical functions are

* Enrollment and counseling
* Curriculum planning
* Assessment
* Research and development
* Learning resources
* Work experience
* Selection and appointment of staff
* Staff development

Procedures would then be written for each of these. A procedure is a clear and systematic method that sets out how a function is to be carried out and who is responsible for each part of it.

Work Instructions

In order for procedures to be easily understood and followed, they must be short and must avoid unnecessary detail. Sometimes, however, more detail is needed to ensure that a job is done in a precise manner. Where this is the case, the extra detail is put into a work instruction. For example, a procedure might contain the paragraph:

> Mini-vans for trips shall be ordered by the trip organizer at least seven days prior to any trip, using Form ABC99.

Form ABC99 then becomes the work instruction which tells the organizer exactly what details are needed and by whom.

The distinction between procedures and work instructions is defined as follows:

Procedures
- Refer to a process that includes many subtasks
- Outline what needs to be done

Work instructions
- Refer to just one task
- Provide detailed guidance on how to complete the task

Quality Review

The final management role is the quality review, which is further emphasized by the self-adjusting nature of total quality systems. The management review is the engine for that process. At its simplest, the review needs to decide:

- What information is needed to be sufficiently certain that the quality policy is being implemented
- What information is needed to decide whether the policy needs amendment
- How frequently these data need to be collected

As ever, it is important to decide what is critical and genuinely indicative of the health of the university. As management requests more data, the less it will be possible to make sense of it. Also, the cost of data collection must be considered. As management requests more data that is not automatically collected as part of day-to-day work, the cost of the quality system will rise. The efficient and economic way to resolve this is to scan the procedures once they have been written in order to identify data that exist in the system that will be of value in assessing the overall health of the university system. There will, however, be two types of data:

- Operational data, e.g., course completion rates, award rates, absentee rates, repeat business rates
- Total quality system data, e.g., percentage of audits completed on time

The management review should contain a sensible balance between the two. Enough data should be provided to assure management that nothing *critical* could be going wrong, but no more.

The Quality System Loop

A final way to check on the role of management is to examine the quality loop and determine whether everything has been included. Because the basic loop in ISO 9000 is difficult to interpret for training and education, Figure 9.5 is provided as a preliminary model to be used as a springboard for discussion.[11]

Module #2: The Quality System

It is one thing to have a policy, but quite another to turn it into a system that can deliver that policy. It is the responsibility of management to devise, promulgate, and monitor such a system. In one sense, everything that is done as part of the ISO 9000 system is part of the quality system, but here we are looking at the specification of that system and the documentation that goes with it.

Where does management start? It starts with the age-old question, "What kind of a business are we really in?" and then with the new total quality question, "What is really critical?"

These two questions must be asked and carefully answered in order to (a) avoid an inappropriate application of ISO 9000 (designed for manufacturing) to training and education and (b) prevent the system from tackling irrelevant detail. *For a total quality system to work well, it is essential that it concentrate on the those items which make a difference.* What might these be? Each university is different, but the following areas might prove critical in most training and education organizations:

- How market needs are identified
- How needs are turned into curriculum or course specifications

Figure 9.5 Quality System Loop for Higher Education. (Source: Freeman, Richard (1992). *Quality Assurance in Training and Education*. London: Kogan Page Limited.)

- How students are recruited and counseled
- How student progress is monitored
- How student achievement is assessed
- How staff are selected
- How staff are developed
- How courses (rather than individual students) are evaluated

Once such a list has been compiled (almost certainly by a bottom-up process involving staff and students at all levels), it is management's job to decide which items are critical and, therefore, for which there will be a quality policy. Most organizations make this initial list too long.

Once a list of critical functions has been prepared, a policy is needed. This will set out in broad terms management's quality approach to each function, e.g., the policy for student recruitment and counseling might be:

> All prospective learners shall receive written details of the courses in which they have expressed interest. These details shall include: the prior knowledge and skills assumed for the course, the course aims and objectives, the learning time, the methods of assessment, the qualification awarded and career/training routes available at the end of the course. Before enrolling, each learner shall be interviewed by an admissions' counselor.[11]

This is a policy statement and is, therefore, short on operational detail. For each functions that has been identified as critical, the policy statement will be followed by a detailed written operational procedure. Although the quality policy should be regularly reviewed, it should not be full of transient detail which requires frequent updating. The goal should be a balance between a policy that is too vague to be meaningful and one that is too detailed.

Module #3: Contract Review

The term *contract review* comes from BS 5750 and is a typical example of manufacturing terminology that is difficult to translate into training and education. In manufacturing, it is common for the manufacturer to make something which has been very precisely commissioned by a customer (often another manufacturer or an assembly company). Hence, most of the work of manufacturers is dominated by contracts which specify what is to be produced and define quality. In training and education, the situation is often less clearly defined.

As with any part of BS 5750, implementation is required only insofar as it is relevant to the nature of the organization and the needs of its customers. Consider the case of a training supplier that has received a contract to supply a program of training for a group of supervisors. BS 5750 then obliges the supplier to carry out the following tasks:

- Make sure that the customer's requirement is "adequately defined and documented"
- Account for any specification changes that the customer may have made to the original requirements
- Check that the organization has the resources to fulfill the contract

- Check that enough detail has been provided for:
  - The learners and their current skills and knowledge
  - The learning outcomes they are to achieve
  - When and where they will be available for teaching and learning
  - The resources to be supplied by the client, etc.
- Ensure that the latest understanding of the requirement is in writing and signed by the client
- Verify that appropriate resources are available, such as:
  - Staff with the proper skills
  - Registration with the appropriate awarding body
  - Appropriate training rooms
  - Appropriate learning materials, etc.

Module #4: Design Control

In training and education, the design process is course planning, including the preplanning necessary for teaching the course. All trainers and teachers would avow their personal commitment to promising a quality service. Quality assurance goes beyond that promise to seek methods by which the quality can be systematically guaranteed rather than arise solely from personal commitment. Nowhere is that assurance more important than in the design stage. If an organization plans the wrong course or develops the wrong course content, whatever the quality of the delivery, the course will still be wrong. Given the tendency of trainers and educators to take a teacher-driven view of their work, this is doubly important for an effective design system.

The main purpose of the design system is to take the identified needs of the identified customer and develop a way of meeting them. Anything which will be used to meet the customer's needs and must be designed is covered by this section. This could include:

- Curriculum plans
- Course plans
- Handouts
- Learning materials
- Assessment materials
- Work placements
- Course visits

ISO 9000 identifies five aspects of design control:

- Design and development planning—deciding who does what in the design system
- Design input—making sure the designers know what the customer wants
- Design output—being clear about the final form the plans should take
- Design verification—checking that the design solution is acceptable to the customer
- Design changes—having a system to ensure that any changes to the design are approved by the appropriate people

Module #6: Purchasing

Assuming that part-time instructors are considered "staff" rather than "suppliers," only a small range of items are covered in this module (part-time instructors will be covered in Module #18):

- Learning materials
- Consultants
- External examiners and assessors
- Awarding body services

For each of the above, the organization needs to consider:

- The standard of performance required
- The selection process
- The records the supplier is to keep
- The resulting list of approved suppliers

Module #7: Purchaser-Supplied Product

The two general areas where this may apply are the supply of materials and the supply of equipment. Basically, the following tasks may apply:

- Ensuring that the correct items have been supplied on time and in usable condition

- Storing and retrieving items safely
- Reporting lost or damaged goods

Module #9: Process Control

The key to this module is to view the "teaching and learning process" from the customer's point of view. To apply this section to training and education, what constitutes *process* must first be identified. The heart of process is everything normally referred to as teaching, training, tutoring, and assessment. This comprises a wide range of activities, including:

- Teaching (the presentation of material)
- Tutoring (assisting individual students with learning difficulties)
- Feedback to the student
- Monitoring student progress
- Adjusting the course to individual progress and needs (or moving the student on to some other course)
- Assessment of the student
- Maintaining suitable records of progress

In other words, anything which teachers are expected to do during the teaching process (as opposed to the preparation process or the evaluation stage) and which is critical to quality is covered by process control. In this context, a process control list for training and education would have to cover:

- Standards for staff selection, e.g., the required qualifications
- How the continuing relevance of staff skills is monitored
- How staff development needs are met

Additionally, it must be determined which of the following processes need formal control:

- Teaching methods
- Tutoring methods
- How feedback is given to students
- How student progress is monitored
- How checks are made to ensure that student needs are still being met

- How students are assessed
- Which student records are kept

In each case, the following are being decided (in addition to whether to control that function at all):

- Is a work instruction needed for this function, e.g., a specified student record format
- Do when and how often a function will be carried need to be specified, e.g., students will be assessed at least once a month
- Does the standard to which something should be done need to be specified

Module #10: Control of Nonconforming Product

This is a rather difficult area to define in ISO 9000 terms, except if students are classified as "products," in which case students who have failed tests and assessments would be included. Other items could include:

- Damaged or out-of-date books
- Teaching material that does not conform to the syllabus
- Incorrect assessment items

ISO 9000 requires that the university take the appropriate steps to ensure that such items are not used for teaching, such as marking them out of date.

Module #17: Internal Quality Audits

The quality policy and the procedures can be well prepared, but this does not guarantee that they will be followed. Auditing is the means by which the organization verifies that the procedures have been implemented. Regular checks (audits) are made in a specific and systematic manner to identify whether or not adherence to the procedures exists. This inevitably involves the potentially threatening process of interviewing the people doing the work, who can easily assume that they are being inspected. However, this is not the case at all. This impression has to be regularly dispelled by reminding everyone involved that it is the procedure that is being audited, not the person.

The entire management review system and the self-improvement nature of total quality systems demand that the system be continually checked to determine whether it is performing according to plan. This checking process is called *auditing*, because the methods it uses are very similar to those in financial auditing.

Auditing works by regularly checking each procedure to determine whether the work is being done as set out in the statement. Any deviations are recorded as *noncompliances*, which then have to be corrected. The process of adjusting a noncompliance is called *corrective action*.

Through the quality management system, a timetable is drawn up which ensures that all procedures are audited on a regular basis. For example, the most important procedures might be audited once a year, while less important ones are audited once in two or three years.

One or more auditors are appointed for each procedure. When it is time to audit that procedure, the auditor visits the section that uses the procedure and, in an auditing meeting, works step by step through each statement in the procedure to check for evidence that the step has been applied.

It is at this point that the difference between good and bad procedures can often become apparent. In a bad procedure, precisely what evidence constitutes compliance may be very unclear. In a good procedure, the nature of evidence of compliance should be obvious. For example, "The trainer shall agree to a list of performance outcomes with the students" is vague because it does not state what constitutes evidence of agreement. If the procedure is reworded, this vagueness can be eliminated: "The trainer shall prepare a list of performance outcomes agreed to with and signed by the students." It is now clear that the auditor will be looking for items on the signed list. These clear-cut pieces of evidence are called *quality records*.

Module #16: Quality Records

It is clear that successful auditing depends on evidence being available to demonstrate that the procedure has—or has not—been followed. Anything used to record compliance is called a *quality record*.

It is possible to introduce a total quality system that specifies numerous new and complex records which will have to be kept as quality records. However, this is not the way to introduce total quality. It results in deep resentment from all the staff who have to run the system and fortifies the belief that ISO 9000 is just additional paperwork.

An efficient and successful quality system will seek every opportunity to use everyday working documents as quality records. Almost certainly, the existing document formats will need some revision in order to become quality records, but the important thing is that the number of documents is not increased.

Module #14: Corrective Action

Even auditing is not enough to ensure that a total quality system works. What happens if the auditing shows that some aspect of a procedure is being ignored? For example, suppose a procedure specifies that each trainer is to receive three copies of any change to the content of a training event before the event starts. Auditing reveals that (a) trainers receive only one copy and (b) the copies arrive a day before the training event starts. The next step is corrective action, i.e., rectifying what has been overlooked or done incorrectly. This can result in one of two actions:

- In some cases, the auditing simply reveals that the procedure is out of date. Perhaps the trainers no longer want three copies of the changes. In this case, the action is to amend the procedure.
- In other cases, it is agreed that the procedure is still appropriate, and the parties involved in the audit must agree on how best to correct the discrepancies. If it is too late to correct the past action, then attention is focused on preventing the problem from recurring.

While everyone might hope that the auditing will reveal complete compliance, noncompliances are not unusual, especially in a new system. The corrective action process is the means through which a noncompliance is corrected. ISO 9000 requires a quality system to have a systematic method for corrective action.

Because there is no guarantee that the corrective action will have been taken at the end of the agreed upon period, the quality system must have a means of acting on failure to implement corrective action. This would normally involve the auditor reporting the omission to someone at a higher level in the management chain.

Module #18: Training

This is another section where training and education do not differ from manufacturing or service. ISO 9000 requires that for those *activities that affect quality*, only properly trained staff be used. This probably includes all staff, because training and education are only deliverable by skilled staff. Therefore, for staff in each area or function deemed critical, a procedure must be established to:

• Identify the training needs of the staff
• Provide the training
• Keep records of the training

This does not mean that extensive skills tests will need to be conducted. In training and education, most jobs are well defined, with clearly established standards or minimum qualifications. For example, a college may require that all lecturers have:

• A first degree or professional qualification in their subjects
• A further education teaching certificate

If this is what is required for the job of lecturer, then records for each lecturer must show that he or she has sufficient qualifications to meet the requirements.

Module #1 Revisited: Management Reviews

The ISO 9000 system begins and ends with the commitment management, and the final part is the management review. A quality council composed of senior management holds regular review meetings to assess how well the system is meeting the needs of the organization and the customer and how well the system is being run. Such a review would receive summary reports on the system, which might document areas such as:

• Adherence to the audit schedule—Are audits being done on time?
• Implementation of corrective action—Are problems revealed by audits being corrected in the agreed upon manner and promptly?

- Procedure review—Are procedures being regularly reviewed by their users and amended if needed?
- Mission—Is the mission statement still appropriate?

The overall approach is self-regulatory and self-improving, with heavy emphasis on documentation and audit, as previously discussed.

IMPLEMENTING ISO 9000

Issues to Consider

Having identified and summarized the major components that constitute ISO 9000 for higher education, it is now appropriate to review the implementation issues. The following is a sample of the types of issues which ISO 9000 will require management to consider (see Table 9.1 for deployment details):

- What management must do in order to effectively run the quality system
- What constitutes a total quality system
- How auditing should be conducted
- Checking customers' requirements
- Controlling course/materials design
- Ensuring that precisely what is needed is purchased
- Keeping track of the learning process
- Using appropriate assessment methods
- Ensuring that out-of-date information and materials are not used
- Helping students after course completion
- Keeping appropriate records
- Maintaining safe working practices

Management Reviews for Implementation

Day in and day out, employees will be carrying out tasks and functions according to the agreed upon procedures and work instructions. At regular intervals (perhaps once a month) some part or the procedures will be under audit. The entire process becomes an integral part of how work is done and how it is managed. However, just as any course or training system needs to be evaluated from time to time, so does any quality system. This evaluation process is called management review.

Management review should be second nature to trainers and educators because it follows the basic principles of evaluating any ongoing training and education system. In training and education, this could be stated as follows:

- Are the objectives being met?
- If not, what action needs to be taken?
- Do the objectives need to be changed?

The management review follows a similar format:

- Are the procedures being implemented?
- If not, what action needs to be taken?
- Do the procedures need to be changed?

As with any evaluation system, if steps are not taken early to collect the data as work proceeds, it may be difficult, expensive, or even impossible to collect the data later. That is particularly important because if compliance with the procedures cannot be proved, noncompliance is assumed. No news is bad news in ISO 9000. This means that management must be explicit about the data to be evaluated in its reviews. Data will tend to be of two types: routine statistical data and ad hoc surveys. Examples of routine statistical data that management may require include:

- Percentage of audits carried out within one week of target date
- Number of noncompliances detected per audit
- Percentage of corrective actions carried out within the time period agreed upon with the auditor
- Percentage of total noncompliances for each procedure
- Average length of time since each procedure was last reviewed
- Number of procedures not reviewed in the past twelve months

All these data are easily plotted on time graphs, so that management can see the trend in performance.

Table 9.1 Deployment Planning Matrix for Integration of ISO 9000 and Higher Education

	Stage		
	Starting an ISO 9000 program	Operating a start-up ISO 9000 program	Sustaining an ISO 9000 program
Module #1: Management responsibility	• Learn the quality values and their implications for education • Develop personal support mechanisms • Develop the overall corporate quality policy framework • Link to broad-based community movement focused on TQM • Provide resources	• Draft the corporate quality statement details • Push the quality policy understanding down to all levels every day • Communicate the quality policy mission and values to the public	• Lead consistently day to day; model learning with staff; see things getting better • Perform quality reviews to ensure that quality policy is being implemented • Decide if policy needs modifying • Determine how frequently data need to be corrected
Module #2: Quality system	• Answer the questions "What business are we in?" and "What is critical to success?" • Identify critical issues by involving staff and students • Decide upon items that need a quality policy	• Develop procedures for every process in the university • Identify accountabilities and responsibilities • Define the quality standard and appropriate quality records that will be needed	• See an integration of QA in all major decisions • Decide where to pursue certification and choose a certification body • Experience a sense of personal transformation
Module #3: Contract review	• Identify areas where contract review is needed and appropriate • Define areas requiring review and ensure that documentation is available	• Review customer requirements to ensure that they are adequately defined and documented • Ensure that changes have been accounted for • Allocate resources to fulfill the contract	• Check that the teachers and staff have the proper skills • Follow up with the appropriate awarding body

Table 9.1 Deployment Planning Matrix for Integration of ISO 9000 and Higher Education

	Stage		
	Starting an ISO 9000 program	Operating a start-up ISO 9000 program	Sustaining an ISO 9000 program
Module #4: Design control	• Identify the product/course to be delivered • Identify the learning process to be followed • Ensure that customer needs are being identified and captured	• Prepare the course design and development plan cycle • Design inputs • Design outputs of the plan • Verify the design with customers • Design changes as required by curriculum development • Build in mechanism of continuous improvement	• Begin working with suppliers of design technology to incorporate latest thinking • Shift the ways that schools provide learning
Module #6: Purchasing	• Classify part-time instructors as either "suppliers" or "staff" • Identify other areas needing purchasing	• Identify the standard of performance required • Outline the selection process • Create a list of approval bodies	• Monitor the performance of suppliers • Work with suppliers to eliminate defective materials • Update approved bidder list
Module #7: Purchaser-supplied product	• Determine whether purchaser-supplied products are relevant	• Check to see if the products are correct • Report any loss or damage	• Eliminate unauthorized access to material and supplies • Create system to report any damage
Module 9: Process control	• Identify processes needing standards • Understand areas needing work function documentation • Synthesize ongoing efforts • Develop measures to track effectiveness and improvement	• Design quality into curriculum development process • Begin working with suppliers • Build in mechanism of continuous improvement (time issues, action research, quality tools)	• Consider how to change to an interdisciplinary curriculum, if applicable • Apply continuous improvement to the ways the university provides learning

Table 9.1 (continued) Deployment Planning Matrix for Integration of ISO 9000 and Higher Education

	Stage		
	Starting an ISO 9000 program	Operating a start-up ISO 9000 program	Sustaining an ISO 9000 program
Module #13: Control of nonconforming product	• Discuss the cost of nonconforming courses and materials	• Begin tracking costs of nonconformance • Consider proper handling and disposition of nonconforming products	• Show consistent trends in data collection • Spend fewer dollars in waste and rework
Module #14: Corrective action	• Specify the system for corrective action • Show how the monitoring system will work	• Take action quickly • Record the action to be taken and initiate correction • Provide feedback on specific problems to concerned parties	• Review procedures and revise as appropriate • Inform those concerned as to changes
Module #16: Quality records	• Set up the requirements for quality records • Decide where to benchmark quality practices	• Document the use of student records, staff records, instructor records, and course design records • Review procedures and revise • Benchmark to set high standards • Make decisions based on quality	• Ask if need for record exists on an ongoing basis • See if an existing record can be-substantiated • Monitor the documentation process • Determine if data are used to drive decisions

The other category of data which a management review group might require is ad hoc reports. For example, the group might review:

• Trainers' views on how well the quality system supports them in their day-to-day work
• Suppliers' views of the quality system
• Sample of quality systems in similar establishments

Table 9.1 (continued) Deployment Planning Matrix for Integration of ISO 9000 and Higher Education

	Stage		
	Starting an ISO 9000 program	Operating a start-up ISO 9000 program	Sustaining an ISO 9000 program
Module #17: Internal quality audits	• Appoint auditors and ensure they have the skills needed • Create the audit schedule • Arrange for special training if needed	• Ensure that audits are carried out as scheduled • Review results and follow-up activities are noted • Ensure that proper audit records are kept	• Follow-up to see that audit recommendations are being implemented • Modify audit plan as required • Indicate system changes as required
Module #18: Training	• Drive out fear concerning loss of jobs from ISO 9000 • Orient all employees in ISO 9000 values, standards, and documentation • Develop a training program for key employees and students	• Attain intended implementation through development of staff and students • Foster professionalism as outlined in the National Board of Professional Teaching Standards (NBPTS) • Obtain feedback on training effectiveness	• Consider modifying the ways that learning is provided • Modify training materials based on audit and staff feedback

Source:Based on the deployment planning matrix concept developed by Randy Schenkat.

Obtaining ISO 9000 Certification

Whether to seek external recognition of the total quality system is a matter of choice. If the decision is made in favor of external recognition, then the system must be assessed against either the ISO 9000 standards or another quality standard such as the Malcolm Baldrige Award.

As discussed earlier, BSI issued the 5750 standard in the U.K. A number of certification bodies have been approved to assess organizations against BS 5750 (ISO 9000). Currently there are about fifteen certification bodies in the U.K. Their role is to assess the quality system in depth in order to determine whether it meets the standards set out in BS 5750. The certification body requires a fee, which is negotiated in terms of the size of the organization and the complexity of its quality system. A Quality Manual and procedures must be submitted, but documentation is kept very simple. The certifying body then:

- Reviews the documentation
- Visits the premises to interview quality staff and other employees and to generally observe the total quality system in practice
- Produces a report which either confirms that the standard has been met or indicates changes needed in the system to meet the standard

Including the certification process alongside the other steps in this chapter, the full process of obtaining ISO 9000 certification is as follows:

1. Obtain the necessary parts of ISO 9000
2. Design the system as set out in this book (in practice, the assistance of an external consultant will probably be required for this step)
3. Choose a certification body
4. Schedule a certification body visit
5. Receive certification or amend the system

Choosing a Certification Body

A list of certification bodies can be obtained from BSI or from the National Accreditation Council for Certification Bodies (NACCB). In choosing a certification body, it is best to identify one with plenty of experience in working with institutes of higher learning. The better this type of business is understood by the certification body, the better they will be able to understand the subtleties of adapting ISO 9000. It is also a good idea to check with other similar organizations to determine which certifying body they used (if any) and what their experience was. If a certifying body with a poor track record is chosen, difficulties can be expected as they adapt to the specific needs of the organization in the realm of total quality in higher education.

EPILOGUE: THE DRIVING FORCE BEHIND TQM

Total quality began in those markets where Japan and the United States were in direct competition. It has continued to expand wherever markets are characterized by an ever-increasing demand for quality and reliability combined with a reduction in price in real terms. Thus, TQM is particularly common in automobile manufacturing, process industries, and electronics, areas where today's products are far more reliable than those of a decade or two ago.[12]

The training and education markets have not as yet experienced competitive pressures of this type. However, as the worldwide privatization trend continues, it is likely that training and education will become more competitive. Particularly with the aid of high-tech media, customers will less and less frequently automatically turn to the nearest local provider of training or education. It is, therefore, reasonable to expect that providers of training and education will increasingly find themselves competing in terms of quality, satisfaction, and price. Mandatory total quality and ISO 9000 could well be on the way.[13] Today's choice may be tomorrow's mandate.

Overall, the goals of an integrated ISO 9000 based total quality system can be summarized as:[14]

- Listen to the voice of the customer
- Focus on the needs of the market
- Achieve top quality performance in all areas, not just in the product or service
- Establish simple procedures for quality performance
- Continually review processes to eliminate waste
- Develop measures of performance
- Understand the competition and develop a competitive strategy
- Ensure effective communication
- Seek continuous improvement

When comparing QA-based ISO 9000 programs to total quality, the most significant difference is that total quality adds customer focus and cost to the quality debate. QA essentially ignores cost (or money in any form), whereas total quality uses cost as a critical performance measure.

It is not the intent here to draw any firm conclusions as to the merits of ISO 9000 versus TQM. Indeed, there is too little evidence of the application of either method to training and education to validate conclusions. What can be said, however, is that training and education cannot expect to escape the current drive toward higher quality and customer focus. Therefore, a more sensitive measure of past performance will be required, as well as a means of improving past performance. However, in phrasing such a need, it points toward some form of quality assurance. Perhaps ISO 9000 will fit that need. Perhaps TQM will, or some combination of the two. If neither does, some other approach will soon be required.

ENDNOTES

1. Freeman, Richard (1992). *Quality Assurance in Training and Education.* London: Kogan Page Limited, pp. 9–12.
2. Partnerships between industry and educational institutions are also helping to promote quality improvement in education. For example, the TQM University Challenge, first proposed by Robert W. Galvin, chairman of the executive committee of the board of directors of Motorola Corporation, is intended to foster the integration of TQM principles into existing business and engineering curricula and into administrative processes that support curricula development. To help accomplish this, the university representatives will complete a week of on-site education at their host companies. A pilot program, the TQM University Challenge, pairs Motorola with Purdue University, Procter & Gamble with the University of Wisconsin–Madison and Tuskegee University, Xerox Corp. with Carnegie Mellon University, Milliken & Company with North Carolina State University and the Georgia Institute of Technology, and IBM with the Massachusetts Institute of Technology and the Rochester Institute of Technology. (Source: Axland, Suzanne (1992). "A Higher Degree of Quality." *Quality Progress,* p. 42, Oct. 1992.)
3. Sprow, Eugene (1992). "Insights into ISO 9000." *Manufacturing Engineering,* p. 73, Sept. 1992.
4. Freeman, Richard (1992). *Quality Assurance in Training and Education,* London: Kogan Page Limited, p. 10.
5. Freeman, Richard (1992). *Quality Assurance in Training and Education,* London: Kogan Page Limited.
6. Sink, Scott (1991). "The Role of Measurement in World Class Quality." *Industrial Engineering,* June 1991.
7. Freeman, Richard (1992). *Quality Assurance in Training and Education,* London: Kogan Page Limited. pp. 12–13.

8. Freeman, Richard (1992). *Quality Assurance in Training and Education,* London: Kogan Page Limited. p. 14.

9. Spizizen, Gary (1992). "The ISO 9000 Standards: Creating a Level Playing Field for International Quality." *National Productivity Review,* pp. 331–346, Summer 1992.

10 Note on traditional quality control: Quality control is a much more widely known term than QA, but the distinction between the two is not always well drawn. Quality control is essentially a method of inspecting for, and rejecting, defective work (although some of its statistical methods can be used to prevent defective work from occurring). In training and education, a quality control system might measure exam or test scores and then penalize the trainers or teachers who fail to achieve defined passing grades. In such an approach, there is no concept of preventing the problem in the first place. QA is essentially *preventive,* as the word assurance implies. It means preventing errors, not correcting them repeatedly.

11. Freeman, Richard (1992). *Quality Assurance in Training and Education,* London: Kogan Page Limited, p. 22.

12. Total quality is based on the assumption that suppliers (in this case, providers of training and education) will only prosper in their markets if they are able to both improve quality and reduce costs. While this concept is not novel in manufacturing, it is perhaps revolutionary in training and education. Teachers frequently request additional resources so that they can improve quality. Total quality says that you must improve quality with fewer resources, because if you do not, your competitor will.

13. Total quality assumes that there is a hidden source of fat in any organization. That source is the cost of quality, also known as the price of nonconformance (PONC) or the cost of not doing things right the first time. In training and education, the cost of quality includes (a) planning a course for ten people, but running it for eight because the time did not suit two people or running it for twelve because of scheduling problems, (b) students starting courses for which they were not ready and dropping out before completion, (c) lecturers having to remark assignments because the initial marking scheme was not adequately standardized, and (d) students failing an assessment because of substandard teaching.

14. Jackson, Susan (1992). "What You Should Know about ISO 9000." *Training,* pp. 48–52, May 1992.

15. Voehl, Frank (1993). ISO 9000 Adapted to Various Business Industries and Institutions of Higher Learning, Unpublished manuscript, Coral Springs, Fla.: Strategy Associates.

16. Ozeki, Kazuo and Asaka, Tetsuichi (1990). *Handbook of Quality Tools: The Japanese Approach.* Cambridge, Mass.: Productivity Press, 1990.

17. According to Dr. Asaka of JUSE, most problems can be classified as follows: (a) Problems related to worker skills or attitudes: pure mistake; not following the operating procedure; skills not yet adequate; concern for quality not strong enough. (b) Problems related to the workplace QA system: the quality characteristic to be assured is not well defined; operating standards are incomplete; management points are unclear; casual attitude about QA methods; quality control process chart not yet complete. (c) Lack of motivation to solve the administrator's problem: no desire to delve deeply into the problem and solve it; administrator's leadership in setting improvement goals and in making improvements is inadequate. (d) Problems in the workplace culture: never delving deeply into problems; blaming the workplace custom. (e) Problems originating in another department: design error; error in determining customer specifications. Asaka believes that if problems are solved in a haphazard manner, a problem might mistakenly be identified as a recurring worker error when the true cause is the daily training and quality control education being provided to the students and workers. Try to create an atmosphere in which everyone is motivated to build quality into their courses and seminars.

An administrator should look for the root cause of any problem that occurs, consider if he or she (not others) is causing the problem, and implement the basic policies needed to correct it.

18. Figures 9.1 and 9.3 and Table 9.1 ©1993 Strategy Associates, Inc.

TECHNICAL SUPPLEMENTS

TECHNICAL SUPPLEMENT 9.1:
ADAPTATION OF THE JAPANESE QA SYSTEM
TO THE UNIVERSITY ENVIRONMENT[15]

The following principles are based on the work of Tetsuichi Asaka and Kazuo Ozeki, as originally documented in the JUSE research materials and writings.[16]

Make Quality the Top Priority

Putting quality first is fundamental to the long-term survival of a university. Those organizations that neglect QA in favor of delivering a product first in a competitive market later discover defects and suffer in the long run. Many companies have failed for this reason. In the twenty-first century, the same will be said of universities.

Built-In Quality

It should be understood that inspections and examinations do not create quality; quality is built in during the curriculum development process. University administrators need to create improvement targets to build quality into the education process. The administrator might set the target at 133 percent or more of the current process capability, and then work with instructors and employees to create and implement a quality improvement plan on a semester-by-semester basis.

Problems Are Opportunities to Improve the QA System

Administrators should view complaints and quality problems as opportunities to improve the organization and attitudes within it and to implement reform. The fundamental principle of quality control is to identify the root cause of a problem so that it will not recur. If the administrator does not search for the root cause and strive to prevent the recurrence of the problem, his or her work becomes haphazard.[17] Search for the root cause thoroughly.

QA Checkpoints for the University

1. Motivating for quality consciousness
   - Are the philosophy and general policies of the university and of top management easy to understand and have they been thoroughly implemented?
   - Have employees been made aware of the damages the university suffers due to poorly prepared students and customer complaints (loss of customer confidence, loss of image, etc.)?
   - Have concrete examples been provided to the staff to show the importance of quality as a shortcut to lower costs, higher student confidence, and a great sense of achievement?
   - Have staff and students been helped to understand the role that quality plays in their work?
2. Objectives and planning
   - Are classroom quality targets clear and well understood?
   - Has the QA improvement theme been clearly set forth?
   - Has each individual and student been given instructions for his or her part in the plan for carrying out the improvement themes that will achieve these targets?
   - Are the plans related to these targets and improvement themes clear?
3. Education
   - Are chances for achieving the goals and plans being improved through education, exchanges with other universities, and participation in events outside the organization?
   - Have the functions that make the offerings useful to the market and the current extent of the product's use in the market been explained?
   - If a problem arises, does someone take charge, give proper instructions for solving the problem, and direct the improvement activities?
4. Practical work and its improvement
   - Are tasks related to the quality characteristics carried out thoroughly?
   - Has a handbook been prepared to summarize work procedures in order to teach employees how to do their jobs?
   - Have workers been taught how to use computers, instruments, and tools and to make revisions and adjustments to the curriculum?

- Are the work methods reviewed to determine that they are performed properly?
- Are workers encouraged to upgrade their technical knowledge and skills? How much time is spent each year per employee?

5. Problem solving and team activities
   - When problems or accidents occur, do workers receive guidance in solving the problem?
   - When on-the-spot emergency firefighting must be done, is the root cause of the problem identified in order to make sure it does not recur?
   - Is the project team directed to work together to solve a problem?
   - Are effective and rational problem-solving methods used, such as the seven quality control tools?
   - If improvements and reforms are needed in organization, systems, or standards to prevent a problem from recurring, do the people directly involved participate in taking the necessary actions?
   - Is careful consideration given to whether the university workplace culture is the problem, and are appropriate measures taken to change the situation?[17]

TECHNICAL SUPPLEMENT 9.2: DESCRIPTION OF SYSTEM COMPONENTS

Procedures

In the quality policy, all the main functions to be controlled as part of the quality system are identified. Because policy statements are far too broad to be used for day-to-day implementation by staff, a procedure is written for each function. In operational terms, the procedures are the most important documents because they control most day-to-day actions and—more important—identify who does what.

A procedure is established for each function and includes:

- The main steps in that function, with special emphasis on the critical interfaces
- Who is responsible for carrying out each function
- The quality standard to which each stage should be taken
- The form in which work is to be passed from one stage to another

- The quality records to be retained to demonstrate that the work was done according to the procedure.

Once the procedure is written and agreed upon, employees should follow it.

No matter how well people know and understand the quality policy, their immediate reference will be to one or more procedures. It is, therefore, critical that procedures satisfy a number of criteria:

- Accurately reflect how the job should be done if customer requirements are to be met
- Easily understood
- Clearly describe tasks in terms of the outcome
- Clearly define responsibilities

For example, the following is poorly worded:

Learners shall be regularly tested.

In checking on whether this wording had been followed, the following would not be clear:

- How often constitutes "regularly"
- What evidence shows that testing has been done
- Who should have done the testing

The same sentence can be modified to include the kind of precision required in a procedure:

At least once a month, trainers shall test each of their learners using one of the tests from the approved test bank. The results shall be recorded by the trainer in the learner's log.

From this it is clear:

- *When* the task is to be done (at least once a month)
- *Who* carries out the task (the trainer)
- *What* the outcome is (a result recorded in the learner's log)

For every task, it should be easy to identify:

- The outcome
- Who does it
- When it is to be done

Anything that fails these three tests must be rethought.

Work Instructions

Procedures should never describe how a task should be done. If that level of detail were allowed, procedures would become so dense as to be useless. It is at this point that work instructions take over. Work instructions can be very detailed— if necessary. Their function is to specify precise detail where such detail is needed.

Creating a good work instruction is often a matter of considering who will use it and how it will be used. For example, consider the task of producing a course specification. A lengthy guide could be written to tell someone how to do the job. Would it be read? Probably not. Would it be followed? Even less likely. The solution is to turn the instruction into a job aid. This makes the user more likely to follow the work instruction because to do so makes the job easier. For these reasons, almost all work instructions are in one of the following forms:

- A form (e.g., an exam entry form)
- A checklist (e.g., a list of points to check in preparing a training form for a training session)
- A list of headings (e.g., the headings under which to collect data for a course specification)
- A diagram showing how to do a task (e.g., how to lay out a page of text for a presentation)

Not only are such work instruction formats very easy to follow, but they are a natural part of the work. Wherever possible, use natural documents and data as part of the ISO 9000 system.

GLOSSARY

Abnormal variation: Changes in process performance that cannot be accounted for by typical day-to-day variation. Also referred to as nonrandom variation.

Acceptable quality (AQL): The minimum number of parts that must comply with quality standards, usually stated as a percentage.

Activity: The tasks performed to change inputs into outputs.

Adaptable: An adaptable process is designed to maintain effectiveness and efficiency as requirements change. The process is deemed adaptable when there is agreement among suppliers, owners, and customers that the process will meet requirements throughout the strategic period.

Appraisal cost: The cost incurred to determine defects.

Benchmarking: A tool used to improve products, services, or management processes by analyzing the best practices of other companies to determine standards of performance and how to achieve them in order to increase customer satisfaction.

Business objectives: Specific objectives which, if achieved, will ensure that the operating objectives of the organization are in alignment with the vision, values, and strategic direction. They are generally high level and timeless.

Business process: Organization of people, equipment, energy, procedures, and material into measurable, value-added activities needed to produce a specified end result.

Business process analysis (BPA): Review and documentation (mapping) of a key business process to understand how it currently functions and to establish measures.

Competitive: A process is considered to be competitive when its overall performance is judged to be as good as that of comparable processes. Competitiveness is based on a set of performance characteristics (defects, costs, inventory turnaround, etc.) that are monitored and tracked against comparable processes within the corporation, the industry, and/or the general business community.

Competitive benchmarking: Comparing and rating the practices, processes, and products of an organization against the world best, best-in-class, or the competition. Comparisons are not confined to the same industry.

Conformance: Affirmative indication or judgment that a product or service has met specified requirements, contracts, or regulations. The state of meeting the requirements.

Continuous improvement: Sometimes called Constancy of Purpose, this is a principle used by W. Edwards Deming to examine improvement of product and service. It involves searching unceasingly for ever-higher levels of quality by isolating sources of defects. It is called *kaizen* in

Japan, where the goal is zero defects. Quality management and improvement is a never-ending activity.

Control: The state of stability, or normal variation and predictability. It is the process of regulating and guiding operations and processes using quantitative data. Control mechanisms are also used to detect and avoid potential adverse effects of change.

Control charts: Statistical plots derived from measuring a process. They help detect and determine deviations before a defect results. Inherent variations in manufacturing processes can be spotted and accounted for by designers.

Corrective action: The implementation of effective solutions that result in the elimination of identified product, service, and process problems.

Cost of quality: The sum of prevention, appraisal, and failure costs, usually expressed as a percentage of total cost or revenue.

Critical success factors (CSFs): Areas in which results, if satisfactory, will ensure successful corporate performance. They ensure that the company will meet its business objectives. CSFs are focused, fluctuate, and are conducive to short-term plans.

Cross-functional: A term used to describe individuals from different business units or functions who are part of a team to solve problems, plan, and develop solutions for process-related actions affecting the organization as a system.

Cross-functional focus: The effort to define the flow of work products in a business process as determined by their sequence of activities, rather than by functional or organizational boundaries.

Culture (also vision): The pattern of shared beliefs and values that provide members of an organization rules of behavior or accepted norms for conducting operational business.

Customer: The recipient or beneficiary of the outputs of work efforts or the purchaser of products and services. May be either internal or external to the company.

Customer, internal: Organizations have both external and internal customers. Many functions and activities are not directly involved with external customer satisfaction, but their outputs provide inputs to other functions and activities within the organization. Data processing, for example, must provide an acceptable quality level for many internal customers.

Customer requirements (also called valid requirements): The statement of needs or expectations that a product or service must satisfy. Requirements must be specific, measurable, negotiated, agreed to, documented, and communicated.

Customer/supplier model: The model is generally represented using three interconnected triangles to depict inputs flowing into a work process that, in turn, adds value and produces outputs that are delivered to a customer. Throughout the process, requirements and feedback are fed from the customer to the supplier to ensure that customer quality requirements are met.

Cycle time: The elapsed time between the commencement and completion of a task. In manufacturing, it is calculated as the number of units of work-in-process inventory divided by the number of units processed in a specific period. In order processing it can be the time between receipt and delivery of an order. Overall cycle time can mean the time from concept of a new product or service until it is brought to market.

Defect: Something that does not conform to requirements.

Document of understanding (DOU): A formal agreement defining the roles, responsibilities, and objectives of all the parties to that agreement. The degree of detail is dictated by the nature of the agreement, but it should always clearly address the requirements of the work product in question.

Effective: An effective process produces output that conforms to customer requirements. The lack of process effectiveness is measured by the degree to which the process output does not conform to customer requirements (that is, by the level of defect of the output).

Effectiveness: The state of having produced a decided or desired effect; the state of achieving customer satisfaction.

Efficiency: A measure of performance that compares output production with cost or resource utilization (as in number of units per employee per hour or per dollar).

Efficient: An efficient process produces the required output at the lowest possible (minimum) cost. That is, the process avoids waste or loss of resources in producing the required output. Process efficiency is measured by the ratio of required output to the cost of producing that output. This cost is expressed in units of applied resource (dollars, hours, energy, etc.).

Employee involvement (EI): Promotion and mechanisms to achieve employee contributions, individually and in groups, to quality and less company performance objectives. Cross-functional teams, task forces, quality circles, or other vehicles for involvement are used.

Employee well-being and morale: Maintenance of work environment conducive to well-being and growth of all employees. Factors include health, safety, satisfaction, work environment, training, and special services such as counseling assistance, recreational, or cultural.

Executive Quality Service Council (EQSC): Comprised of members of executive management and union leadership who oversee the quality effort from a corporate view and set strategic direction.

Facilitator: Responsible for guiding the team through analysis of the process. Also concerned with how well the team works together.

Failure cost: The cost resulting from the occurrence of defects (such as scrap, rework/redo, replacement, etc.).

Functional organization: An organization responsible for one of the major corporate business functions such as marketing, sales, design, manufacturing, or distribution.

Human resource management: Development of plans and practices that realize the full potential of the workforce to pursue the quality and performance objectives of the organization. Includes (1) education and training, (2) recruitment, (3) involvement, (4) empowerment, and (5) recognition.

Implementer: An individual working within the process and who is responsible for carrying out specific job tasks.

Indicators: Benchmarks, targets, standards, or other measures used to evaluate how well quality values and programs are integrated.

Information system: A database of information used for planning day-to-day management and control of quality. Types of data should include (1) customer related, (2) internal operations, (3) company performance, and (4) cost and financial.

Inputs: Products or services obtained from others (suppliers) in order to perform job tasks. Material or information required to complete the activities necessary for a specified end result.

Involved managers: Managers who have responsibility for the day-to-day activities and tasks within the process.

Just-in-time (JIT): The delivery of parts and materials by a supplier at the moment a factory needs them, thus eliminating costly inventories. Quality is paramount because a faulty part delivered at the last moment will not be detected.

Kaizen: See Continuous improvement

Leadership: The category of the Baldrige Award that examines personal leadership and involvement of executives in creating and sustaining a customer focus and clear and visible quality values.

Management for quality: The translation of customer focus and quality values into implementation plans for all levels of management and supervision.

Measurable outcomes: Specific results that determine, corporately, how well critical success factors and business objectives are being achieved. They are concrete, specific, and measurable.

Measurement: The methods used to achieve and maintain conformance to customer requirements. Measurement determines the current status of the process and whether the process requires change or improvement.

Mission: The core purpose of being for an organization. Usually expressed in the form of a statement twenty-five to fifty words in length.

Operating plans: Specific, actionable plans which, if carried out successfully, ensure that critical success factors are met, which in turn ensures that corporate business objectives are met. They are tied to critical success factors, are detailed, and contain measurements of success.

Operating Quality Service Council (OQSC): Comprised of activity management and their direct reports, and many include union and staff representation. The council oversees the quality effort within an activity and ensures that quality strategies support the corporate strategic direction.

Organization for quality: Structuring organizational activities to effectively accomplish the company's objectives.

Outputs: The specified end result, materials, or information provided to others (internal or external customers).

Pareto analysis (or Pareto chart): A statistical method of measurement to identify the most important problems through different measuring scales (for example, frequency, cost, etc.). Usually displayed by a bar graph that ranks causes of process variation by the degree of impact on quality (sometimes called the "80/20" rule).

Prevention activity: Elements of prevention activity include (1) education in process quality management and (2) process management (ownership, documentation/analysis, requirements activity, measurements including statistical techniques, and corrective action on the process).

Prevention cost: Costs incurred to reduce the total cost of quality.

Process: The organization of people, equipment, energy, procedures, and material into the work activities needed to produce a specified end result (work product). A sequence of repeatable activities characterized as having measurable inputs, value-added activities, and measurable outputs. It is a set of interrelated work activities characterized by a set of specific inputs and value-added tasks that produce a set of specific outputs.

Process analysis: The systematic examination of a process model to establish a comprehensive understanding of the process itself. The intent of the examination should include consideration of simplification, elimination of unneeded or redundant elements, and improvement.

Process capability: The level of effectiveness and efficiency at which the process will perform. This level may be determined through the use of statistical control charts. Long-term performance level after the process has been brought under control.

Process control: The activity necessary to ensure that the process is performing as designed. Achieved through the use of statistical techniques, such as control charts, so that appropriate actions can be taken to achieve and maintain a state of statistical control.

Process elements: A process is comprised of activities and tasks. A process may also be referred to as a subprocess when it is subordinate to, but part of, a larger process. A subprocess can also be defined as a group of activities within a process that comprise a definable component.

Process management: The disciplined management approach of applying prevention methodologies to the implementation, improvement, and change of work processes to achieve effectiveness, efficiency, and adaptability. Critical to the success of process management is the concept of cross-functional focus.

Process model: A detailed representation of the process (graphic, textual, mathematical) as it currently exists.

Process owner: Coordinates the various functions and work activities at all levels of a process, has the authority or ability to make changes in the process as required, and manages the process end-to-end so as to ensure optimal overall performance.

Process performance quality: A measure of how effectively and efficiently a process satisfies customer requirements. The ability of a product or service to meet and exceed the expectations of customers.

Process review: An objective assessment of how well the methodology has been applied to the process. Emphasizes the potential for long-term process results rather than the actual results achieved.

Quality function deployment (QFD): A system that pays special attention to customer needs and integrates them into the marketing, design, manufacturing, and service processes. Activities that do not contribute to customer needs are considered wasteful.

Quality Improvement Team (QIT): A group of people brought together to resolve a specific problem or issue identified by a business process analysis, individual employees, or the Operating Quality Service Council. A group of individuals charged with the task of planning and implementing process quality improvement. The three major roles in this task force are team leader, team facilitator, and team member.

Quality management: The management of a process to maximize customer satisfaction at the lowest overall cost to the company.

Quality management system: The collective plans, activities, and events established to ensure that a product, process, or service will satisfy given needs. The infrastructure supporting the operational process management and improvement methodology.

Quality planning: The process of developing the quality master to link together all of the planning systems of the organization. The objective is to follow all areas of achievement of the vision, mission, and business objectives and to operationalize the strategy by identifying the requirements to achieve leadership in the market segments chosen. Includes key requirements and performance indicators and the resources committed for these requirements.

Quality tool: Instrument or technique that supports the activities of process quality management and improvement.

Requirements: What is expected in providing a product or service. The *it* in "do it right the first time." Specific and measurable customer needs with an associated performance standard.

Resource allocation: A decision to allocate resources, capital, and people to support specific operating plans, tied to the budget process.

Results: Results are, quite simply, a measurement of how well corporate business objectives are being met. Results require that standards and goals for performance are set and the results of processes and performance tracked.

Robust design: Making product designs "production-proof" by building in tolerances for manufacturing variables that are known to be unavoidable.

Root cause: Original reason for nonconformance within a process. When the root cause is removed or corrected, the nonconformance will be eliminated.

Six-sigma: A statistical term that indicates a defect level. One-sigma means 68% of products are acceptable, three-sigma means 99.75, and six-sigma means 99.999997% perfect or 3.4 defects per million parts.

Sponsor: Advocate for the team who provides resources and helps define mission and scope to set limits.

Stakeholder: Individual or department who either has an effect on the process or is affected by it.

Statistical process control (SPC): The use of statistical techniques, such as control charts, to analyze a work process or its outputs. The data can be used to identify deviations so that appropriate action can be taken to maintain a state of statistical control (predetermined upper and lower limits) and to improve the capability of the process.

Statistical quality control (SQC): A method of analyzing measured deviations in manufactured materials, parts, and products.

Strategic quality planning: Development of strategic and operational plans that incorporate quality as product or service differentiation and the load bearing structure of the planning process. Includes (1) definition of customer requirements, (2) projections of the industry and competitive environment for identification of opportunities and risks, and (3) comparison of opportunities and risks against company resources and capabilities.

Subprocesses: The internal processes that make up a process.

Suppliers: Individuals or groups who provide input. Suppliers can be internal or external to a company, group, or organization.

Taguchi methods: Statistical techniques developed by Genichi Taguchi, a Japanese consultant, for optimizing design and production.

Task: The basic work element of a process activity.

Total quality management (TQM): The application of quality principles for the integration of all functions and processes of the organization. The ultimate goal is customer satisfaction. The way to achieve it is through continuous improvement.

Variation: The degree to which a product, service, or element deviates from the specification or requirements. Quality in service organizations deals with identifying, measuring, and adjusting to variability resulting from interactions with customers, while manufacturing organizations are focused on bringing product variability under control.

Vision: The long-term future desired state of an organization, usually expressed in a 7- to 20-year time frame. Often included in the vision statement are the areas that the organization needs to care about in order to succeed. The vision should inspire and motivate.

INDEX